THE CREW

By

Marc Wilder

THE CREW

Copyright © 2025 Marc Wilder

This book is intended for informational and entertainment purposes only. The content is provided "as is" and reflects the author's personal opinions and interpretations. While every effort has been made to ensure accuracy, the author and publisher make no representations or warranties of any kind, express or implied, regarding the completeness, accuracy, reliability, or suitability of the information contained herein.

The material in this book should not be considered as professional advice (legal, financial, medical, or otherwise). Readers are encouraged to consult with qualified professionals before making any decisions based on the content. The author and publisher disclaim any liability for any loss, damage, or inconvenience arising from the use of this book.

No part of this book may be reproduced, distributed, or transmitted in any form or by any means, including photocopying, recording, or other electronic or mechanical methods, without the prior written permission of the author, except in the case of brief quotations embodied in critical reviews and certain other non-commercial uses permitted by copyright law.

Dedication

This book is dedicated to the good, the bad and the ugly that I've sailed the seas with throughout the years. Without experiencing your energy – good or bad, this book would not have been possible.

THE CREW

Table of Contents

Dedication iii
Introduction 1
Chapter 1 The Crazy Gang 3
Chapter 2 White Suits and Black Money 11
Chapter 3 Bleary Eyed and Battered 21
Chapter 4 All That Glitters Is Not Gold 28
Chapter 5 Muddy Geysers 35
Chapter 6 Gold Diggers 42
Chapter 7 Hedonistic Tendencies 52
Chapter 8 Kindred Spirit 60
Chapter 9 May the Force Be with You 72
Chapter 10 The Bigger They Are the Harder They Fall 83
Chapter 11 The Panda-Eyed Goon 89
Chapter 12 Priapism 103
Chapter 13 Escort the Escorts 113
Chapter 14 Initiation by Fire 125
Chapter 15 He Speaks the Language Like A Native 135
Chapter 16 All You Need Is a Good Ashtray 141
Chapter 17 Don't You Just Love the Smell of Puppies? 152
Chapter 18 Cruel to Be Kind… Or So He Thinks! 161
Chapter 19 Swine Rodeo 173
Chapter 20 Live Fast, Die Young and Leave A Good Looking Corpse 182
Chapter 21 Inspiration Comes in Many Forms 193
Chapter 22 We Are Us 206

Chapter 23 Nature Has the Answer 225

Chapter 24 What Goes Around Comes Around 246

MARC WILDER

Introduction

My name is Marc Wilder, I'm 37 years old, and I'm a qualified Master Mariner. Over nearly two action-packed decades, I've worked on an array of ships, each offering unique and unforgettable experiences. My career has seen me serve as a Navigation Officer on government vessels, crew square-rigged sailing ships that take individuals with disabilities to sea, navigate vast cruise liners, and even work aboard a millionaire's private yacht, to name just a few.

My journey to the sea began with what can only be described as an epiphany. One day, as I sat gazing at the ocean near Captain Cook's statue in Whitby, North Yorkshire, I felt an undeniable calling. From that moment, I've travelled, worked, and played across the globe. I embarked on my career as a Merchant Navy officer cadet with the Ministry of Defence in the early nineties, starting at the age of 18.

One of the highlights of my career was working as Chief Officer on a luxurious private motor yacht based in Monte Carlo. As second-in-command, I oversaw the deck department and managed the crew on behalf of the Captain. The yacht travelled to some of the most glamorous locations in the world, including the French and Italian Rivieras. My time at sea has been filled with unforgettable and often outrageous experiences—from extravagant private parties to drug-fuelled orgies, encounters with Russian gangsters, and interactions with the most stunning escorts money can buy. I've shared many of these adventures with a crew of colourful characters.

Every story in *The Crew* is inspired by true events, condensed into one of the dirtiest, sexiest, and most rock 'n' roll charters imaginable. I hope you enjoy the wild ride—it's been an exhilarating journey for me.

When I'm not at sea, my favourite things include travelling, savouring extra leg room, indulging in a good steak, hiking in the nature and spending time with my kids. And enjoying Guinness and Jack Daniels (preferably in generous amounts). I also cherish spending quality time with my beautiful partner.

THE CREW

As a young boy, a well-known clairvoyant once told me that I'd write a book someday that would bring fame and fortune. This is my first book… let's see if she was right.

MARC WILDER

Chapter 1
The Crazy Gang

'Chicken nuggets? You've got to be kidding!' shouts Tom. It's clear that Tom is a little upset by the request.

'Sorry, mate, the Captain has just told me,' I say, trying to calm him down.

He's pissed off because his shift is nearly over, yet he now has to transport a box of chicken nuggets by boat to the owner's multi-million-dollar mega-yacht anchored in Monaco.

'I don't fucking believe these twats. They hire a state of the art mega-yacht for $250,000 a week and what do they eat... shit!' Tom throws his hands in the air. 'What a pair of dickheads!'

'I'm pretty sure it's for their kid, mate,' I say, still trying my best to calm things down. 'Foie gras and lobster must upset his stomach, I guess.'

'I'll upset the little fucker when I bury my size ten boot up his arse. And I'll tell you another thing, boss – his bloody dad upset me watching him play football last weekend; fucking stupid haircut as well. How many millions is he supposed to be worth? What a fucking joke!'

Tom was always straight to the point, his sentences often laced with enough expletives to make a sailor blush. He was a great guy, and everyone always knew exactly where they stood with him. For years, he'd been travelling the world—usually solo—and living life to the absolute fullest. Recently, he'd spent a good chunk of time backpacking around Bolivia, embracing an alternative lifestyle and generally being a bit of a reprobate. Tom stumbled into the world of millionaires' mega-yachts after his ferret business spectacularly crashed. The downfall began when his prized ferret apparently decided it was gay and refused to screw the females. He still curses the little critter for letting him down. In one particularly memorable conversation, he confessed that, in a moment of utter frustration, he pulled the ferret from its cage, put a shotgun to its head, and seriously considered ending the standoff once and for all. 'Are you telling me that you shot your prize ferret because you thought it had turned fruit?'

'Nah, mate, that would have been too cruel,' he said in a softer voice.

'Oh, that's all right then,' I said, feeling a little better.

'So I drowned it!' Tom added before taking a big drag of his cigarette.

This was one of many conversations I had with Tom during his time aboard the yacht. He'd have me laughing my arse off on an hourly basis. I liked him a lot because he wasn't your average guy. He'd never been affected by the bullshit and one-upmanship that plague the yachting world, and he never pretended to be someone he wasn't. I was his boss, and fairly often I had to give him a bollocking over one thing or another, but I always found it difficult to stay pissed off at him for long. Solid as a rock, that was Tom, and I respected him for it.

Another character aboard the yacht was a strapping Scotsman called Jock. Born and bred in one of the rougher parts of Glasgow, he had a heart of gold but very few social graces—especially after a few beers. The term *'social hand grenade'* fit Jock perfectly; he was pure local colour.

Jock had grown up on a tough housing estate, the kind of place where even the rats wouldn't walk down the streets after sunset. Coming from a broken family, he'd regularly witness his dad stumbling home pissed, either beating his mum or turning on Jock if he got in the way. Survival in those days meant doing whatever it took, including stealing cars and flogging rave tickets to gullible students.

His scam was as audacious as it was effective. He'd print off thousands of tickets for a supposedly organised outdoor rave, borrow his mate's battered Escort van, and drive around the country selling them. We're talking thousands of tickets at around £10 a pop—this was the 1990s, after all. Jock would charm his way into student bars, target naïve, spotty students, and offer them the tickets at half price—provided they bought a minimum of 20 or so.

With cash in hand, he'd tell them to wait by a specific phone box at an arranged time. The plan was that they'd receive a call with details of the rave location. The only problem? The phone call never came. By the time the poor sods realised they'd been had, Jock was already flying down the motorway, en route to scam another city—thousands of pounds richer and without a care in the world.

He got away with this and other ingenious scams for quite a while, until he underestimated a particular shady character in a northern city. For God's sake, he should've known better when he got the go-ahead to meet the guy in his local where he did business. Jock turned up with 3,000 tickets and was greeted by a man the size of a pie shop, with a face that looked like it had been through regular panel beating. There were three vicious-looking pit bull terriers and three equally hard-looking sidekicks. They were all wearing dark jackets, even darker shades, and had pug-like expressions. Jock should've realised, when he walked into this scenario, that he should listen to the little voice in his head screaming, 'Don't fuck with these guys!' Disregarding that warning in situations like this is a mistake you make at your peril.

True to form, Jock decided not to listen. He did the deal and high-tailed it, just like all the times before. Everything went well until the night of the supposed phone call. He was at a nightclub, gearing up to scam another city, when he met a girl of dubious morals. He figured if he hung around and did the verbal spadework, he wouldn't be sleeping alone that night, and he'd leave the city on a high note the next morning. Ten o'clock passed and still no call, for obvious reasons. Eleven o'clock came and still no call. By this time, Mr Scary had realised he'd been shafted. He had a lot of explaining to do to the other gangsters he'd sold tickets to, as well as a couple of thousand party-hungry clubbers. He'd lost face and a shitload of cash, and he was obviously pissed off, to say the least. Loss of face + loss of cash = disaster for our Jock!

Meanwhile, everything seemed to be going well with Jock and Miss Slack-Knickers, and around one in the morning, after sucking face with her, he decided to hop in a taxi back to her place for some fun between the sheets. Jock liked to call it 'slimy pump-pump action'. As he was leaving the club, Mr Nasty arrived with his entourage. Jock was immediately spotted and greeted with, 'I'm gonna rip your fucking face off!' by one of the henchmen. Without missing a beat, Jock ejected the 38G blonde from the taxi and pleaded with the driver to put his foot on the pedal. Mr Nasty jumped into another taxi in hot pursuit. Jock threw a handful of cash at the driver and told him to head down a country lane and slow down just enough so he could jump out and leg it across a field. The driver grudgingly agreed, Jock threw himself out, and the taxi carried on. The only problem was, Mr Nasty and the gang had seen him. They stopped their taxi and chased after Jock on foot, fuelled by adrenaline and anger.

Jock ran and jumped like a gazelle over rocks, fences, hedges, and various other obstacles, not to mention fields of bulls. He was being pursued by a psychotic mob and an enraged Aberdeen Angus. Running as hard as he could, he managed to put about a hundred yards between them. Jumping into a ditch, he took refuge in a pipe that ran under the road and decided to crawl along it on his hands and knees until he was safely out of the area. He stayed there all night and emerged from a manhole around ten the following morning, right in the middle of a busy high street, still dressed in his clubbing gear. He lifted the manhole cover, climbed out, calmly stretched, yawned, and told an astonished pedestrian that he lived down there to save money on poll tax. Then, he walked across the road and into a McDonald's for brunch. Priceless and typical Jock antics.

Then there's Robbie. Robbie was the quiet one of the yacht's crew, but you know what they say about the quiet ones. He kept to himself mostly but absorbed everything around him. He wasn't sensible by any means, but he wasn't as loud as Jock. Then again, who was? He was a man of very few words, but when he did speak, it was usually something either really funny or really philosophical, and you'd be thinking about it all day. He was just an ordinary guy, but he was too intelligent for his own good, and that sometimes got him into trouble. He'd quit school early because lessons bored him, probably because intellectually, he was way ahead of the others. In fact, he was probably ahead of the teachers. He didn't stay at school long enough to take any exams and left with no formal qualifications.

He had a problem with substance abuse back then, probably as a form of escapism. Nothing too heavy—just pills, weed, and drink. He once worked in an old folks' home to make ends meet and noticed that, at Christmas dinner, none of the residents were talking. Most of them looked like they wanted to die. In a moment of madness, the silly sod took pity on the poor old folk and wondered what he could do to inject a bit of party atmosphere. Sometimes, he just let his emotions rule his head without really thinking about the consequences of his actions, and he laced the old folks' chocolate cake with a little speed.

Half an hour later, one granddad was bouncing around like a kid on a pogo stick, laughing his wrinkly old face off. Everyone else was chatting away like mad, and he couldn't get a word in edgeways. The two resident spaniels, who'd also had some of the cake, were going ballistic, running around like lunatics chasing their tails and barking their heads off. The place was in complete fucking mayhem. Robbie felt genuinely great that the atmosphere had picked up and everyone was enjoying themselves. He was happy he'd brought a few moments of joy into otherwise dreary and dishevelled lives.

He decided to sit down with a few of the old boys, put some music on, and share a joint with them. Everyone was having a blinding time until the manager walked in and discovered Albert buzzing his arse off, while the normally orderly dining room had turned into a place that smelled like a Moroccan hashish den. That was the end of Robbie's career caring for the elderly. He swears blind that, while shopping in town one day, he bumped into one of the old boys who tried to score some hash off him.

'By crikey, it was cracking stuff that, son. Took all my aches and pains away! You wouldn't have any more, would you?'

It was a bloody silly thing to do, though, thankfully, everyone was fine. Still, it does make you think about the subject of narcotic substances. Robbie and I come from the same basic background when it comes to work and travel. We've both travelled extensively and worked in most countries around the globe. One night, after a few pints in the pub, Robbie shared his thoughts on the use of party prescriptions, and it made remarkable sense to me. Robbie believed that using certain substances in small quantities, within a safe environment, could help free your mind, lower your guard, and make you incredibly creative. One thing he noticed while travelling was that most countries and cultures, among other things, share one common trait: they all have some way of getting high!

Somebody famous once said that the only way to discover the limits of the possible is to go beyond them into the impossible. Another person believed in a prolonged displacement of the senses to attain the unknown. Robbie, however, favours a quote from William Blake: *"When the doors of perception are cleansed, things will appear as they truly are – infinite!"*

* * * *

The yacht was a stunning, state-of-the-art masterpiece – a top-of-the-range beauty. Weighing several hundred tonnes and measuring about half the length of a football field, she was a sight to behold. Her teak decks, gleaming stainless steel, and tastefully chosen, expensive furnishings exuded luxury. She could accommodate twelve guests in utter opulence, with a crew of twelve or thirteen catering to their every whim.

The upper deck, or sun deck, boasted a large Jacuzzi, a barbecue, and a fully stocked bar. She also carried two rigid inflatable speedboats capable of seating six to eight people each, used for waterskiing, fishing, and wakeboarding. At the stern, in the garage known as the lazarette, the crew stored all the "toys" – two immensely powerful 1300cc jet skis, scuba gear, a sailing dinghy, and various inflatable water toys.

Walking into the crew room on board, I found the team gathered around the table.

"You'd better keep out of the Captain's way today, everyone," I warned. "He's definitely not in the best of moods."

Robbie sighed. "Tell me something new. That man was born an arsehole and just grew bigger."

"What's the matter with Thrush today, then?" Jock chimed in. "Thrush" was Jock's nickname for the Captain – because, as he put it, "just like thrush, he's an irritating cunt." The first time Jock shared that quip, I was mid-sip of tea. I laughed so hard I burnt myself.

The Captain was a cold, skinny, sour-faced man in his late fifties, utterly devoid of warmth or any grasp of man management. He had recently joined the yacht after the owner of his previous vessel died. That particular yacht had a notorious reputation, largely because its owner had a rather questionable penchant.

"He'd fuck the crack of dawn if he could get up early enough," was the crew's general consensus. "He'll shag anything with two legs – or sometimes four." It was also rumoured he often tried it on with the crew, especially the officers.

Tom loved to imagine Thrush's tenure on that yacht. "I bet his arsehole looked like it'd gone through a bloody mincing machine by the time he left!" he'd joke. "I can see it now – the owner making him show up at his cabin every morning, trousers neatly folded over his forearm, ready to assume the position."

Thrush had no enthusiasm or passion for anything beyond belittling people or being a general arsehole. He was nothing more than a cold-hearted businessman.

Captains on mega-yachts can earn an absolute fortune. The bigger the yacht, the higher the salary, with most captains pulling in between £5,000 and £15,000 a month, tax-free, alongside expenses. Charter yacht captains often enjoy additional perks, such as tips from guests – anywhere from five to twenty percent of the total charter bill, which typically runs around $200,000 a week. Crew members also receive tips, usually tax-free, but the distribution depends on the captain's discretion.

THE CREW

A good captain divides tips equally among the crew. However, some take a larger share for themselves, as they're often the only ones who see the final bill. Thrush was one of those captains.

He also controlled the accounting, deciding what came in and what went out. Depending on the yacht, captains often arrange for food, fuel, and other supplies from their own contacts, earning kickbacks of five to ten percent. Unsurprisingly, when I asked to stay informed about expenses, I was bluntly told to fuck off. Thrush was clearly on the take and had no intention of sharing.

The crew despised him, and this often made my job difficult. Thrush was romantically entangled with Olga, a Polish stewardess who was equally disliked. She acted as his eyes and ears when he wasn't around. If a conversation stopped abruptly when she entered the room, you could be sure whatever was said would reach the Captain.

The rumour was that he'd met Olga on an "Eastern European brides" website. She pampered him excessively, calling him "Puppy" – much to the crew's amusement.

Chapter 2
White Suits and Black Money

One thing you can guarantee about anyone hiring a mega-yacht for a charter is they're stinking rich. We're not just talking people with a couple of million in the bank; we're talking people with a couple of hundred million or even a few billion. You often find that many of them are crooks in some way, shape, or form. Sure, there are the legitimate businessmen and showbiz personalities, but some come from pretty dubious backgrounds.

For the next charter, we picked up a bunch of Russians and Japanese in the port of Nice. The crew had just spent the past twenty-four hours working their arses off to get the yacht in pristine condition to create the right impression. This included washing, sponging, and leathering the entire exterior by hand. Then, they had to wash and treat the wooden decks, polish the stainless steel, and scrub the white speedboats. If they'd just finished it, and it rained that awful red sandy rain from the Sahara, they'd have to do it all over again. It was a ball-ache of a job!

We'd just changed into fresh uniforms and were standing by the passerelle – yacht jargon for the gangplank – waiting for the guests to arrive. It was a beautiful sunny day, and Jock already had a sweepstake going on what tip we'd get at the end of the charter.

Zecky, the Chief Stewardess, is gorgeous and great fun. She's 'one of the lads,' a head-banger in her time off but very professional when she needs to be. She's partied around the world and has become a legend. She got into yachting, thinking the sea air would sort her head out after years of clubbing… bless her.

Zecky radios from the hired limo, saying she'd met the guests at the airport and they'd be with us in ten minutes.

'Oh, and by the way, they're not what you were expecting.'

'What do you mean?' I ask, intrigued.

THE CREW

'You'll see, but there's some eye candy for you boys.'

Two sleek black limos edge around the corner and slowly pull up to the yacht. The doors open, and huge bodyguards in designer suits and shades climb out. They give the area a quick 360-degree scan before leaning back into the car to give the all-clear.

The crew watches silently, holding their breath, waiting to see who it is that needs this sort of security. We've been told no cameras are allowed onboard – clearly, whoever it is doesn't want any evidence of them being here with the other guests.

First, a shiny, high-heeled shoe steps out. Then, a beautifully toned and waxed leg appears, followed by another from a second limo. Two stunning women stride towards the yacht. One's a blonde with blue eyes, like a taller, classier Pamela Anderson. The other's a black Latina with wavy jet-black hair, long legs, and that South American sexiness you just can't put into words. Both are so beautiful they could bring traffic to a halt.

Robbie's mouth is wide open, like a goldfish at feeding time.

'Close your mouth, mate – you look like a gormless twat,' I say quietly.

'Ha! Sorry, mate, it's just...' Rob mutters, jumping back into work mode.

'I know, I know. Give your marks out of ten, then – what would you give them?'

'Marks out of ten? I'd give 'em one!' Rob grins.

'I guess I walked into that one. Seriously though, what do you reckon?'

'Well, put it this way, boss. I'd crawl ten thousand miles through scorching desert, along a winding pathway, over broken glass, naked, just so I could put matchsticks in her shit!' he whispers.

I find this hilarious and have to control myself at the worst possible moment. However, the thing with me is that I just can't help my eyes – they've got a nasty habit of dropping me in the shit every time.

The two girls walk up to the yacht, and I greet them with a warm handshake. The blonde leans forward, and she smells divine. She kisses me on each cheek.

'I'm very pleased to meet you,' she says in an Eastern European accent, giving me a cheeky wink.

Next, the dark-haired girl struts towards me with that supermodel walk they use on the catwalk. I've no idea how they make their hips move like that, but it's a delight to see. She plants two kisses on my cheeks, but instead of moving on, she stops for a chat.

She gives me a polite two-handed shake, standing so close that if she gets any nearer, I'll end up needing a condom. She chats away in a husky Brazilian accent, her huge chocolate-brown eyes locked on mine while stroking my forearm. Then it happens.

'Oh fuck! No fucking way... not now!' I scream silently to myself. I'm getting an erection – she's just my type, and there's nothing I can do about it. Consciously, I want her to stop stroking my arm, but subconsciously, I'm thinking, 'Let's get naked.'

I'm trying to concentrate on what she's saying while thinking about dead puppies nailed to trees to stem the blood flow to my groin. But let's face it, chaps – men can't do two things at once at the best of times, let alone with a boner. You know what they say: when there's a boil-up in the loins, there's a freeze-up in the brain.

She eventually moves on, but to my horror, the main guest – who we came to refer to as 'Mr Big' – is now standing right behind her.

In all the excitement, I hadn't noticed him approach. I'm flustered and still sporting a not-so-discreet hard-on as he greets me with a handshake.

'I'd gladly sell my soul to the Devil right now if I could only stop what's happening in my pants,' I think.

Mr Big is dressed in a pristine white suit, puffing on a huge cigar, and dripping in enough gold to put Mr T to shame – a proper vulgar display of wealth. He nods a pleasantry and walks on by.

THE CREW

'Thank God for small mercies,' I think. That's three guests down and about half a dozen to go.

Just as I think I'll get away with it, the last bodyguard takes forever to walk up the passerelle. My bulge is only getting worse. He finally stops in front of me, bends to put his briefcase down, and clocks the bulge in my pants. For a moment, he stays there, my boner inches from his face.

I'm silently screaming 'DEAD PUPPIES!' but it's no use. He stands up slowly, removes his shades, and gives me a steely stare before asking sternly to be taken to the ship's safe.

My beetroot-red face says it all. 'Escort this gentleman to the Captain's cabin, please,' I say firmly, trying to maintain my professionalism.

'If you'd like to follow me, sir,' says Jock, ushering him away.

As soon as they're out of sight, I bolt for the toilet, walking hunched over for obvious reasons. Just as I reach the corner, the blonde appears out of nowhere.

'You help me, please?' she asks, pointing to the suitcases by the steps.

With no one else around, I grab two suitcases and follow her. When we reach the stairs, she turns around, her eyes locking onto my crotch. A grin spreads across her face.

'Fuck! That's two guests and Jock who've noticed it,' I think.

Finally, I hand over the suitcases, dash into the toilet, and close the door behind me. Dropping to my knees, I shove my fist into my mouth and let out an almighty 'Ahhhhhhhhhhhhhh!' of pure embarrassment.

* * * *

It turns out the guy in the white suit has brought about $450,000 in cash on board with him. It doesn't take a genius to figure out this is more than likely 'black' money, and the Captain would soon be rubbing his hands at the sight of it. It's not unusual in this game for this sort of thing to happen. These people usually have a complete disregard for money—it runs through their hands like sand. Once they're settled aboard, the guests give directions to start the engines and head for St Tropez, where they want to anchor off the beach until morning.

St Tropez is the destination of the rich, famous, and those who 'want to be looked at.' In summer, dozens of gleaming white mega-yachts are moored in the harbour or anchored off the beach. There's a real party atmosphere—it's a hotspot for celebrities, partygoers, wannabes, and fashion junkies. Cafés and bars line the bustling beach. One of the most famous of these is Club 55, where you can practically smell the money.

People go mad for cash around here, but I've still got my feet firmly on the ground. As far as I'm concerned, all I want is enough to enjoy a few simple pleasures. I learned a long time ago that money alone won't make you happy. I've stacked shelves in supermarkets, earning about £100 a week when things were rough. I've also had one of the top ten jobs in the world, earning fantastic tax-free cash on private yachts. After some serious soul-searching, I've realised that my overall happiness isn't directly proportional to the amount of money in my account.

When I was in my twenties, growing up and trying to figure out the world, I believed money was all you needed to be happy. Now that I've experienced both ends of the spectrum, I know that's complete and utter bullshit. I've worked with and known billionaires who were depressed because they had nothing left to strive for. They're like caged wild animals—trapped, with everything they need handed to them on a silver platter. Over time, the fire leaves their eyes, and their souls begin to wither. Many of the seriously rich I've met fall into the trap of sex and drugs to escape the tedium of life. It's a classic case of escapism.

I once had a chat with the owner of the yacht about his life and how money had changed him. The man is worth about £800 million. After getting to know him well, I asked if money had changed him negatively as well as positively. He lit a cigarette, took a deep drag, looked me straight in the eye, and said:

THE CREW

'More than you'll ever know, mate.'

'Why's that, sir?' I asked.

'If you're chasing money just to make yourself happy, you've lost the plot. Sometimes, it's a fucking menace. Every day, I have problems trying to figure out people's intentions and whether they're fleecing me. I'm always on guard, and I find it very difficult to trust anyone. My life's actually become more stressful because of money. You end up mixing with people constantly trying to outdo each other—it gets really petty. I'm hassled all day long.

'A few years back, before I got really wealthy, all I wanted was to make a million pounds. After a couple of years, I made that. Then it was ten million, then fifty million. I call it the Del Boy Effect. Do you remember the end of that TV comedy *Only Fools and Horses*?'

'I think so, but remind me.'

'Del Boy had spent his life wheeling and dealing, always saying, "Rodney, this time next year we'll be millionaires!"'

'Oh yeah, I remember.'

'When he finally got the money, he didn't know what to do with it. Next thing you know, he's telling Rodney, "This time next year we'll be billionaires."'

'So, where does it end? What's the secret to happiness?'

'The key to happiness is finding pleasure in life's simple things. Discover the exotic in the everyday, and you won't go far wrong.'

'Like what?'

'I don't know—the smell of a flower, a setting sun, the wind in your hair, the sound of the ocean, or the smile of your girlfriend. It's about living in the moment and having the freedom to bring as much variety into your life as possible.

'I watched a film once—*American Beauty*. It had this brilliant explanation about what we're talking about. It basically said you should have fantasies, but make sure they're impossible to attain.

Because the day you get what you've been fantasising about, you won't want it anymore. It's not the fantasy itself that excites you—it's the fantasy of the fantasy.

'Your desire makes you long for something crazy, but we're only truly happy when we're daydreaming about future happiness. It's sick but true. Remember: the hunt is much sweeter than the kill, so be careful what you wish for. Appreciate every second of your life and don't chase fool's gold.'

I ponder this for a moment before replying, 'Does that mean I can have your cash then, boss?' I say, joking.

'Fuck off! The wife would kill me! I'm not kidding—lost my bank card the other day and seriously considered not reporting it.'

'Why's that?' I ask, confused.

'Because whoever finds it will probably spend less than my wife!'

We shared a laugh, but I pressed him further.

'What does it all mean then?'

'Think of it like this: happiness can be imagined as your hand in front of you. Like the five digits on your hand, you need five things for complete happiness. Sure, you can do without a finger or thumb, but your hand won't be 100% healthy—just like your life. For me, the five "musts" are health, wealth, variety, companionship, and peace of mind. Have all of these, and you'll have happiness. Think about each one and imagine what life would be like without them.'

'Fairly crap, I'd say.'

'Well put, mate. Enduring both good and bad times in equal measures is a sure way to find that elusive thing called happiness. Just like the tides, happiness and pain go in and out. There's no good without bad. The hardest thing in the world is not so much getting what you want, but appreciating what you've got when you've got it! They really are vitamins and minerals for the soul. Whatever you remember from what people tell you, promise me you'll remember that.'

'Yeah, OK. It seems like valuable advice to me.'

'Believe me, if you listen to what I've just told you, your soul will be richer than any bank account that I have.'

* * * *

The yacht is just out of the port of Nice, en route to St Tropez, and the two stunners are on the sun deck, rubbing baby oil into their surgically enhanced bodies. They're sitting on the side of the Jacuzzi when I escort Mr Big to join them. He's dressed in nothing but very tight white Speedos, and I'm thinking if he sneezes, he'll cut himself clean in two.

'Can I get you anything?' asks Zecky.

'Three bottles of Cristal,' he replies. His eyes are firmly planted on the girls as they beckon him over.

'Will that be all, sir?' I ask.

'Yes, for now,' he answers in a thick Russian accent. Ten minutes later, Zecky joins me in the crew lounge and tells me that all three of them are at it like rabbits. I look at her with a grin like the Cheshire Cat.

'What, all three of them?!'

'Yeah, I couldn't fucking believe it. Ménage à trois, I believe it's called.'

'What happened, then?' I ask, barely able to control my curiosity.

'Well, I went down to the fridge to get him the champagne and some strawberries, and when I came back, our friend Vladimir is shagging the blonde in the Jacuzzi and snogging the other. They're getting passed around like peace pipes!'

Jock seizes this opportunity to fire into me. 'You aren't going to get another boner, are you, mate?'

Tact and diplomacy weren't Jock's strong points. 'Let's never talk about this again, Jock,' I tell him, joking. 'Go on, Zecky, carry on. I'm bloody dying here.'

'Well, I walked up on the sun deck and caught them at it, and I didn't know where to put myself.'

'Didn't you join in, Zecky?' Jock shouts over. 'Thought you might be into gangbangs. Who wouldn't want to be the meat in that sandwich?'

'For fuck's sake, Jock!' I say, apologising for him.

'Second thoughts. I know you've got a packet of condoms with my name on it, darling,' says Jock, beaming and stroking her shoulder.

'What, Durex Extra Small?' Zecky fires back.

Jock does this every time Zecky is around. It's all good-natured banter on his part, but Zecky puts him down every time with a witty comment. Jock seems to love it, though.

Zecky continues her story. 'Anyway, I put the tray down where the dark girl is pointing on the table, right next to them. Then she looks sideways at me and gives me a wink. All this happens, and he's still shagging the other. They all knew I was there, but none of them gave a shit!'

'Some people, eh?' says Jock.

'Bloody hell, this is going to be an eventful charter,' I say.

Jock slips away, and I take a stroll up to the wheelhouse to tell the Captain that everything is in order. Thankfully, he doesn't know about the explosion in my pants earlier on the passerelle. Well, not yet, he doesn't, anyway.

'Have you seen Jock anywhere?' I ask him.

'I'm far too busy up here to keep an eye on your crew,' he shrugs.

I turn around and walk away from the spineless goon. I haven't really got the energy for another argument with him at the moment. I head down to the Jacuzzi pump room, where the heating and lighting are controlled, because I want to check everything is perfect for the guests. Not that the Jacuzzi needs heating up, considering the action that is going on up there at the moment. As I walk in, I can't believe my eyes. Jock is sat down in a chair with his back to me. He's looking through the underwater Jacuzzi window at the rampant trio getting up to mischief, and he's having a wank.

'For fuck's sake, put it away, you dirty bastard,' I say, putting my hand over my eyes and turning away.

'Just give me a minute, mate,' he gasps urgently.

'What?'

'When am I ever going to get another opportunity like this without having to pay for it?' he says, looking over his shoulder and laughing. Jock really is one crazy fucker!

Chapter 3
Bleary Eyed and Battered

The next morning, the yacht is anchored a few hundred metres off the beach at St Tropez. The guests had an almighty party last night – pretty normal for the first night of a charter. Whoever is on deck-cleaning duty gets up a couple of hours before the guests surface from their slumber and makes sure the exterior guest areas are cleared and cleaned. This means scrubbing the decks, polishing the stainless steel, rearranging or washing the cushions, and uncovering the seats.

Tom and Robbie get up at 5.30am, a little earlier than usual, because they don't really know what they might find. They sort out the barbecue deck first. This is the area where the guests usually congregate because it's the most comfortable and offers easy access to the bar and lounge. They can also watch the huge plasma TV screen there. The crew always makes sure to approach this area with extreme caution in the morning. A couple of times, they've found half-naked guests curled up on the sofa after a heavy night, or they've walked in on a guest snorting coke off the coffee table. It can be embarrassing for all concerned. We certainly don't condone the guests taking drugs, but we don't pretend that it doesn't happen. You can't really tell a guest who has paid around $250,000 for a charter that he can't snort a line of coke or smoke a spliff if he wants to. At the end of the day, money talks, and theoretically speaking, these guests are treated like a 500kg gorilla – they do what they want.

The clean-up doesn't take too long, and the place is shipshape after a couple of hours. The worst they find is a little bit of vomit on the sunbed. It's no big deal in the whole scheme of things. All they do is bite their tongues, hold their noses, and think of the tip.

We're still trying to figure out who these guys and girls are. I usually run the guests' names through Google, but I get nothing this time. I also ask around the yachting fraternity if anyone knows anything, but again, come up with nothing. One thing is for sure, though: whoever the main man is, he is off the map and untraceable. He's probably a drug lord or a Russian gang boss, or something along those lines.

The guests finally start to wander out onto the sun patio around midday, and amazingly, their breakfast consists of ice-cold vodka and lines of coke. All of them are at it, with the exception of the bodyguards. I heard somewhere that "the road to excess leads to the palace of wisdom." If that's the case, then this bunch must be fucking Einsteins!

I tell the boys to make themselves scarce and stand down on the lower deck, but to make sure they keep an eye and an ear on what's going on. Tom tells me that the guests want to go jet skiing this morning, so I take out the lazarette. I tell Tom about the Jacuzzi incident last night, and he has a good chuckle.

"What are they doing now?" Tom asks.

"Snorting coke and necking vodka shots."

"They haven't even had breakfast yet!"

"That is their breakfast, mate."

"Pretty hardcore bunch, eh?"

"And then some," I tell him, raising my eyebrows. "I think we're going to have our hands full this charter, so I'd keep on your toes, mate."

"So have you discovered anything about this lot then?" Robbie asks me.

"Yes, I caught one of the bodyguards checking himself out and flexing his muscles in the mirror last night."

"You're kidding? Me too! The one with the swallow tattoo on the side of his neck?" says Robbie, looking surprised.

"Yeah."

"I caught him talking to himself while he was combing his hair on the sun deck."

"What was he saying?"

"He was combing his hair while looking at himself in his pocket mirror and saying 'very nice' or something like it."

"Hey Rob, he's so vain, I bet he shouts his own name when he comes!"

"Probably," Rob says, joining in the laughter.

"I've got a feeling they'll want to go on the jet skis to wake up, so we'd better get them in the water and check the engines. Hopefully they'll be OK, but I'll have to give them a safety demonstration on how to handle them."

"Rather you than me, mate. Calming down a bunch of coked-up, bleary-eyed and battered Russian gangsters who only speak pigeon English isn't going to be child's play!"

It's the same story every time the male guests get on these powerful machines. They forget everything they've just been told, and within seconds of putting their fingers on the throttle, they're out of control or going way too fast. It's a mixture of the male ego, excitement, testosterone surges… or a shitload of coke. The machines have 1300cc engines, and they accelerate like missiles. It's the same-sized engine as a small car, but they weigh next to nothing. They're lethal in the wrong hands, and even in the right hands, if you push the envelope of safety.

I get the machines in the water, and Mr Big spots them from the barbecue deck. The next thing, he's running down the outside steps with the South American hooker in tow. He jogs up to me, reeking of booze, and his pupils are huge and black.

'We go now!' he says, jabbing his finger at the jet ski.

'Certainly, sir, but first, I must give you a very quick safety brief,' I say. It falls on deaf ears.

'No… no… we go now. I know, I know!' he says impatiently.

I'm thinking I should've placed a bet on this happening. I've been here before, though. It's my neck on the line if I let him go, and there's an accident, or worse, he kills himself. In his state, it's very likely. I take his arm and tell him, as politely as possible, that I don't want anything to happen to his precious girlfriend, so I must give him the brief. I can't tell from his eyes if he understands what I'm saying or if he's about to shoot me, because his eyes have no soul.

They both follow me back up to the barbecue deck, and I grab the lifejackets on the way up. All the guests are out, and the music is pretty loud. The bodyguards are just changing into their swimming shorts to accompany their boss, and the other hooker is making out with one of Mr Big's entourage. I apologise and turn down the music so I can be heard. Robbie is standing next to me, trying his best to model the life jacket like an air stewardess.

'Excuse me, please. Sorry to disturb you. If I could just take a few moments of your time,' I say to them. 'We've got the jet skis out as you requested, and they're ready for you. They're very powerful, and there are a few local laws around this beach you must obey, so I'll just quickly explain them to you.'

The hooker is still making out with the guy, eagerly watched by Robbie, and I don't think any of them are paying attention or understand any more than ten per cent of what I'm saying. I'm about a minute into my speech, pointing out the safety features of the lifejacket, when I notice that Mr Big and the girl have vanished. I turn to Robbie and quietly ask where the other two are, but he's got his blinkers on.

'Robbie!' I say, a little louder to wake him from his dirty daydream.

I'm still met with silence.

'Robbie, where are the other two guests?'

'Oh sorry… what other two?' he says, turning towards me, startled.

'The other two!' I shout urgently.

Robbie is barely through his 'but they were here a minute ago' speech when there is a roar, and the jet ski speeds away from the yacht with Mr Big and the girl on the back. She's holding on for dear life. Everyone stops what they are doing to watch. They start giving Mr Big further encouragement by yelling and whistling. Mr Big loves it, and he's flying around like a man possessed. He's doing doughnuts, zigzagging and circling the yacht at speed. She's laughing hysterically and holding on to his hairy pot belly. Robbie and I look at each other, and we can see that carrying on would be futile, so we just leave them to it and hope for the best.

'Well, that went well, don't you think, Rob?' I say sarcastically.

'I don't think they understood a word.'

'Yeah, I know. It doesn't help that they're coked off their tits. You'd better get the boat in the water as a safety measure.'

'Right, mate. I'll be on the radio,' says Rob.

I walk up to the bridge to grab a pair of binoculars so I can see where they're heading. As I open the door, the Captain has already heard the commotion and has beaten me to them. The jet ski is flying along only a few metres from the beach, running parallel to it at full speed. This is really dangerous because of swimmers and children, not to mention the noise it makes. Bad news all round!

'Didn't you tell him about keeping his distance?' says Thrush.

'I tried, but he vanished before I could finish,' I say innocently.

'So, you didn't finish the safety brief,' he says in a condescending way.

I can tell by the tone of his voice that Thrush is in one of his moods again. There's a saying that you have to kiss a little arse before you can kick it, but unfortunately, I'm not made that way. I hold back the impulse to grab the scissors off the chart table and drive them through the back of his head. This kind of thing really annoys me about this prick: he makes out that he's the blue-eyed boy and never makes any mistakes, but in reality, he's the most incompetent, mealymouthed, passionless dickhead I've ever had the misfortune to meet.

I take a deep breath and slowly let it out to help me stay calm, but I can feel my fist tightening uncontrollably. I nearly call him 'Thrush' out of habit, but I remember just in time.

THE CREW

'Listen, Captain, when we first arrived on deck this morning, they started snorting coke and drinking vodka shots virtually immediately. I don't even think they've sobered up from last night.'

'If he crashes the jet ski or hurts anyone, I will hold you fully responsible,' Thrush tells me.

'Now hang on a minute. You told me, and I quote, "Give them anything they want at any time. They are paying a lot of money for this charter, so whatever they want, they get." Did you or did you not tell me that yesterday?' I say, losing my calm.

There is a short silence, then, still looking through his binoculars, Thrush just says, 'That will be all.'

I storm out of the door, and I need to vent my anger before I knock a wall down or something. I decide to take it out on the punchbag in the crew quarters. I imagine the bag is Thrush's ribs, and after five minutes of punching at an intensity that would put Mike Tyson to shame, I feel just about human again.

Jock's heard the noise and pops his head round the corner. 'Don't worry about the skipper, boss – he's not worth it. Everyone knows he's a prick!'

I turn around with red knuckles and face him. 'Oh… hi, mate, I'm just venting a bit of anger.'

'I do that all the time, boss.'

'I didn't know you came down here, Jock?' I say, a little puzzled.

'I don't. I've barely got enough energy to eat my dinner at the end of my day.'

'So how do you vent your anger then?'

'I've got a much better way,' Jock smiles.

'What?'

'Special coffee.'

'Eh?'

'Special coffee. He's always fucking telling me to go make him a coffee, so that's exactly what I go and do. It helps me in ways I can't explain. It's twice as good as wasting energy punching the shit out of that bloody thing.'

'I'm not with you, mate. How does making the old man a coffee make you feel better?'

'Because, my dear buddy, before I pour the coffee in the cup, I pull my foreskin back and rub the end of my dick around the rim of the cup.'

I look at him, unable to control my laughter. 'You sick fucker!'

'I prefer to make him frothy cappuccinos if I can persuade him to have one, because you can hide so much more in it.'

'Go on then,' I say, not sure if I really want to hear it.

The foam, for example. I can make the foam out of anything really. Spit, phlegm, spunk, or all three if he really pisses me off,' Jock explains with a poker face expression.

'Jock, for fuck's sake!' I feel I'm about to be sick.

However, it's so funny that I don't know what's worse – retching or laughing really hard. I find my composure after a minute or so, walk over and pat Jock on the shoulder.

'Jock, that's not the sort of behaviour I expect from my lads. But well done, that really is outstanding work, fella!'

Chapter 4
All That Glitters Is Not Gold

After the crew drop off the guests at the beach, they spend the rest of the day cleaning the boat from top to bottom. The yacht is washed with freshwater and dried with a leather rag. By late afternoon, she is gleaming in the setting sun.

Mr Big and his hooker make it back in one piece—wet but uninjured. She looks like a drowned rat, and I don't think she's all that happy with him. She probably spent an hour or so that morning applying makeup to her beautiful features and blow-drying her jet-black hair, so you can imagine she wasn't best pleased.

The interior staff spend most of the day cleaning and polishing the lounges and cabins, as well as hand-washing the guests' party clothes. All of us on the deck crew do feel for them sometimes. We get to work in the sunshine and fresh air, whereas the interior staff spend most of their time inside, apart from an hour or so at lunchtime. It must be tough for them, seeing the same walls every day while outside the weather is glorious. They also have to deal with guests when they return drunk, which isn't easy at the best of times.

The interior staff are all female, and as you can imagine, it can be a nightmare when they're menstruating at the same time. Robbie calls it 'mad cow syndrome.'

Tom once asked him why he doesn't trust women.

'You should never trust a species that bleeds for one week of every month and doesn't die!' he once told me. Interesting point!

The deck crew get to do the boys' stuff—taking guests wakeboarding, jet skiing, diving, and waterskiing—which is always good fun. They also stand on security patrol on the quayside in some of the classiest places on the planet, including the Bahamas, the Caribbean, the Amalfi Coast, the Greek islands, and the Italian and French Rivieras. I'd be lying if I said it doesn't feel fabulous when the yacht arrives at the quay to an audience of hundreds of spectators. You feel a bit like a film star.

If the yacht is only docked for one night, you can be sure that most of the deck crew will try to get passerelle duty so they can watch the world go by on the quayside. It's been known to be good for pulling girls—they can't help but be impressed by all the bling and crisp, white uniforms.

* * * *

The crew receive a call from the guests at around eight o'clock, just as the sun is setting. The best time to be at the beaches around St Tropez is a couple of hours before sunset. The temperature cools down, the party atmosphere starts to heat up, and the beach bars blast out dance music. The beautiful people and the 'wannabe seen' crowd emerge from the woodwork to party and dance. The booze flows, the music pounds—and so does your head the following morning.

Ginger Spice, Victoria Beckham, and Robbie Williams have all been spotted here, among other stars. From what the crew hear, Robbie is a great guy and a lot of fun—the kind of celebrity they enjoy looking after. They like people who are up for a good time but aren't full of themselves with delusions of grandeur. Having money doesn't make someone a better person; it just means they have more in their bank account. Some celebrities, however, believe their own bullshit, and they are a real pain in the arse.

I once heard a story about a charter on another yacht where a very famous American pop singer came on board and demanded that the yacht's freshwater tanks be emptied and refilled with bottled Evian mineral water. That's tonnes and tonnes of water, for fuck's sake! She also insisted that the carpet leading to her stateroom be ripped up and replaced with red carpet. Apparently, she even wanted candles placed all the way from her stateroom, across the deck, and onto the quay. When the captain informed the yacht's owner, who was at home in Monaco, he refused point-blank. He told her to vacate his beautiful yacht immediately and never return.

THE CREW

Life is too short to entertain these divas, but many do—for the money. Plenty of yachts will do anything their guests demand, no matter how ludicrous. This is never more apparent than in St Tropez during silly season or at Cannes during the Film Festival. One year, we worked on a well-known charter yacht moored on the quay at Cannes. All the large, ludicrously oversized yachts were there, and celebrities commuted back and forth between them.

Dozens of parties took place on the yachts, with all the major players in the film industry strutting their stuff. One story that has made the rounds in the yachting world concerns a yacht owned by a beer company, which hosted a party for the rich and famous in Cannes. Naturally, these yachts are furnished with incredibly expensive and luxurious interiors, so guests are typically expected to obey certain house rules—such as no smoking inside.

This particular yacht had a 'No Smoking' sign posted at its entrance on the quay. The staff also reminded all those boarding—including many Hollywood elites—of the rule. The story goes that a stewardess offered a very famous actor a glass of champagne. When he turned around, he had a cigarette hanging from his mouth, the ash about to drop onto the carpet. He looked high as a kite on something (allegedly). The stewardess gently and tactfully reminded him that smoking wasn't allowed on board.

The actor, as the story goes, looked her up and down before replying sarcastically, 'Where am I supposed to go?'

'You're welcome to smoke at the entrance in the foyer, sir,' she replied.

Allegedly, he then took a deep drag of his cigarette, blew the smoke slowly into her face, and said, 'Do you know what? I don't think I will,' before turning his back on her and continuing his conversation as if she didn't exist.

Another well-known tale concerns a famous model and her notorious tantrums. It's said that she was offered a glass of champagne and, after taking a sip, spat it out and threw the glass down. She then furiously berated the stewardess, complaining that the champagne wasn't Cristal.

But for every diva and egotistical actor, there are famous people who are seemingly lovely. Cuba Gooding Jr, Brad Pitt, Angelina Jolie, David Coulthard, Kevin Spacey, and Cameron Diaz are just a few who are known to be genuinely down-to-earth. From what the crew have seen and heard, they are respectful, easygoing people who, despite their millions, remain grounded. I take my hat off to them.

If anyone asked us to name the most interesting celebrity we've encountered, we'd probably say Quentin Tarantino. We saw him at the Cannes Film Festival one year while working at a party he attended. There are many ways to describe the man, but 'mad wizard' sums him up perfectly—and we don't mean that in a bad way. At first, he comes across as fairly quiet, but get him to a party and give him a few drinks, and he transforms into an energy whirlwind, bursting with incredible ideas as if they're being fed to him from a higher source. It's mesmerising to watch—his creative mind just explodes in front of you. Jock always says he'd love to hypnotise him and figure out what makes him tick. Then again, maybe the world isn't ready for that yet…

Other entertaining personalities include Eddie Irvine, the former Ferrari Grand Prix driver, and the family of the Sultan of Brunei. Eddie was a legendary playboy. The pressure to perform at Ferrari must have been immense, yet he still managed to embrace the high life of fast cars, beautiful women, and endless cash. His yacht used to moor right next to the circuit during the Monaco Grand Prix. There were much bigger and flashier yachts in the harbour, but the press and public flocked to his like seagulls around a fishing trawler, hoping to catch a glimpse of something exciting.

He lived the dream—high-speed racing, luxury, and fame. Let's be honest: you have to respect the guy. He was under incredible pressure, yet he still found time to enjoy life. Not many people could have handled it!

THE CREW

As for the Sultan of Brunei, the story goes that either he or his brother owned two yachts, aptly named *Tits 1* and *Tits 2*... and that's all that needs to be said about that.

When the average person meets a celebrity or someone of status, they often become star-struck and fall to pieces. Sometimes, this can be highly entertaining. Jock once heard a story about a deckhand working on a yacht when the Duke of Edinburgh was a guest aboard. The deckhand was kneeling down, polishing some brasswork on deck, when the Duke suddenly popped his head around the corner. Looking up, he found himself face-to-face with the formidable Duke.

'Good morning, young man. What are you up to there?' the Duke enquired.

Startled and completely in awe, the deckhand leapt to his feet—only to hit his head on the heavy stainless-steel bell above him. He struck it with such force that the bell rang loudly, cutting his head in the process. In his dazed state, he completely lost the plot—curtsying to the Duke while clutching his bleeding head, followed by an impromptu tap dance, presumably due to the pain.

Then, realising with horror that only women curtsy, he panicked and attempted to correct himself—this time giving the Duke a deep Japanese-style bow while apologising profusely and addressing him, incorrectly, as 'Your Lordship'.

To make matters worse, he then seized the Duke's hand and shook it vigorously—using his bloodied right hand. Not a great day at the office. The Duke, apparently, gave him a look that said a million words and muttered something under his breath. For the rest of the cruise, whenever their eyes met, the Duke gave him a look of sheer despair.

One common illusion about people with vast wealth is that whatever they say must be correct simply because they are rich. Another is that they must be more intelligent than the average person. This couldn't be further from the truth. I've lost count of the number of times crew members have been asked the most outrageously stupid questions.

I was once asked by a female guest whether the stairs on the yacht went up or down. Another asked, in all seriousness, 'How long is the power cable from the mains on land to the boat to keep the lights on at night?' We were a few hundred miles out to sea at the time—she had clearly never heard of onboard generators.

On one transatlantic voyage, another guest enquired, 'Excuse me, what time does the helicopter come to take you all home at night?' The poor woman had no idea that the crew lived and slept aboard for months at a time. One of the Australian crew decided to play along, replying that he had to bring an extra-large packed lunch every day to sustain him on the journey back to Australia each night. Cheeky bugger!

Jock was once asked by an elderly lady about an island a few miles ahead of the yacht: 'Young man, how do you keep track of where all the islands are when they're floating around all the time?' The same woman later dropped her expensive watch overboard and demanded that he dive down and retrieve it. He politely pointed out that the water was several hundred feet deep. Undeterred, she insisted that a fit young man like him should be able to hold his breath long enough to fetch it. These people are not of this planet!

A guest once informed the Captain that they no longer wanted to spend three weeks sailing from Monaco to St Tropez (France), then to Marbella (southern Spain), on to Croatia (the Adriatic), and back to Monaco.

'OK, madam, where would you like to go instead?' he asked politely, despite having spent the best part of a week organising the trip.

'Oh, we still want to go to all those places,' she replied, 'but I'd like to do it in four days instead of three weeks.'

This was, of course, impossible—the total distance was a few thousand miles, and the yacht's top speed was only 14 miles per hour.

I am frequently amazed that some of the rich and famous can run a bloody bath, never mind their lives or a money-making business. It's utterly baffling that society continues to idolise these people simply because they appear in films, on TV, or have inherited wealth. To be fair, most of the crew can see the irony. Have we lost our minds?

There's a saying that familiarity breeds contempt, and sometimes, it's true. Perhaps the crew have simply heard too many absurd stories over the years. That said, they're not all like that—many of our guests are intelligent, successful, and perfectly reasonable.

Chapter 5
Muddy Geysers

It is seven o'clock in the morning, and the yacht is moored alongside the quay in St Tropez. The guests are still asleep in their cosy bunks, recovering from another late night. Despite this, the decks remain immaculately clean—once the yacht was moored, the guests went clubbing ashore and partied the night away, meaning they weren't on board to make a mess.

The crew are making their way to the crew room on the lower deck for breakfast, all except the watchman and the stewardess, who had to stay up until the guests returned. Jock is in high spirits and still trying to worm his way into Zecky's affections.

"Morning, sexy! You know what, Zecks? If I saw you naked, darling, I'd die happy," he says with a cheeky grin.

Zecky gives him a look of pity. "Well, if I saw you naked, Jock, I'd die laughing."

"Easy, sweetie. Stop playing hard to get," Jock replies dryly.

"I don't want to shatter your illusions, sunshine, but if you and that flea-bitten old mongrel on the quay were the last two living creatures on Earth, I'd be over there trying to shag Fido."

"I love it when you talk dirty—it makes me want you even more, you saucy minx."

"Want all you like, sunshine, because you're not getting it." Zecky really was the queen of put-downs.

Jock starts making his breakfast, cracking a couple of eggs into a sealed plastic container before popping it into the microwave. Two minutes later, they explode, splattering the entire interior.

"For fuck's sake! How many times have I told you to prick the yolks and cook them on low power? I must have told you a million times already!" Zecky yells at him. She looks at me and raises her eyebrows.

THE CREW

I can't help but chuckle at his culinary incompetence—I mean, how difficult can it be to cook a fucking egg?

"Honestly, on average, fifty million sperm are released at conception, and I can't believe he was the quickest," Zecky says, pointing at Jock.

Jock looks up and frowns. "What's that supposed to mean?" he asks, looking hurt.

"It means if your brains were dynamite, you couldn't blow your fucking nose," she says sharply. "Now go and sit down."

Jock doesn't argue. Feeling suitably chastised, he does as he's told. "I was going to clean it up, you know," he mutters under his breath.

"I've seen your tidying up—it'll be quicker if I do it."

He winks at me from across the room. "She's a right feisty one, our Zecks." He loves the ear-bashings she gives him; I think it makes him feel wanted.

The rest of the boys arrive, making toast and discussing their jobs for the morning. Meanwhile, Tom and Robbie are deep in debate over which of last night's hookers had the best tits and who was filthier in bed.

"It's no contest, Robbie. You can tell by the look in her eye and the way she walks that the blonde could suck a golf ball through fifty metres of hosepipe. That girl is just one hundred per cent sex. How does the dark-haired one beat that?"

Robbie puts his knife down, finishes chewing his toast, then leans forward, looking Tom directly in the eye. "Because, Tom, my dear boy, once you try black, you never go back."

"What?"

"Black women are genetically blessed by the hands of God—it's as simple as that."

"Explain," says Tom, intrigued.

Everyone is now listening intently.

"All right, think about it. Take Naomi Campbell, for example. She is physically built for pleasure. Her ivory-white eyes contrast effortlessly with her dark ebony skin. She has those big, full lips that you'll only ever see naturally on a black girl—unless they're surgically enhanced. Just imagine what they could be used for…"

"That's it?" Tom interrupts.

"I've not even started yet. Then there's the muscle tone and the high, pert bums, not to mention the natural dancing rhythm that white girls can only dream about. All in all, it's just a much more attractive physical package—that's all I'm saying."

Robbie leans back, takes another bite of his toast, and looks satisfied, convinced he's proven his point.

"He paints quite a picture, doesn't he, mate?" I say to Tom.

"Whatever," Tom responds, feeling dejected.

I'm just about to go into detail about the morning jobs when Thrush walks in. There are no pleasantries and no light-hearted morning banter.

"My toilet's blocked. Get your lads to sort it out first thing," he demands.

The boys look startled at his rudeness, exchanging glances before rolling their eyes.

"OK," I say, forcing a smile.

I look up at Jock and give him a sly wink. "Could you make the Captain a coffee, please, Jock? Some of that new special brand you were telling me about?"

"Absolutely, no problem," he says, jumping up from his seat and disappearing with a spring in his step.

"Would you like to sit down, Captain? I'll take you through this morning's schedule," I offer.

"After my toilet, of course," Thrush replies sharply.

THE CREW

"Yes… after your toilet."

He sighs and glances at his watch as if it's an unbearable effort. "Yes, all right, I suppose I can spare you five minutes."

I'm pissed off but keep it hidden. Thrush will spend an hour on ship's business, then watch TV or surf the net for the rest of the day. I start explaining the rota and work routine when a strange noise comes from down the alleyway where the 'special coffee' is being made.

It sounds like the deep, throaty gurgle of a coffee machine.

"When did we get a coffee maker?" Tom asks Robbie.

"We didn't."

"Then what—?"

"Shhhh," Robbie says, kicking him under the table. He puts a finger to his lips and signals for Tom to keep quiet.

The noise grows louder, sounding like someone clearing their throat. Then there's silence, followed by the clanging of a toilet seat and a flush.

I try to focus on the work briefing, but my mind keeps drifting to what Jock might be doing to that coffee. "So, after that, we'll be testing the fire alarms, Captain," I say, struggling to concentrate.

A few minutes later, Jock returns, looking slightly flushed, and hands Thrush the coffee with a big smile. "There you go, Captain. Made you a special frothy coffee—pretty unique flavour, I think you'll find."

The Captain barely manages a quiet "thank you" before taking a large gulp.

Robbie, Tom, and I glance up at Jock, who is standing behind him, grinning. He points to his crotch and makes a crude hand gesture. Then he gestures to his backside, making a circular motion with his finger. Finally, he lifts both hands to his mouth, dangling a long thread of saliva from his lips like a shoelace.

The Captain, oblivious, takes another sip. I feel my stomach churn and cover my mouth, pretending to cough.

Thrush sets the cup down, his top lip coated in slimy, brown froth. I struggle to hide my revulsion as he peers at me over his glasses.

"You all right? You don't look well," he asks.

"Oh, just a bit of an upset stomach, Captain. It seems to be going around," I say, forcing myself not to gag.

"No doubt I'll be next," he mutters.

Jock, Tom, and Robbie get up to leave.

"There's nothing surer," Jock says, smirking as he walks out.

I wrap up with Thrush after about twenty minutes. Usually, I'd be quicker, but I want to make sure he finishes every last drop of that coffee.

Moral of the story: never piss off the people who make your food and drink—you never know what they might do to it.

* * * *

I meet the boys in Thrush's cabin to see what the problem is with his toilet. As I walk into his en-suite bathroom, Robbie is plunging away with all his might using a suction stick, but with little effect. Tom is holding the seat up with one hand and pinching his nose with the other.

"Jesus, what's been coming out of his arse—fucking bricks?! It's well and truly blocked, mate," Robbie tells Tom.

"Give it here, Rob. Let's get the job done and get the fuck out of here," replies Tom impatiently.

Tom starts plunging at the U-bend with renewed intensity, and after a couple of minutes, a loud gurgling noise suddenly comes from the pipe running along the wall to the toilet. Tom and Robbie, standing directly over the bowl, turn their heads and look at each other, their faces inches apart. The noise is moving quickly towards them, and whatever's coming is headed their way. They know it. I know it.

THE CREW

I spin around and leap out of the bathroom, just managing to escape while Rob and Tom scramble to follow. But in their panic, they wedge their shoulders in the narrow doorway, getting stuck. As they turn to each other in horror, their eyes instinctively shift towards the toilet—just as it belches out its contents with the force of a Yellowstone geyser.

I glance back, momentarily speechless. They stand there like scarecrows, their faces frozen in terror and disbelief. The walls, the ceiling—everything, including them—is covered in faeces, urine, used tampons, cotton wool, pubic hair, and God knows what else. It's in their hair, on their clothes, on their faces, dripping from the ends of their noses. They just stand there, silent.

Tom eyes Robbie in horror, no doubt wondering what he looks like himself. Robbie stares back, terror-stricken, his eyes welling up as if he's about to cry.

"KNOCK ME OUT!" he demands through gritted teeth.

"What?" Tom asks, bewildered.

"YOU... KNOCK... ME... OUT... NOW!" Robbie enunciates loudly, slowly, and deliberately.

He's barely using his mouth to speak, more from his throat, while making a punching motion with his hand.

"Why?" Tom asks, watching a dribble of dirty urine trickle down Robbie's nose.

"'CAUSE I THINK I'M GONNA LICK MY LIPS!"

I shouldn't have laughed, but I did—so hard that I couldn't breathe for what felt like a lifetime.

They spent the next hour in the shower, scrubbing themselves raw with a wooden brush and strong antiseptic, cursing Thrush with every insult under the sun. By the time they emerged for the passerelle watch, every inch of their exposed skin was red raw.

As they approach, I turn to Jock and say, "There's a funny smell around here."

Jock starts sniffing the air. "Yeah, can't quite place it."

"What do you reckon it is?"

"Dunno. Smells a bit fragrant to me… That's it—Eau de Toilet!"

"Fuck off, you two. My skin's so sore I can barely move," Robbie groans.

Tom is clearly suffering too, but he tries not to show it. Instead, he takes a swipe at Robbie to shift the focus.

"I don't know, Rob. You've got no big-match temperament for the dirty jobs," he teases.

"I just don't like starting my day covered in a layer of shit," Robbie snaps, losing his temper.

"All right, boys, calm down. I've got some good news that might put a smile back on your faces."

"What's that? You've won us both a skin graft?" Robbie grumbles.

"Well, the guests will be back for an hour or so today, then they're gone until tomorrow night. That means we can go for a few beers tonight—if you're up for it. First few are on me, all right?"

That afternoon, the guests return, quickly wash and change, then get picked up by a limo and whisked away to one of their associate's hillside villas overlooking St Tropez.

That's it for the day. The crew have a rare night off.

It's time to party!

Chapter 6
Gold Diggers

It's not very often that the crew get time off in the middle of a busy charter, so when they do, they grasp it with both hands. Just having a night off is good news in itself, but getting a Saturday night ashore in St Tropez during the summer is the icing on the cake. The boys are looking forward to a few hours of quality time with each other. They all get on well, but yachting is hard work, and the hours are long. Privacy on board is virtually nonexistent since they all share small cabins, so after a while, even the smallest things start to annoy them. Getting off the boat, out of uniform, and sinking a few cold beers—away from the arsehole of a captain—feels like heaven. Everyone can blow off steam and let their hair down, at least for a few hours.

The boys gather in my cabin early in the evening, and I open a bottle of tequila to set the mood. We're all dressed in our 'going ashore' gear, and Jock is wearing the most outrageously bright green shirt. He calls it his 'falling-down shirt' because he only ever wears it when he's planning to get drunk.

'Are you wearing that for a bet, Jock?' Tom asks cheekily.

Jock looks down at his shirt and strokes one of the sleeves.

'I'll have you know this cost me seventy quid, you cheeky bastard.'

'HOW MUCH?! Fucking hell, they saw you coming, mate. I wouldn't wipe my arse with that! You look like that green bird hand puppet.'

Robbie looks up from fastening his shoelaces. 'What... Orville?' he laughs.

'Yeah, that's him... Orville!'

'You're only jealous, you bunch of fucking losers! Anyway, grab your tequilas, boys!' Jock says, slapping Tom on the back.

We each take a drink to toast the evening—it's a bit of a tradition before we head out on a mad one. Raising our shot glasses, we chant:

'Here's to you, and here's to me,

The best of friends we'll always be,

But if by chance we disagree,

Then fuck YOU, and here's to ME!'

We knock back our shots, and Robbie quickly pours another round. The next tradition is that each of us states our aim for the night or shares our planned party tricks.

'Right, boys, your radical agendas for the night, please!' I shout.

Robbie goes first, adopting the voice of a loud US Marine Drill Sergeant. 'First, I'm going to stomp a few brain cells, followed by a howl-at-the-moon session, finished off with a game of "hunt the cunt"!'

'Excellent! Right, Tommo, what's yours?' I ask, clinking my glass against his.

'To get my kicks before the whole shithouse goes up in flames!' he says, doing his best Jim Morrison impression.

'OOOOOOOORRRRRRRAAAAAAAAA!' everyone screams, while Jock starts howling like a wolf.

'All right, Fido, cool your jets for a second,' I tell Tom, laughing.

'Your turn, Jock!' Robbie says, pointing his shot glass at him.

Jock puts on a news presenter's voice, using a wall poster of a naked woman as his 'map'.

'Intentions for tonight: to satisfy my primal instincts to the limit, with my trusty comrades beside me, creating absolute mayhem. I intend to empty my bollocks into anything remotely female, and wet patches can be expected specifically in the areas here… here… and here,' he says, pointing to various parts of the female anatomy on the poster.

'Beautifully put, Jock. OK, boys, let's finish the bottle and put the cat among the pigeons.'

THE CREW

We leave the cabin with a tequila glow. On our way to the passerelle, we pass Thrush, who's holding his stomach.

'We're just going ashore for a few hours, Captain. See you in the morning,' I say as we walk past.

'Well, don't be late. I might sleep in an hour longer, so if you don't see me at eight, you'll know why.'

We all stop momentarily before walking off the yacht.

'Something wrong?' I ask.

'I'm not feeling well—sickness and diarrhoea,' he groans, clutching his stomach.

'Drink plenty of fluids to replace the ones you've lost, Captain,' Jock says, unable to resist taking the piss.

'I'll make you plenty of coffee in the morning,' he adds with a smirk.

'Yes, OK,' Thrush replies wearily.

'See you in the morning,' I say as we walk down the passerelle. We can't help but snigger at Thrush's expense.

'Looks like your special coffee worked quicker than expected, mate,' Tom says to Jock.

'Oh, yeah. It's potent, and it was lovingly prepared!' Jock grins.

The quayside is bustling with tourists and locals admiring the yachts. It's a beautiful, balmy night, and the harbour front hums with chatter and music from the nearby bars and restaurants. As we step ashore, people gather around the passerelle, checking if any of us are famous. A group of young, tanned girls catch our eye—clearly not locals. I elbow Jock in the ribs.

'There you go, mate. Your first target—blonde, blue-eyed, and five-foot-five. Just your type.'

'Oh yeah... nice. Very nice.'

'Now, remember, Jock—softly, softly, catchee monkey. Put in the gentle spadework first. Don't scare them off like last time!'

'I didn't scare them off.'

'Yes, you fucking did! After a few beers, you forget you're not talking to the locals in Glasgow. You speak at a million miles an hour, and your volume goes through the roof.'

'Shit! Really? I didn't know I was doing that,' he says, scratching his head.

I make eye contact with one of the girls and beckon her over. They huddle for a moment before one steps forward.

'Hola!' she says, then asks me something in Spanish.

Jock looks confused because he doesn't speak anything but English (or, rather, Scottish).

'Does she come with subtitles, mate?' he asks me.

I explain to her that we only speak English—a fact I'm deeply embarrassed about—and she quickly slips into our native tongue.

'That is a very nice yacht,' she says in fairly good English.

'Thanks very much,' says Rob. 'We bought it between us a couple of days ago.'

We see the dollar signs light up in their eyes. They lead us into the nearest bar, and I order some drinks. The girl nearest Jock is wearing the tightest black leather trousers he's ever seen. They look like they've been sprayed on—but she does look great in them.

'Bloody hell, how the hell do you get into those?' says Jock, as direct as ever.

'Well, you can start with a glass of champagne,' she responds with a wink.

No sooner are the words out of her mouth than he's at the bar with a big grin on his face, ordering champagne. From her thick accent, we guess she's from the Newcastle area. She's very pretty but as rough as

THE CREW

arseholes! We can all tell a mile off that they're a bunch of gold-diggers. They're easy to spot, and we've developed an eye for them—especially in the South of France, where there's no shortage of money.

The girls are getting stuck into their drinks, and it's becoming increasingly obvious that these particular gold-diggers are trying to get as much money spent on them as possible. The way they look, the way they act, and the fact that they repeatedly ask us questions about how much money we have—none of it leaves much to the imagination.

After about twenty minutes, the girls head off to the toilet to freshen up and, no doubt, discuss a plan to relieve us of some hard-earned cash. Jock and I follow them and listen in from around the corner.

'OK, let's get them to buy some more champagne,' says one.

'Yeah, we're on holiday, and they can afford it,' says another. 'We'll have to find out what they do.'

Then the Geordie exclaims, 'Eh, fucking hell! All I want is a few inches, and there's fucking yards of it out there! I'm definitely having that Scots lad's cock tonight!'

Jock and I look at each other and burst out laughing.

'She's a classy one, that Geordie girl,' I say sarcastically as we head back to the boys.

'Just my type, mate. Don't think I'll need much spadework there. I think I'll nickname her Marg.'

'Marg? Why Marg?' I ask, puzzled.

'Marg, as in margarine… because she'll spread easy!'

'I don't know where you get them from, mate. You're right, though. I reckon the only reason she wears knickers is to keep her ankles warm.'

Jock tells the boys what we've overheard, along with his nickname for the Geordie girl, which Tom finds hilarious. At that moment, we decide to turn the tables and play the first game of the night.

MARC WILDER

We'll make up a story that we're rich businessmen in pharmaceuticals. Since they're after our money, we bet on who can act the most unattractive in full view of everyone and still end up with the girl at the end of the night. We're using their perception that we're millionaires to keep them interested and to test just how far they're willing to go for money alone. Time will tell.

The girls return a few minutes later, looking as thick as thieves. The first thing they ask for is a couple of bottles of champagne. We oblige, and after a while, the boys give me the wink to start the game.

I dream up a plan to be this really unattractive, cold-hearted businessman—a bit like Thrush, but worse. This man has no respect for animal life and questionable hygiene habits.

The Spanish girl takes a sip of her drink, looks up at me, and starts questioning me about money.

'So, what do you do to afford a yacht like that? You must be very rich!'

I immediately let out a loud belch, followed by a bit of genital-scratching through my jeans.

'Well, I basically test beauty products on animals to see if they damage them before they're fit for human use,' I say, keeping a straight face.

'Oh… erm… that must be interesting work,' she says, looking quite worried.

'Yeah, once you get used to the blood and the rancid warts caused by the products bursting on you, it's a breeze, really.' *Fart.*

The girl now looks horrified.

'Doesn't that hurt the animals?'

Belch. 'Hurt… Who? The beagle puppies? Yeah, it's bloody agony for the barking little fuckers. You know that lipstick you're wearing?'

'Erm… yes,' she says, looking even more worried.

'That gave me a heap of trouble. I ended up burning the faces off two dozen beagles before I got the mixture right on that one.'

'OH MY GOD… that's awful!' she gasps, covering her mouth with her hand.

'Serves them right for shitting everywhere.'

I glance over at Tom, who's trying not to laugh.

Meanwhile, Robbie is talking to one of the other girls. As he speaks, he suddenly develops a bad nervous twitch while grabbing handfuls of peanuts and ramming them into his mouth. She notices a few peanuts have dropped into his beer, and her look says it all. He just shrugs and says he prefers them mushy because it's easier on his dentures.

Then he starts picking his nose—really getting in there—and slowly removes his finger, revealing its contents in full view.

Tom is a bit slow off the mark, so to encourage him, Jock tells the girls what a fantastic dancer he is. This couldn't be further from the truth. Tom dances like old people fuck.

I tell him to take his girl for a dance, so he takes her hand and leads her to the small dance floor.

He starts moving, but he's as out of sync as you can get. There's lots of arm-waving, crotch-thrusting, and leg-shaking—and then he starts body-popping. He looks more like he's having a fit than busting some moves.

The whole time, he keeps this serious expression—the kind a chimpanzee makes when it's concentrating—and the girl's face is pure embarrassment.

When the song ends, they head back to the bar, and she downs her champagne in one go, presumably to numb the humiliation.

We order more drinks, and after a couple of hours, everyone is wasted. After a while, when we're sure the girls think we're a bunch of fucking idiots and are starting to lose interest, we start the game again—this time, talking about how much cash we're all worth. Sure enough, they perk up, suddenly happy to put up with our awful habits.

"What a sick world we live in," I whisper to Jock, barely believing what I'm seeing.

We have a few more drinks and decide to raise the stakes, just to see how far we can push the envelope. We bet a hundred euros on who can make the first girl walk away—without being offensive or rude in any way. Everyone pulls out their best tricks, and Tom even launches into some spontaneous barking.

Jock, never one to be outdone, whips out his testicles and grips his ball sack between his thumb and index finger, shaping it to look like a small brain. But somehow, this only seems to turn the Geordie girl on! She's laughing away, looking at him with unmistakable 'come to bed' eyes—much to Jock's disappointment. Undeterred, he rolls up a napkin, sticks one end between his arse cheeks, and I set fire to it. He then attempts to run to the far wall and back before it burns him. We call it 'the dance of the flaming arseholes'. It's always wise to have some ice cubes on standby. I remember a few poor souls in the past who didn't make it back in time—they were walking like John Wayne for a week afterwards.

By the time we all start getting a bit randy, we give up on the games and come clean to the girls. We tell them that, actually, we were just playing a silly game and that we're all fairly normal—Jock being the possible exception. Then, we head off to a club, dancing the night away and making out.

Towards the end of the night, the girls invite us back to their hotel, and we figure we're not going there to play dominoes.

The girls' rooms are next to each other, so we all gather in Jock's room first—it's in the middle, with Rob and me on either side. Later, in my own room, I get undressed, thinking about the fun I'm about to have with my sexy girl, who's in the shower. But the bedroom walls are paper-thin, and suddenly, I hear loud giggling from next door, followed by a thick Geordie accent yelling at Jock. She wouldn't be the first.

"Ehhhh, tiger! Tits first! Have you got no manners?" she shouts.

THE CREW

This is followed by loud fumbling, the sound of furniture crashing over, and then even louder moans and shrieks. At one point, I'm convinced the bloody headboard is going to come straight through the wall. It honestly sounds like she's being murdered in there.

My girl comes out of the shower, and we attempt to get down to some fun, but after ten minutes, I give it up as a lost cause. The racket next door makes it impossible to concentrate. I get up, grab my clothes, and step out into the corridor—where I find Robbie and his girl sitting on the floor, heads in their hands, laughing hysterically.

I point back towards my room and, between fits of giggles, tell them there was just no way I could carry on. Rob looks up, tears in his eyes, and says he had the same problem. After a while, we decide to head back to the yacht and leave Jock to rid himself of his sexual energies. Tom has also joined us by now, and we kiss the girls goodbye.

Halfway down the corridor, I suddenly realise I've left my wallet in Jock's room. After some discussion with the boys, I decide I can probably open the door, reach in, and grab it off the shelf—without being noticed. The hellish din from inside suggests they'll be too busy to pay me any attention.

I quietly open the door and lean in to grab my wallet. That's when I see him.

Jock, with his back to me, jeans around his ankles, wearing her knickers on his head while shagging her from behind. She's bent forward over the back of an armchair, and he's going at it like a man possessed.

As he's pummelling away, she looks over her shoulder and gasps, "No... no... not from behind! I want to see your face!"

Jock, utterly plastered and wearing a pair of panties on his head, stops for a split second. Then, in a moment of pure genius, he pulls his picture ID card out of his shirt pocket, turns around, holds it up in front of her face—and carries on where he left off!

I snatch my wallet and nearly fall out of the door, struggling to contain my laughter.

That's the beauty of Jock. His coltish behaviour and thought processes—especially when drunk—have to be seen to be believed. There is simply no filter between his conscious and subconscious brain. Whatever comes up—comes out.

Chapter 7
Hedonistic Tendencies

The next morning, we meet on the bridge for a recap of the previous night's activities and for me to assign the day's jobs. The boys turn up bang on time—they're really good that way. They work hard and play hard, and I have full respect for every one of them. We all went overboard with the partying last night, yet not a single one complains about having to get up and graft on deck in the sweltering sun.

However, they don't resemble the crew I worked with yesterday. Every one of them looks like living proof of life after death.

'Morning, chaps!' I say, trying to sound bright and breezy.

'How are we all doing?'

'SHIT!' comes the unanimous reply.

'Well, you're not the only ones. I don't know if I'm Arthur or Martha today. I fancy a cigarette, but I fear my breath is too volatile at the moment. These nights off are hard work, aren't they?'

I have to question Jock about his ID card moment last night—only he could pull a stunt like that and think it perfectly reasonable.

'How do you know about that?' asks a puzzled Jock. 'I was alone.'

'Ha! You thought you were. Interesting headgear, that, Jock, but I'd stick to the company baseball cap if you're on deck today. Very fetching, though, mate!'

We tell him about the missing wallet and how he was caught going at it like a rabbit on amphetamines.

'What time did you get back?' I ask, fearing the worst.

'About an hour or so ago.'

'I bet you were sorry to leave, weren't you?'

'Quite the contrary. Bit embarrassing, really, mate,' he says, looking at the floor and turning bright red.

'Why... what happened?' I ask, barely able to contain my curiosity.

'Well, I woke up around six, still fairly pissed, and figured I'd better get my arse back here on time. Geordie's not in the room, and all my clothes have gone—along with my cash, bank cards, and everything else I had in my pockets. I'm not thinking straight because of the drink, and I'm in a bad mood because I'm already late. Then it dawns on me—she's got up and left the hotel with all my gear.'

'You thought she'd robbed you?' asks Rob.

'Fucking right, I did! I thought she'd checked out while I was asleep and fucked off with everything!'

'So what did you do?'

Jock starts to laugh nervously. 'Well, I just lost the plot. I'm thinking I'm going to have to walk back to the yacht naked, in broad daylight. I start swearing at the top of my voice and jumping up and down on the bed, calling her every name under the sun, when I realise she's standing there in the doorway.'

'She came back to the room in the middle of your tantrum?' asks Tom, laughing.

'Yeah, she's stood there in the doorway with a cup of tea for me in one hand and a croissant in the other. She'd put my clothes in the wash.'

'You're fucking kidding me!' shouts Rob.

'No, I'm not! I felt like a complete wanker, stood there naked in the middle of the bed with my morning glory hard-on, I can tell you.'

'So what did you say to explain?' I ask.

'What could I say? I'd just been calling her a fucking thieving gypsy cunt at the top of my voice! I just blushed, took my clothes, and fucked off sharpish.'

'I take it you won't be seeing her again, then?'

'Errrr... no, mate.'

* * * *

THE CREW

I clap my hands to get their attention.

"Right, boys, let's get back to business. We're expecting the guests back at around 3 p.m., and they've said they want to head over to the millionaires' playground—otherwise known as Porto Cervo."

"Where's that?" asks Tom.

"It's over on the north end of Sardinia. It's a purpose-built resort with a very wealthy clientele. We'll motor over there tonight. We may or may not fit in a bit of scuba diving, depending on time. There's a great little reef with loads of fish and plenty to see, so they should be happy."

Tom leans back, putting his arms behind his head and grinning. "I'm getting paid for this! It sure beats the hell out of watching ferrets shagging."

"Yes, indeed. Anyway, get the boat rubbed down and be in your uniforms by 1:30, all right?"

Just as the boys are getting up, Thrush walks onto the bridge. As usual, there's no preamble.

"The guests just called to ask about the weather for the crossing to Sardinia. I checked the forecast and told them it's going to be quite rough."

"They're not going to like that," I say. "I suppose I'd better nip ashore and get some sea-sickness tablets."

Thrush rolls his eyes and sighs, as if I've just suggested the most idiotic thing in the world.

"Well, if you'll let me finish, I'll tell you why you shouldn't. They won't be coming with us. They're staying at the villa tonight and will fly over to Sardinia tomorrow or the day after to meet us there. They don't fancy rolling around for twelve hours being sick. Two of you will need to take some suitcases up to the villa as soon as they're ready. The girls are preparing them now."

Jock exchanges a glance with me and rolls his eyes. "I don't believe this lot. He's shelling out a fortune to charter a yacht, and he's hardly on it! Less work for us, I suppose."

"That's one way to look at it."

Before leaving, Thrush turns to me. "Can you come to my cabin, please?"

"Sure," I reply, wondering what he wants.

In his cabin, Thrush tells me the limo will be here in half an hour. Then, he gives me some instructions.

"Right, the chauffeur knows where he's going, but this is the guest's mobile number just in case."

He then picks up a very large Jiffy bag full of used banknotes and hands it to me. I look inside—it's all $100 bills. I guess there's probably about $40,000 to $60,000 in total. As he hands it over, he fixes me with a stern look.

"It's very important that you don't lose this. Keep it on you at all times and hand it over to the guest personally," he says in his usual condescending way.

I just about manage to hold back a sarcastic "Oh really? I was just going to leave it on the dashboard, you fucking scrotum!" but think better of it.

* * * *

I take Robbie in the limo, and within a few minutes, we're headed for the villa with a few suitcases containing God knows what—plus a Jiffy bag full of hard cash. On the way, I quietly tell Rob what's in the bag.

'You know what, Rob? This is the edge. Did you ever think you'd be in this position when you were growing up?'

'Not in a million years, mate. You?'

'Nope. You know, we could just vanish with the cash and never be seen again. What do you reckon?' I joke.

THE CREW

Rob laughs before replying, 'I think I might decline. I don't really fancy waking up with a horse's head on my pillow—or my own severed dick in my mouth, if you know what I mean.'

'You're not wrong, mate. I can't imagine our friend Mr Big would let us off with a slap on the wrist.'

Rob leans forward towards the cocktail bar in the back of the limo.

'Don't even think about it!' I warn. 'You've only just got rid of the smell of booze from last night. You're on your best behaviour today.'

'I was just having a look,' he protests.

'Likely story! I know what your "looks" end up as. I always know when you've been snooping around my cabin when I'm not there, you know.'

'How so?'

'Because the porn drawer is always left open, there's piss on my toilet seat, and beer seems to go missing from my fridge. I've got your number, sunshine!'

Rob is silent for a few seconds, then bursts out laughing. 'I thought I always got away with that.'

Eventually, the limo pulls up at the security gate in front of the villa. A guy in a suit approaches the window and peers in. The chauffeur explains that we've brought some of Mr Big's things from the yacht and that he's expecting us. The suited man steps back and radios the staff at the villa, speaking in Russian. I notice a bulge at his waist—he's definitely carrying a weapon.

He presses a button on his remote control, and the two enormous black-and-gold iron gates swing open. As we drive through the immaculately manicured gardens, up the winding driveway, we pass marble statues, peacocks, and water fountains. The villa sits atop a hill, its grand colonnade dominating the front.

'Fuck me! I bet this place cost him a bit,' Robbie splutters, looking around wide-eyed.

I'm equally awestruck. 'You're not kidding—especially in this neck of the woods. I reckon a good few million, at least.'

We step out of the limo onto the marble steps at the entrance. Rob moves to the boot and starts unloading the cases. Mr Big's heavies emerge and take them off his hands. I ask where Mr Big is so I can deliver the cash personally. One of the bodyguards nods towards the door.

'By the pool, in the garden,' he says gruffly.

Robbie and I walk up the steps and into the villa's entrance hall—huge, elegant, and dripping with wealth. We make our way through a set of side doors and out to the pool area. It's like a cross between Hugh Hefner's Playboy Mansion and the Garden of Eden.

A large swimming pool is surrounded by palm trees, a sunken Jacuzzi, and a bamboo pool bar. Reggae music drifts through the air, and around twenty people—an equal mix of men and women—are lounging, drinking, and partying. The women look like supermodels, their tanned, oiled-up bodies barely covered by tiny bikinis. The men, dressed in shorts and designer shades, exude wealth and power.

The atmosphere is electric—booze, coke, and hired female company setting the tone. A charge of sexual tension hangs in the air. I notice that all the men share the same tribal tattoo on their right shoulders. A gang symbol, perhaps?

On the far side of the pool, Mr Big signals me over. He's sprawled on a padded sunbed, two stunning women attending to him. I greet him with a polite nod and hand him the Jiffy bag. Without hesitation, he opens it in full view of the girls. Their eyes widen at the sight of the cash.

Mr Big peels off a few $100 bills and hands them to Rob and me for our trouble, then casually slides the bag under his sunbed. He doesn't even bother to count it. Lowering his sunglasses, he fixes me with a bloodshot, coked-up stare.

THE CREW

'I trust it's all there, gentlemen?' he says, his heavy Russian accent laced with menace.

'Of course, sir. It never left our sight.'

'Because if it isn't... this is what you get.'

He grins and slowly drags a finger across his throat, winking. The girls giggle sycophantically, mimicking his gesture.

I force a smile, unsure of the correct response. Mr Big then shouts to the bodyguard behind the bar to pour us a couple of drinks. After that throat-slicing display, Rob and I could definitely use one.

We thank him and make our way to the bar, slipping into the shade. Behind us, one of the Japanese guys grabs a bikini-clad girl and jumps into the pool with her. This sparks chaos—suddenly, all the men are chasing after the women, diving in with them. The music cranks up, and soon the pool is a cauldron of splashing water, squealing girls, and rowdy gangsters.

The bodyguard hands us two large, ice-cold vodka shots. I say "shots" in the loosest possible sense—these aren't the stingy ones you get down the pub. These are Russian-sized—quadruples, at least.

'You have two of these, and this will help your problem,' the bodyguard says.

'Problem?' I frown.

The bodyguard points at the nearly naked girls in the pool—then at my crotch.

'The girls... they make you crazy down there.' He nods towards my drink. 'And this stops your problem,' he chuckles.

Rob grins. 'Might help prevent another trouser explosion like the one on the passerelle when the guests boarded the yacht.'

The bodyguard removes his sunglasses, and my stomach drops. It's the same guy who was carrying the briefcase earlier.

Fuck.

'Oh, right. Thanks a lot,' I mumble, my face burning. I down the vodka in one, mutter another thank you, and grab Rob's arm.

'Come on, you—we're off.'

As we turn to leave, the bodyguard shouts something to his colleagues. A ripple of laughter spreads through the group. Then, in unison, they raise their forearms and make the universal 'boner' gesture at me.

Brilliant.

This definitely isn't your average office job.

Chapter 8
Kindred Spirit

Back on the yacht, heading out to sea for Sardinia, I bump into Zecky and tell her about the afternoon we've just had with Mr Big.

"My God, you see some sights!" she says. "I've definitely chosen the wrong department to work in on a yacht. I just see the same walls every day."

I know what she means. She must get sick of laundry, polishing, and serving food.

"Well, at least you don't get sunburnt, sweetheart. We wouldn't want that soft complexion of yours getting old and leathery, would we? Jock would no longer find you the sexual magnet he thinks you are now."

"If I thought that would work, I'd be on the sunbed 24/7 and turn into a prune, I can tell you that!" she laughs.

"You love it, really… I know you have a soft spot for the boy."

"Ha!" she grunts.

"Come on, Zecks—don't tell me you're not just a little bit curious?"

"I'm curious why men think it's funny to fart in their girlfriend's face, but no, I'm not curious about Jock. Now bugger off! I've got the beds to make."

I hear what she says, but I think there's some element of curiosity about Jock there.

I go up to the wheelhouse to make sure Tom is happy with the navigation plan for the voyage to Sardinia and that he doesn't have any problems.

"Hey, Tom, how's it going?"

"Hey, mate. Had a good afternoon, have we?"

"You wouldn't believe me if I told you."

"Why's that?" Tom asks, curious.

"Without going into too much detail at the moment, let's just say Mr Big is some boy."

I'm just in the middle of explaining more when someone approaches from behind. Tom quickly changes the subject to a work-related topic and starts waffling on about jet ski maintenance.

"So… after how many engine hours' running do you need to change the plugs?" he asks me with a knowing look.

I know the look, and I automatically pick up from his question. It comes as second nature now because we've done it so many times before. I can feel Thrush approaching from behind me, and I can smell his ridiculous aftershave—the kind only worn by teenagers who are trying to pull.

As usual, he just barks what he wants.

"There's been yet another change of plan for the next couple of days," he says in a weary voice. Thrush doesn't like surprises.

"What now, Captain? Have they decided to come with us after all?"

"No, but whatever they're doing at the villa, they seem to be enjoying it because they're not coming over to join us until at least Friday."

"I'm not surprised. They all seemed to have smiles on their faces when we left," Rob butts in.

"I guess that gives us a break for a couple of days then," I say, half confidently.

"Unfortunately not, because Mr Thomas is in town, and he'll be visiting Cannes tomorrow with a couple of friends. He's heard about the guests and wants to come aboard for drinks on the aft deck."

"Who's Mr Thomas?" Rob asks me quietly.

"He's the owner of the yacht and the guy who pays your salary."

The Captain carries on his brief:

THE CREW

"Anyway, we're to go immediately to Cannes and prepare the yacht for them. We'll arrive first thing in the morning. If there's anything you need, let me know, and I'll put an order in with the agent."

He then disappears as quickly as he arrived, presumably to play on the internet and pretend to work in his cabin.

"I'd like to order a new personality for him, boss," says Tom.

"Urgently required, eh?" I add with a wink.

"And then some, mate… and then some!"

We arrive at the Cannes port limits just after sunrise on a beautifully calm summer's morning. We pass other luxury yachts at anchor in the bay, gleaming in the morning sunshine—including a mega-yacht owned by Roman Abramovich, the Russian billionaire owner of Chelsea FC.

The huge yacht—377ft—is probably his finest. She's a state-of-the-art motor yacht but looks like a mini cruise ship. She has every conceivable luxury and allegedly costs $250,000 just to fill the fuel tank. She also has a missile-tracking system, just in case someone decides to assassinate the rich Russian—maybe an Arsenal fan. She cost $300 million and has a crew of forty-six. She's not your average sailing dinghy.

We reach our anchorage only a few hundred metres off the Promenade des Anglais.

"Let go the port anchor," barks the Captain as he puts the engines astern.

Jock releases the brake on the winch, and the anchor chain rushes out with a clatter. The engines drag the chain out along the seabed, and after a few minutes, she is riding to the anchor nicely.

"That's the anchor brought up, Captain," I report.

"OK, go about your business then," he tells us before turning his radio off—without even a "well done" or a "thank you." His rudeness becomes almost funny after a while.

"And a very good morning to you, Thrush!" says Jock, shaking his head. "He's got all the warmth of a graveyard, that man."

We both look at each other and raise our eyebrows in disbelief.

"Maybe you should warm him up with some of your special coffee, eh?"

"Pleasure… consider it done."

Jock and I walk back into the accommodation for a spot of breakfast before launching the ship's guest tenders to refuel them ashore. As we walk down into the crew room, Tom and Robbie are talking about how much cash Roman Abramovich makes in interest alone, based on what the newspapers say he's worth.

"Right, Tom, hand me the calculator," says Robbie. "If we take this figure he's reckoned to be worth, multiply it by this average percentage rate, divide it by 365, we'll find out approximately how much cash he earns a day in interest."

"Pass me the paper, I want to see," says Jock.

He takes a quick glance, puts the paper down, holds up his fingers and thumbs, and starts counting.

'Christ, he'll be getting his toes out next,' laughs Zecky. 'What are you going to do when those run out?'

'Well, I've got one more appendage on me I could use in an emergency, but that one's gift-wrapped for you, sweetie,' he says.

'In your dreams, sunshine.'

'Anyway, that's about £90 million a year in interest or roughly 246,000 quid a day,' Jock announces, as if it's the most obvious thing in the world.

We all exchange glances, then Tom works it out on the calculator.

'Bloody hell! It works out at £246,575 a day… Jock, you were nearly bang on!'

THE CREW

We all look at each other again in disbelief. Zecky, more than anyone, can't believe it.

'It must have been a fluke… surely?' she says, shrugging. 'So, what's £15 times 96, times 31, minus 395, smartarse?'

A bit of finger movement and a few seconds later, Jock confidently tells her, '£44,245.'

Zecky looks over at Tom for the answer on the calculator.

'Well… is it?'

Tom slams the calculator down.

'Fuck me, Jock, you should be on *Countdown*!'

Zecky has her mouth wide open in shock.

'Is he right?'

'Bang on!' I say, leaning over to check the calculator. 'He'd give Carol Vorderman a run for her money.'

It's the first time the boys have ever seen Zecky genuinely impressed by Jock. It's as if she's uncovered the equivalent of $E=mc^2$, and he knows it.

'I didn't think you took that much notice in the short period you went to school, Jock,' I say, scratching my head in amazement. 'You must have got on well with the maths teacher, eh?'

'No, he wouldn't let me in his class for the last year.'

'How come?'

'I was trying to chat up the girl next to me, and he lost his patience and threw the blackboard rubber at me.'

'So what did you do?'

'I threw it back, and it hit him square between the eyes!'

'Is this the same teacher who suspended you for pissing in his petrol tank?'

'No, that was another one.'

'I blame the parents,' jokes Robbie.

Jock suddenly moves into philosophical mode.

'Well, you know what they say—for every action, there's an equal and opposite reaction.'

'That's Newton's Third Law,' I tell him.

'That's right. Well, it's just karma getting back at him for all the shit he gave me!'

'So come on, then—how did you learn to do that so quickly?' asks Tom.

'My brother and I virtually lived in the bookies in our younger days, and that's when I discovered a use for maths. We used to play a lot of darts for cash in the local afterwards if we won, so working out numbers kind of came naturally after a while. The only other use of maths I found was geometry for snooker and pool, which we'd play for pints, so there was a bit of motivation there.'

'You're definitely a one-off, I'll give you that,' sighs Zecks.

The eggs that Jock put in the microwave a minute or two earlier suddenly detonate, and everyone is startled for a second before they realise what it is.

We look at each other, and 'For fuck's sake,' echoes around the room.

'You still can't microwave an egg, though, can you, sunshine?' I say, putting my arm around his shoulders.

'If I were you, I'd stick to cornflakes. It would save you a lot of time and effort in the long run,' Tom tells him.

'Just think of your cholesterol level as well,' Zecks says with fake concern. 'You don't want to be popping your clogs from a heart attack before your time, do you? Because you know that would break my heart.'

Jock shakes his head before answering.

THE CREW

'Ahhhh, it's a load of bollocks, that healthy eating lark. Take my granddad, for example. He was a miner from the age of 17, and he inhaled soot and dirt all his life. He smoked sixty Woodbine cigarettes a day, lived on bacon, and polished off nearly a bottle of whisky a day. He died at 84. Health and fitness? Load of old bollocks!'

'What did he put his old age down to, then?' I ask. 'Positive thinking and other men's wives?'

'He always said thought creates form, and if you think you'll achieve something for long enough, it will happen. He said it was the law of cause and effect. He believed there are mysterious forces at work in the universe that conspire to give you the things that you want, and all you have to do is want them enough. I, for one, believe in it.'

'So what did he put other men's wives down to, then?'

'I don't know. I guess he liked to get his rocks off, but he did once give me some advice about marriage.'

'Oh yeah? What was that?' asks Zecks.

'He told me, *don't be a fucking idiot*. Why buy the chicken when you get the eggs for free? It's in a man's interest to delay marriage as long as possible, and it's in a woman's interest to get married as soon as possible.'

'What did he mean by that?' says Zecky, looking a little confused.

'I guess he meant the eggs represent the sex, but I haven't really thought about the last bit.'

Tom suddenly jumps in. 'Maybe he's trying to say that men never really grow up, and they want to be kids for as long as possible. I guess men can father kids into their seventies, and when they start getting older with a few wrinkles, they just look windswept and interesting. So maybe he's saying, why should men rush into getting married if it's not in their interest?'

'He's got a point,' says Robbie. 'After all, the only real reason a bloke gets married in the first place is because he wants his kids to have his name. If it fails, he loses half of everything he's worked hard for.'

'Bit unfair really, isn't it?' says Zecks.

'Well, yeah, it bloody well is!' says Tom.

'You should've been born a girl then, shouldn't you?' Zecky tells him.

'You're bloody kidding!' says Jock. 'You can keep your menopause, childbirth, raging hormones, dieting, and periods. I'm quite happy being a bloke, thank you very much.'

'So what do you reckon he means by "a woman should get married as soon as possible"?' I ask.

'Goes without saying, really,' answers Robbie. 'They get married as soon as possible because the clock's ticking, and they want to have a family while they still can. That, and the fact that they're an altogether better proposition when they're young, wrinkle-free, firm, and bendy!'

Jock stops cleaning the microwave for a second. 'Well, yeah, he's right. Nobody wants to look at an old granny with her tits down to her knees!'

'Honestly, you men are so bloody simple. All you think about is what you can put in your belly or on your dicks!' mutters Zecks, looking at the other stewardess for back-up.

Jock jumps in again. 'Well, at least we don't think shopping is a sport, eating the odd packet of crisps is overeating, and the world revolves around diamonds. At least we admit we're simple creatures!'

'Tell me more about your grandfather,' I say to Jock. 'He sounds like a bit of local colour.'

'Tell him about the night out, Rob,' says Jock, starting to laugh.

Robbie sits up in his seat and remembers the story. 'Bloody hell, he was an original kindred spirit, that one. I did a safety course back in the UK a few years back, and Jock and I took him for a quiet pint one night. Granddad has half a dozen Stellas, all with whisky chasers, and decides to paint the town red. He's matching us drink for drink, showing no signs of slowing down. In fact, he seems to be speeding up.

'By closing time, Jock and I are wasted, but the old boy gets the horn and takes us to the local pole-dancing club. We don't really want to go in, but we think we'd better keep an eye on him and walk him back after the booze hits him. So we're in the club, and Granddad's sat at a table with a Cuban cigar and yet another Stella and whisky chaser, getting a table dance from this hot little blonde minx. He's loving it—has three lap dances with three different girls—then tries to borrow another thirty quid off me to see if she offers extras behind the curtains. Remember, he's in his eighties!

'We eventually get him to leave the club after much persuasion and promising him more whisky back at the house, so we take a wander over to the taxi rank.'

'This is where the fun begins,' interrupts Jock. 'We fancied a cigarette before we got in the taxi, so I lit one up, and we all had a chat about the night. Granddad turns to me, looks me up and down, and asks if I have anything stronger than nicotine on me. I laughed my ass off. He then mutters about the "bloody youth of today" and starts unscrewing the top of his walking cane. He reaches down into a hollowed-out cavity and pulls out this fucking huge spliff made from his own plants!'

'You're kidding?!' exclaims Zecks, laughing out loud in disbelief.

'No! We aren't… I'm telling you, he's some boy!'

'How old was he again?'

'About 81 or 82,' says Jock.

'Fucking hell! How the hell does he do it at that age?' asks Tom.

'I know! I used to nickname him "Duracell" because he just goes on and on.'

'Where did he get the weed from?' asks Zecky.

'He grows his own in his room at the old folks' home. The staff don't know what sort of plants they are, but they're very pleased he isn't causing trouble anymore. All they know is he's calmed down, so they leave him alone, smoking in his room, and let him get on with his new hobby of botany. The manageress even brings him fertiliser for his plants. They put his good behaviour down to good care and attention, when in reality, he's stoned off his tits most of the time!'

'That's brilliant! So what happened then?' asks Zecks.

'Well, we're all having a smoke of this lethal spliff, and Granddad's talking about us all spending a weekend in Amsterdam for his next birthday when he suddenly stops mid-conversation.

'"I don't fucking believe it… the little toe rag," Granddad mutters, staring at the taxi at the front of the row. We ask him what's up, and he explains that the driver is also a dodgy local electrician. Apparently, he'd been round his mate's house and done some shoddy work that caused something to short out and start a fire.'

'So what did he do?' Tom asks.

Both Jock and Robbie start laughing hysterically, and it takes them a minute or so to calm down enough for Jock to finish the story.

'Granddad walks to the taxi at the back of the queue, which is about ten cars in length. He leans in through the window of each taxi and asks each one of the taxi drivers—all men—for a blow-job. Furious, all of them tell him to piss off, or words to that effect.

'When he gets to the front taxi, where this guy he's got a problem with is, he leans in and asks if he wouldn't mind taking a weary old man home. The driver agrees, and Granddad jumps in the front seat. He shouts through the window at us to take our time finishing our smoke, then he tells the driver he's dropped some coins on the floor by his feet. He asks him if he wouldn't mind leaning over to pick them up, 'cos he's got arthritis in his spine. The taxi driver agrees, and as soon as he bends his lap over to pick up the coins, all hell breaks loose in the taxis behind him.

'The other drivers are hooting their horns and calling the guy all the names under the sun. Rob and I haven't got a clue what's going on because we're now pissed and lethally stoned. After a couple of minutes, Granddad steps out of the taxi with a huge smile on his face, pretending to do up his fly. He then walks over to us, takes a big drag of his spliff, and asks us to get in. The taxi then heads off with the driver looking confused as to what all the fuss was about.

'After a couple of miles, Rob starts to feel a bit ill from the effects of the monster spliff. He winds down the back window and is sick into the road. A bit sticks on the outside of the door, and there's a bit of carrot where the window comes up inside the door. The taxi driver goes apeshit and pulls over. He locks us all in the car so we can't get out and calls Rob a dirty bastard. He then tries to get Rob to cough up a lot of cash for fouling his vehicle.'

'So what did he do?' asks Zecky.

'Well, Rob does the decent thing, apologises and takes his shirt off to clean the door. He's trying to lean out of the window to get to it, but he can't reach. Then a police officer walks up to the cab, and the taxi driver tells him what happened. The policeman is no mug, but he informs us that the law states there is a cash fine for anybody who fouls a taxi, inside or out. We could all tell by the way he told us, and by the look on his face, that he knew the taxi driver was taking the piss.

'Suddenly, Granddad leans over to Rob and me, tells us not to say a word, and that he'll handle the situation. He politely asks the police officer if we can all get out of the vehicle to discuss the problem, and the officer agrees.'

'I still can't believe what Gramps did next,' says Robbie, with his head in his hands.

'What did he do then?' asks Zecks eagerly. 'Did you do a runner?'

'No, not at his age. He leans over to the copper and clarifies what the maximum fine is for fouling the inside of the vehicle, and the copper tells him.

"'Right, no problem," says Granddad, who's as cool as a cucumber.

'Then he walks round to the driver's side of the taxi, opens the door, sticks his fingers down his throat and pukes all over the driver's seat, steering wheel, and dashboard. He calmly closes the door, walks back round to the policeman, and hands him the cash.

"'I like to get value for money, officer, and that was worth every penny!" he announces, walking off into the moonlight and bidding us goodnight. He's a kindred spirit, that one!'

Chapter 9
May the Force Be with You

The next day, we finish our breakfast in the crew room and head out onto the deck for the morning walkaround.

"OK, lads," I say. "As you're all aware, the boss is flying down to Cannes today, and we've got a new crew member joining."

"Anyone we know?" asks Jock.

"No… he's only 19 and he's never worked on a yacht before. He's fresh out of his college induction, so he'll be as green as grass."

"Ha! Fantastic!" declares Jock. "A bit of fresh meat for us!"

"Jock, this is mainly directed at you—go easy on him. I've heard the stories about the stunts you pulled on the cadet on your last boat. Anyway, he'll be waiting on the quay by the steps at two this afternoon. You go over there, Jock, collect him, and bring him back to the boat. Tom and I will take the car to the helipad to pick up the boss.

"Before we get changed, has anyone not met the boss before, apart from you, Rob?"

"I've only seen him once on the quay about a year ago, so fill me in on the details," says Tom.

"No problem. He's a property tycoon, late fifties, usually wears Savile Row suits, bald-headed, about five-eight, average build. He lives in a huge villa in Monte Carlo in the summer and St Lucia in the winter. He's a decent bloke, from humble beginnings in London's East End, so he's a down-to-earth guy—but never forget who he is.

"His main interests while he's on the yacht are drinking whisky, having barbecues, and smoking cigars in the whirlpool spa on the sun deck. He likes his Jacuzzi at exactly 33.0°C."

"How much is he worth?" asks Tom, straight to the point.

"Thrush told me it was around £750 million at the last estimate, but it's probably more than that now."

"What kind of car does he drive?"

"He doesn't drive any of them. He's a multi-millionaire—he gets someone else to drive him."

"Ask a silly question, I suppose…"

"Yep! What kind of mood he's in and where he's travelling to will determine what car he wants us to drive."

"Wants us to drive?" says Tom, perking up.

"Oh yeah. I usually pick him up and drive him to and from airports, but I also take him up to the country club in his guard's red Ferrari 360 Spider. He's also got a jet-black Bentley convertible, a platinum Porsche Carrera 996 Turbo, and a Range Rover for when his back's sore and he doesn't feel like bending down. All brand new, of course."

Tom is crazy about cars, and I think the news that he may get to drive one of these machines is a bit too much to handle. He's grinning like a Cheshire cat.

"We'll be picking him up in the Bentley today because he's got quite a bit of luggage with him," I tell him.

"Tell them about our race around Monaco," says Jock.

"OK, but this goes no further. Jock and I once went to pick up the boss's son and his friend from Nice Airport, but they decided not to come. We didn't get the message, so we hung around the airport until midnight waiting for them. We finally got told they weren't coming, so we took the Ferrari and the Porsche back to Monte Carlo.

"We'd driven both cars there because they'd planned to take them from the airport to a mate's villa near St Tropez. It was past midnight, the roads were virtually empty, and we decided to see what the cars were made of… so we had a bit of a race back along the motorway."

"We were proper flying, though!" Jock tells everyone proudly. "We were side by side at 150 mph on the long flat bit."

"Fucking hell! What about the speed cameras?" asks Rob.

THE CREW

"Oh, it was OK," I say with a grin. "We couldn't really see them long enough to worry at that speed, could we, Jock?"

"We come off the motorway and cruise down the hill into Monaco. Like he said, the roads are empty because it's around one in the morning, so we reckon since we're in two of the most prestigious cars in the world, we might as well have a race round the Grand Prix circuit while we're at it."

"No way!" laughs Tom.

"Yeah, seriously. We thought it'd be something to tell the grandkids. Anyway, the Grand Prix track is basically a circular route on public roads, so it wasn't like we had to break in anywhere. We started racing at the roundabout next to the tunnel, heading towards the marina, and did the circuit three times at speed!"

"Including the famous hairpin outside the Rascasse Bar," adds Jock.

"It was pretty crowded at that time, and by the third lap, a few people had lined the barriers and were applauding!"

"So that's our claim to fame, mate. We raced each other around the actual Monaco Grand Prix circuit, and we were the only cars on it!" beams Jock.

"Ha! That's wicked. You'll have to take me next time," adds an envious Tom.

"There won't be a next time, mate. That was definitely a one-off," I tell him. "Right, we'd better get our skates on then. Jock, go get changed, and we'll get the show on the road. Just give me a ring on my mobile when you're on your way back, so Tom and I can make our way down to the boat and head over to the car."

"No worries, mate," says Jock.

An hour passes, and Jock calls to say he'll be alongside the yacht in ten minutes.

"Have you picked up the new boy?" I ask.

"Yeah, he was waiting where he should've been."

"What's he like?"

"You'll see, boss. I just hope his mum knows he's playing sailor boy, bless him."

The guest tender approaches the yacht, and the new arrival comes into view. He looks about 16 and five-foot-six. His freckly face hasn't a hint of facial hair, and he still has remnants of puppy fat. He's dressed in a shirt, tie, and blazer.

Thrush joins me to help with the luggage—quite decent of him for a change. I hold out my hand and help the lad from the boat onto the yacht.

I hear him thanking Jock for helping with his bag. He's got quite a high-pitched, upper-class but nondescript English accent.

"Hello, are you the Chief Mate?" squeaks the new arrival.

"Why? Do I owe you money?" I say, trying to lighten the atmosphere and settle his nerves.

"Errrr… no… I don't think I've met you before," he says innocently.

I look at Tom, and he's trying not to laugh. "You'll be happy to get here then?" I ask.

"Oh yes, but I must admit I've heard some bad things about the Captain. He's supposed to be, excuse my French, a bit of an arsehole!"

My welcoming smile vanishes as I grit my teeth and signal to him with my eyes that the gentleman standing two feet to his right is the Captain. I quickly bid him farewell and make a swift retreat to the boat with Tom.

"I'm off with Tom to pick up the owner, Mr Thomas, but Rob will settle you in," I tell him as we leave.

As Tom and I look back on the way to the quay, the Captain is staring at the new arrival like he's just stolen something from him. Not the best of starts for the new kid, and he's not going to last two minutes with any of the boys, especially Jock—the ultimate piss-taker.

THE CREW

Tom and I get a taxi to the garage to find the Bentley. "We'll get the cleaning gear out of the boot and give her a rubdown so she's spotless for the boss. I'm not sure if his wife will be coming along as well, but if she does, open and close the door for her and ask if she has enough air in the back. She's a nice enough lady, but she likes to be fussed over a bit, if you know what I mean. Give her a bit of special attention."

"Anything else I should know?" asks Tom.

"He usually wants to know the latest football scores and what his wife's movements are for the weekend. They're not the best-matched couple, to say the least, and apparently, she changed the instant he married her."

"Did she turn into a professional nag or something?"

"They all do that, mate! My guess is that now he's in this predicament, he doesn't want to lose millions in a divorce settlement, so he tolerates her."

Tom and I spend the best part of half an hour dusting down the Bentley, and it's spotless by the time we see the helicopter coming over the horizon. It thunders onto the landing pad, and the pilot helps the boss down the steps—but there's no sign of the wife. Two of the staff pull his two pieces of luggage from the hold and walk behind him to the car, where I greet him with a warm handshake.

"Good afternoon, sir. How was your flight?"

"Not bad. How's yourself?"

"I'm OK, thanks."

"Haven't seen you in a while. I thought you might have buggered off to work for an Ibiza club owner by now and got rid of an old fucker like me," he joshes in an unmistakable East End London accent.

"Ha! Maybe next year, sir, if you're lucky."

I've worked for him for over a year now, and we've developed a good rapport. He's a totally different person when his wife isn't around—always a grumpy old sod when she's with him.

"No wife today, sir?" I enquire.

"Thankfully not. I think she's doing something back in Monaco or off to watch an opera or something."

Tom and I take him straight to his hotel, where he's meeting a few friends for a reunion. They're in town for a couple of days playing golf, so he thought he'd catch up with them for a round or two and a game of poker. He must be pretty fond of them because he's flown down from Bern to Monaco in his private jet.

"This is Tom, sir—you've never met him. He works on your yacht with us. He's originally from Australia."

"Good to meet you, sir," Tom says, leaning round to shake his hand.

"G'day, me old cobba," the boss says, doing the worst Australian accent Tom has ever heard. They both laugh because it's such a shit impersonation.

"I think you've misunderstood, sir. I'm from Australia, not Pakistan," says Tom with a smile.

The boss finds this quite cheeky but funny.

"I see sarcasm is another service yacht crews are offering nowadays! Perhaps I'd better stick to making money instead of impressions."

"I think that would be a wise move, sir," I chuckle.

"I visited Australia a couple of years ago. I went down in a cage with the white sharks and ate kangaroo meat at a restaurant," says the boss proudly.

"Oh yeah? How did you get along?" asks Tom.

"The sharks bloody terrified me! I tend to lose my sense of humour when I'm bottom of the food chain."

We pull up at the front door of the hotel, and the bellboy rushes out to take the bags. Tom jumps out just before the vehicle comes to a stop so he can open the door for the boss.

"All the best then, sir, and have a nice time," I tell him.

THE CREW

He hands me 100 euros, but it's a pleasure to work for a guy like this, so I hand it back immediately.

"I'm very grateful, sir, but you pay me enough already… it's been a pleasure, really."

He looks genuinely touched and holds my stare for a second. I'm thinking I might just have helped restore his faith in human nature a little bit.

As Tom and I jump back in the Bentley, a few of his friends meet him at the door. They all look like they're in a very jovial mood—or should I say half-cut.

"I think he's going to have a sore head tomorrow," I tell Tom. "They look like they're up for a party."

"He certainly seems in good spirits. Is he always like that?"

"He is usually, when he's away from the wife! He calls her 'the ball and chain.'"

"So how did he make his money, then? I take it he's into dodgy dealings, eh?"

"I don't know all the details, but from what I heard, he started out quite young, taking a lot of financial risks. He borrowed money on his house to put a deposit down on another one and renovated it with his own hands. He sold that for a profit, then bought two more and did the same on those. He kept on doing this for a few years until he'd generated several hundred grand, then invested that in the stock market and online gambling. That kept making money, and as he carried on investing in different concerns, he became a multimillionaire after twenty years. He keeps his affairs private, but apparently, he has a lot of money in various football clubs. He's incredibly shrewd, but he's quite a relaxed, funny guy."

I'm happy that everything has gone to plan so far, and the boss has been picked up and delivered without a hitch. So, before we head back, I let Tom drive the Bentley along the coast road as a treat. I can tell he's been dying to get his hands on the wheel from the moment he saw the Bentley. He's been asking me questions about how she drives, how easy the steering is, and how comfortable the driver's seat is.

"Cheers, you're a star! I've been itching for a drive of the beast."

"Now remember, if you bend it, you mend it. This car costs more than your average family detached house, so you'll be working your hands to the bone for the rest of your life if you damage it."

He's only been driving for about ten minutes when a car full of young lads pulls up parallel to us in the next lane. They're driving a customised sports car with a dodgy paint job, a cheap body kit, and one of those nasty spoilers on the back that looks like it was stuck on as an afterthought. Tom and I look over at them, and they start trying to bait us into racing.

"Just ignore the little shits, Tom... Kids, eh?"

"I know, mate," he says, looking straight ahead, not giving them any attention.

A few minutes pass, and they're starting to get really irritating. Then, a doughnut hits Tom's window, and they're leaning out of the car, giving us the one-fingered salute. Tom's got that look in his eye that just shouts, *LET ME!* I hesitate for a second or two, then tap him on the shoulder.

"Are you going to let them get away with that?" I ask.

"Do you know what, boss? I don't believe I am!" Tom replies, now smiling, flipping the gearbox into sport mode and putting his foot to the floor. We charge off, and even at 60mph, we leave the other car standing like it wasn't moving at all.

"Fucking hell, what's that rumbling and shuddering?" I shout.

He looks at me, laughing. "That's the rear wheels spinning."

"But we're doing nearly 70mph!"

"I know! Fucking awesome, eh? Look out the back window."

THE CREW

There are two thick tyre marks along the road where we've just accelerated. Tom is still high on adrenaline as we motor down the last stretch of road heading back to the port. Even though the car full of lads is no longer with us, he's going a little too fast for the speed limit.

As we pass a fuel station, a police patrol car parked in the slip lane zaps us with a radar gun. The laughing and joking stop abruptly as we both look in the rear-view mirror to see if they're following us. Suddenly, the patrol car pulls out, and its roof light illuminates.

"Bollocks, he's after us, Tom."

"How fast do you think we were doing?" he asks, looking worried.

"How fast do *you* think you were doing?"

"I don't know… 80 or 90?"

"Fuck! Well, that's a whole lot faster than the speed limit, mate. My guess is we're in the shit, so you'd better pull over."

Tom isn't the best person to be pulled over by a copper; he absolutely hates them and can't resist taking the piss. To make matters worse, he swerves the car across the road as he heads to the lay-by because he's looking at the patrol car in the rear-view mirror and not where he's going. The omens aren't good, and I get the gut feeling things will go pear-shaped soon.

Tom winds down the window, and the police officer strolls up to the Bentley. He says something in French, but we are both clueless. Tom looks up at the officer.

"Do you speak English?"

The officer turns his head away and sighs, as if he's done this many times before. We're sure he has – there are probably more foreign drivers on the Côte d'Azur than French in peak summer season. The officer is wearing dark shades. It gives him a menacing aura.

"Monsieur, your licence and registration," he says in English but with a strong French accent.

"I don't have it on me, mate," says Tom.

It might be fine calling an Aussie copper *mate* because things are a lot more laid-back there, but it's not the kind of thing you do on the Côte d'Azur.

"Is zis your car, monsieur?" the officer asks, pointing at Tom.

"Nah, mate. We found it unlocked and thought we'd take her for a spin," Tom says, laughing.

I know what's coming, but there's bugger all I can do except look the other way. The officer takes a few seconds to register the dialect and process what he's just been told.

"Soooo… you are zee driver of this vehicle… yes?"

"I know it's an automatic, mate, but I've still got to fucking be here."

Silence.

"Do you know what gear you were in coming down zee hill?"

"Oh, you know… white shirt, black pants, and hush puppies!"

Silence again.

I nudge the piss-taking Tom on the arm.

"Mate, I don't think you—" is all I get out before he pushes me away. I swear quietly under my breath.

"Sir, you were going 78 in a 60 limit," the officer tells Tom, reaching for his ticket book.

"That's a bit disappointing. We reckoned we were doing at least 80 or 90. Can't you make it 100? I'm trying to sell the motor!"

I'm thinking we're in the shit, but I can't help but chuckle to myself at the bloody front Tom has sometimes. The officer puts pen to paper to write him a ticket.

"So… what is your name, monsieur?"

"Walker."

"Walker?"

"Yep, Walker... W-A-L-K-E-R... Walker."

The officer writes it down.

"And what is your first name?"

"Luke... L-U-K-E... Luke."

"And your middle name?"

"Sky... S-K-Y."

The officer writes it down, then after a few seconds, he realises what he's written. He rips up the piece of paper and opens the door.

"You two... step out of zee vehicle," he says in a sharp tone.

I look at Tom and whisper, "Shit! You've really done it now, you bloody comedian!"

After twenty scary minutes, a body search, a vehicle search, a fine, and lots of sweet-talking, I explain to the officer that Tom gets nervous and that's where the jokes come from. Complete bullshit, of course, because Tom just likes to take the piss. Eventually, the officer believes me and sees the funny side. We are cautioned again and allowed to get on our way.

We bid the officer farewell, but Tom can't resist one more taunt before we leave.

"May the force be with you," he tells the officer, waving his imaginary lightsabre at him.

"The force was strong with that one," I say as I accelerate up the road on the way back to the yacht.

Chapter 10
The Bigger They Are the Harder They Fall

Tom and I drive straight back to the quay and notice the yacht's tender moored up alongside the floating pontoon, but Jock is nowhere to be seen.

"Give Jock a shout and see where he is, mate," I say to Tom, fearing the worst.

Tom reaches into his pocket for his mobile and thumbs in Jock's number. It rings six times before going to voicemail. Jock's voicemail informs us that, unfortunately, he's been called away on a matter of national security, but we should leave a message, and if he returns alive from his heroic adventures, he'll call back.

"Just ask him where he is and tell him we're waiting by the boat," I tell Tom. "Ask him to call back as soon as he gets the message."

Tom leaves the message and hangs up. We sit on the tender, smoking cigarettes for ten minutes, until Tom's crazy frog ringtone sounds.

"Mate, where are you? We're on the tender waiting for you," says Tom.

"I'm at the bar on the main road. It's behind the quay."

"You're in the bar?! Fuck's sake, Jock!"

"I've only been here an hour. Take a walk over, I've just got a pint in."

Tom hands me the phone and shakes his head.

"Jock! What the fuck are you doing? Don't move – we're coming over."

"Aye, OK, I'll get you both one in. By the way, you wanna see the tits on the barmaid. It's like a photo finish in a zeppelin race!"

The phone goes dead—Jock has hung up.

"Trust him to find the boozer at this time. Still, how much can one man drink in an hour?" asks Tom.

At the bar, Tom and I spot Jock, who is talking to a young guy I haven't seen before. I walk up to Jock and tap him on the shoulder.

"All right, chaps!" he says cheerily, passing pints along the bar to us. "This is Nick, my new mate from New Zealand. He's only 18, and he's just polished off four shots of tequila."

"Oh yeah? What's the celebration?" I ask Nick.

Before he has a chance to answer, Jock throws an arm around his shoulder.

"Nick went out in St Tropez last night and had his first blow job."

"Oh… errr, congratulations!" I tell Nick, sniggering as I shake his hand.

"Yeah, the poor fucker still can't get the taste out of his mouth, so he's trying a whisky this time!"

"Hey, piss off, Jock – he's only kidding," Nick retorts.

I turn Jock around and give him a bollocking for leaving the tender unattended. But there's no harm done, so we have a few laughs in Nick's company before dragging Jock away from the bar to a food table. I hope he orders something solid to soak up the four pints and whisky chasers he's downed—before we have to get back to the yacht.

"Bloody hell, Jock, are you on a mission to push your luck or something?" I ask him. "If the Thrush smells that on you, he'll have your arse kicked into the middle of next fucking year."

"Well, one beer led to a bit more—you know how it goes. Anyway, I'll order you all some grub to make amends," he says, waving over to the waitress, who's standing at the bar with an order book.

She walks over to the table and smiles. Jock looks up at her, his alcohol-flushed face shining, and proceeds to order in a very slow, very loud voice, using lots of hand movements. Clearly assuming she doesn't speak English, he lays it on thick.

"CAN I… (pointing to himself)… HAVE ONE (holding his digit up in front of her face) EXTRA LARGE (now doing circular movements with his arms) TUNA (pointing to a fish ornament on the bar) PIZZA… and TWO (sticking his fingers inches from her face) MOOO… MOOO… BEEF (now holding two fingers up on his head like horns) PIZZAS… and THREE (again holding fingers up under her nose) GRANDE… GRANDE (holding his arms outstretched) BEERS (pointing to his glass)."

The waitress looks at Jock and repeats his order—in an unmistakable Essex accent.

"So, you want three beers and three pizzas—one tuna, two beef, yeah?"

Jock stares at her, open-mouthed.

"Errr, yeah. Sorry, darling… thought you were a foreigner."

"Clearly. But why you thought I was stupid and deaf is more of a mystery."

"Oh, right… I just looked over, and you seemed that way."

"What? Stupid and deaf?"

"No, foreign, for fuck's sake," says Jock, holding his head. "Can we start again? Where are you from?"

"Essex."

"Essex girls, eh? I've heard about your reputations… Well, it's nice to see one upright and not lying on her back for a change."

"Are you trying to be funny?"

"Ha! Yeah!" says Jock, slapping her on her arse.

"Well, I hope you find this funny!"

She grabs his wrist, twists it painfully behind his back, then throws a fist at his nose. Jock stumbles backwards, gripping the seat of his chair—now sitting in exactly the same position, but facing the ceiling, blood trickling from his nose.

THE CREW

The waitress screams at him to stay put before storming off into the back room.

Tom, sitting across from me, folds his arms and grins.

"I told you these were good seats, didn't I? We find a bar with the only psychotic Essex girl on the Côte d'Azur."

Tom and I lean down to have a word with the flattened Jock.

"I must admit, you've got that off to an art form," I tell him.

"Uhhhh… uhhhh… what?" Jock groans, still stuck in the same position.

"Making a cunt of yourself! You should've opened your mouth a little wider—then you could've put the other foot in. How to win friends and influence people, Jock. Style, eh?"

"Fucking hell, mate—she's got a punch like a steam hammer!" groans Jock.

"Just wait till I tell Rob you got bitch-slapped, mate. You haven't a snowball's chance of living this one down," says Tom.

"Bit of an overreaction, I thought," says Jock.

"Come on… We'd better get out of here, they're coming over."

Jock gets up slowly with a helping hand from Tom, and they start walking towards the exit. The waitress stomps out of the door at the end of the bar to intercept them. She's accompanied by the chef—over six foot, shaven head, built like a brick shithouse.

"Oh fuck! Here we go," I say to Jock.

"Yeah, I see him," replies Jock quietly. "No prizes for guessing who he'd like a word with."

"Hey, you!" shouts the chef.

Jock stops in his tracks and turns around.

"My girlfriend says you touched her up when she came over to serve you."

"That's not quite how it happened, I was just—"

"Nobody touches my girl. Now you're gonna get touched up, you fucking prick!"

I can't help intervening, because I have to back Jock up. "Look, mate, he was just having a joke with her and she took it the wrong way and hit him. He shouldn't have touched her on the arse, but it was innocent enough."

I'm in the middle of explaining when he tells me to shut the fuck up.

"So, you did touch her, then?" says the chef, who's getting angrier by the second.

"Well, yeah… but everything's been taken out of context, mate."

"I'm not your fucking mate. I'm your worst enemy. Now get your arse outside, because I'm gonna kick it off this fucking planet!"

Tom tries to calm things down but gets the same treatment as me. Jock suddenly gives me a wink and holds his hands up in the air.

"OK, OK, you win. I'll come out into the back alley with you. But you're a big lad and I don't stand a chance, so at least let me neck a tequila before we go."

"You fucking what?!"

"To kill the pain."

"Whatever," the chef snarls.

Jock walks over to the bar and orders a tequila from a very embarrassed French barmaid. The chef stands inches away from him, spoiling for a fight.

"Tequila—make it a large one, darling," says Jock. He picks up the shot glass, standing almost nose-to-nose with the chef. There's barely enough room for him to bring the glass to his lips.

"OK, I'll just bolt this, and then you can take me outside. But I don't want to fight you… as long as you know that," Jock tells the chef.

THE CREW

"Well, you don't have much choice now, do you, dickhead?"

"OK, if that's what you want..."

Jock slowly pours the tequila into his mouth—then blows it out straight into the chef's face and eyes. He does it with such force that a fine mist lingers in the air between them.

The chef stumbles back, hands over his eyes, blinded.

"MOTHERFUCKER!!!!" he screams at the top of his voice.

Jock then aims a very hard, very accurate punch at the chef's unprotected balls. The bloke folds over like he's been shot in the gut. His deep voice shifts to a high-pitched squeal as he clutches his balls, blind and in agony.

Tom and I look at each other in astonishment, half-expecting the chef to recover and rip Jock a new arsehole any second. But the guy is in too much pain to move—and Jock knows it.

Jock takes a step back, raises both arms in the air, stands on one leg, and starts humming the theme from *The Karate Kid*. Then, with perfect timing, he pulls off the film's signature move and kicks the chef square in the forehead, knocking him out cold.

Cool as a cucumber, Jock winks as he strolls past us towards the exit.

"The bigger they are, the harder they fall."

"Well, let's just hope he stays fallen," I say. "Now let's get the fuck out of here."

We don't waste time. We leg it back to the tender, cover up the name in case we're spotted, and gun the throttle, speeding back to the yacht as fast as it'll take us.

"I'm kinda thinking Jock might have done that party trick a few times before," Tom says quietly to me. "It looked a little *too* well-practised to be spontaneous."

"I think you're right," I sigh. "Crude—as only Jock can be—but very effective."

Chapter 11
The Panda-Eyed Goon

On the yacht, Robbie is giving the new cadet the mandatory safety tour. You can tell by the look on the lad's face that he's blown away by the beauty and class of the yacht. It's also easy to see that he's clueless, though. He's calling the bow the 'pointy end' and the wheelhouse the 'cockpit'. He's also bemused by the helm—or the 'steering wheel', as he calls it—which is a ten-inch-long, half-moon-shaped metal rig. In practice, navigation officers rarely use it because they usually alter course with the autopilot, unless they're in traffic or navigationally restricted waters. The cadet seems amazed at this—he was clearly expecting a huge, six-foot wooden wheel like you see in old pirate films.

Robbie enjoys showing the new arrival around the yacht. The boy's inexperience is very entertaining, and Rob is sure the crew are going to get hours of entertainment winding him up. I disappear below deck for a quick coffee and hear the stewardesses giggling away to each other. They're wondering if the new crew member will be 'fit', but they're in for a shock—he's barely out of nappies.

I go back on deck to see how Robbie is getting on and check the standard of work that's been done this morning. He's kneeling down, polishing the stainless steel winch, listening to his iPod, and singing away. I tap him on the shoulder to grab his attention.

'How's it going, Rob?'

'OK, mate.'

'Where's the kid?'

'Jock's got him into a job below deck. He took him away as soon as you went for a coffee.'

'Jesus, I wonder what he's up to now. I'd better go and try to save him from the crazy sod! What do you reckon he's got him doing?'

'God only knows… probably making him clean his cabin, I reckon.'

'He's been aboard less than half an hour, for fuck's sake! If he comes back up, don't be too harsh on him just yet. Let him settle in for a few days before we initiate him.'

'It's not me you have to worry about, is it, boss?' he says with a knowing look.

'You're not wrong there, mate. By the way, we're moving alongside the berth in three hours, and we'll be staying overnight until the boss leaves in the morning.'

'So he's definitely coming down, then?'

'Yep, and the crowd he's met up with look like they might be up for a boys' party, so it could be an eye-opener.'

'Well, we aren't exactly short of eye-openers this trip, are we? I could've done with an early night tucked up in my wank chariot instead of standing at the passerelle.'

'I know, mate. Plus, the weather will be shit for the crossing over to Porto Cervo tomorrow, so you won't get much kip then.'

'It's fucking typical, that! We hug the coast away from all the crap weather and seas for most of the summer, and the one time we've got to make a crossing, the weather turns shit.

The hits just keep on coming!'

'That's sod's law for you. Anyway, I'll catch you later.'

I go back below deck to see what mischief Jock is into. I'm not let down. Walking along the alleyway, I hear a shrill, painful moaning from Jock's cabin. Jock has the kid in a headlock under his left arm and is playfully knocking on the top of the kid's head with his knuckles.

'What do you mean, you've not brought any porn with you?' yells Jock.

'Sorry... I... didn't know... ouch!' gasps the kid.

'What about booze? You must have brought some booze with you!'

As I walk into the room, Jock turns and sees me. 'You'll never guess what, boss...'

'I heard—and I think the rest of the yacht did as well. Let him go, for fuck's sake. He hasn't been aboard more than an hour! Go and help Rob finish up and then sort yourself out for moving the yacht to the berth.'

I hold out my hand, and the cadet shakes it warily.

'Hi, mate! I didn't catch your name when we first met.'

'It's Tarquin, sir.'

'Fucking hell! How did you end up with that name? Mum and Dad a bit rich and posh, are they?'

'Well, erm... yes, they are, as a matter of fact. My mother is a merchant banker, and Daddy is a maritime lawyer.'

'No shit! Don't tell me you've got a double-barrelled surname—that would really take the piss.'

'Er... well, actually, my surname is Worthington-Smythe.'

'Oh, for fuck's sake! Tarquin Worthington-Smythe, eh? Jock's going to rip you up for arse-paper. Anyway, Tarquin Worthington-Smythe, I'll call you "Tar" for short. First things first, I'd better give you a few house rules. Unpack and settle in as soon as you can, and don't take Jock too seriously. Treat everything he asks you to do with extreme caution. He'll take the piss and play all sorts of pranks on you, but accept it because we all go through it in one way or another when we first go to sea. Jock's a good 'un underneath, but he's a rough old diamond. Just remember, it isn't the changes in life that are difficult—it's just the transitions. Remember that, and everything will be cool, OK?'

'Right... OK.'

'Number two: I run my department my way, and that way is a mishmash between the right way, the wrong way, the book way, and two decades of experience. If you do exactly what I say, when I say it, you'll be OK. The last thing I want is to be condescending, but you're still a young kid, and there's a lot you don't know.

'And thirdly, don't call me "sir", because every time you call me that, I think somebody important is standing behind me.'

'OK.'

'Oh, yeah – I nearly forgot: whatever happens between us in our department stays between us. Don't mention anything—rumours or otherwise—to or in front of Thrush.'

'Who's Thrush?'

'That's our nickname for the Captain. You know, the guy you insulted before you even stepped aboard.'

'Oh yes, I'm really, really sorry about that.'

'Sorry, my arse, mate. We all hate the fucker, and to be honest, when I heard you say that, I felt very close to you.'

'Why do you call him Thrush?'

'Because, like thrush, he's an irritating cunt. He's only out for himself, and he'll drop you like a sack of shit if you fuck up. Treat him like a mushroom.'

Tarquin looks up, a bit lost. 'Erm… treat him like a mushroom?'

'Yeah, feed him shit and keep him in the dark.

'As for the lads, they're a good bunch. If you treat them fairly and you're loyal and truthful, they'll eventually return the favour—once you gain their respect. Just remember, they can be your best friends or your worst nightmare, so it's completely up to you.

'Are we clear, then?'

'Erm… yes, I think so.'

'Nice one. Right, sort out your shit and go and see Zecky, the Chief Stewardess, for some uniform. I'll see you in the wheelhouse a bit later when we go into port, OK, mate?'

'Yes… thank you. Just one thing I'd like to ask.'

'Shoot.'

'Where is my cabin?'

'You're in it.'

'Oh, no—I think there's been a mistake. I was expecting a cabin to myself.'

'Well, you expected wrong then, didn't you? Everyone bunks up with a buddy except the Captain, and you'll be taking the only bunk that's spare.'

'Who am I sharing with?'

'You're in the top bunk, in here with Jock.'

'But this place is the size of a cubby hole!'

'Well, what were you expecting—a master suite? You're crew, remember. Anyway, it may be small, but it's clean and modern, and the only time you'll be in here is when you're getting your head down for a few hours.'

'But how am I supposed to climb up to the bunk?'

'I must admit, you are a bit of a short-arse, aren't you, Tar? How tall are you? You look about five-foot-four.'

'I'm five-foot-five, actually.'

'Have you thought about being a burglar as a career move, Tar? You'd be fucking great at it.'

'A burglar? Why a burglar?'

'Because your arse would rub your footprints out, and they'd never catch you.'

'Oh, right.'

'Come on, Tar, smile—I'm only messing with you. You'll crack the fucking mirror with that face!

THE CREW

'Right, I'll call you to the wheelhouse when we go into port so you can see what it's all about and get the best view.'

'Oh yes, the best view of the port entrance and navigation light formations… I learnt about all that at college.'

'No, mate. Tits on the beach. They're far more interesting than lights. You'll get a real eyeful as we go in if you're lucky!' I say with a wink.

'Oh!'

'I'll see you in a bit.'

* * * *

I leave Tar rubbing his sore head and take a slow stroll up to the wheelhouse. As I walk in, I catch Thrush and his girlfriend on the sofa. She's stroking his hair like a lapdog, and it turns my stomach to watch the pathetic pair. He spots me and breaks away from the caress like a schoolboy caught with his trousers down. Clearing his throat, he stands bolt upright, the bottom of his white shirt sticking out of his fly. She quickly disappears off to the storeroom, and I'm in two minds about whether to say anything. Eventually, I decide not to—we can all have a few laughs out of this one, and I just want to see how long he'll walk around like that before he notices.

For once, Thrush decides to keep me in the loop and gives me a work brief.

"OK, we'll be going to the berth shortly, so get on with the pre-sailing equipment checklist, and I'll phone down to the engine room to give them half an hour's notice for departure. Make sure the cadet is up here for when we sail so he can see what we do."

"He's already been told, and he'll be up as soon as I call him."

"You'd better call him shortly then. And by the way, I didn't appreciate his comment about me when he boarded. I don't like his attitude."

"He's just wet behind the ears and lacks life experience, that's all. We'll all take him under our wing, but don't expect miracles—he's got a lot to learn."

"Well, you'd better make sure he learns quick, or I'll hold you personally responsible."

I don't say anything back because I don't want to get into a slagging match, but mentally, I'm calling him all the names under the sun.

I call Tar, and he arrives on the bridge a few minutes later, wearing his new uniform, still creased from the packaging. He's sweating, and it's obvious he's nervous as hell. He looks bewildered at all the gadgetry and electronics, so I do my best to calm him down.

"You look very smart, Tar… the boss will be proud."

"Thank you, sir."

I scowl and make a show of looking behind me, as if checking whether someone important is there.

"Oh, sorry—you don't like to be called that."

I give him a wink to put him at ease.

"That's all right, mate. Like I said, when you call me 'sir,' you make me nervous. And besides, I actually work for a living. Right then, Tar, the first piece of equipment I'm going to show you is definitely the most important."

"Oh, OK… is it the radar?"

"No, it's the kettle. Here are two cups, and mine's a coffee—milk with two sugars."

"Oh, right."

"You've got to start from square one, and this is it… learning how to make a decent brew."

He asks if he should make one for the Captain, but I tell him Jock will make him a special one later. Then I take him through the pre-departure checklist.

When we're at the radar, he notices the Captain's shirt sticking out of his fly and glances at me, unsure if he should say something. I quickly put my finger over his mouth.

"Don't say a thing, Tar," I whisper. "I know he makes you nervous, but this will make him seem more human to you. Every time he bollocks you or talks down to you from now on, just remember that shirt tail and what a twat he looks. It's a great leveller, don't you think?"

"You're right, he does make me nervous. I think I let myself down a bit when I first came aboard and made that comment about him."

"Don't worry—what you said was bang on the money. It was just unlucky he was stood next to you, that's all. What happened to you is nothing compared to what I did."

"I can't imagine anything worse than what I did. What did you do?"

"Well, I'd been on a ship about a day and a half, and we'd just departed the port at night. Nobody had told me you weren't allowed to smoke on the wheelhouse wing. It's technically an open-air area outside on either side of the wheelhouse.

I was on watch on my own at night and decided to have a crafty cigarette next to the doorway so the smoke wouldn't get inside and stink the place out. So I'm puffing away, and I decide to flick the almost-finished fag over the side of the ship. I stick it on my thumb and flick it with my middle finger, but as it shoots out over the side, the wind catches it and blows it back on deck."

"What happened then?"

"Well, I heard this loud 'Aaaahhhh!!' The Captain was walking up the outside of the accommodation, and it hit him on his right cheek, just underneath his eye. The bloody thing was going at a fair speed when it exploded on his face."

"Crikey! What did he say to you?"

"Well, put it this way—he wasn't impressed. Anyway, we'll have even more fun in a minute."

"Why?"

"Because that box next to Thrush contains his new binoculars. They only arrived this morning, and I took them out of the box and smeared black boot polish around the eyepieces. He'll look even more of a clown than he does already after he uses them for the first time. He'll look like a fucking panda!"

"You'll never get away with it."

"Won't have to, mate—I'll just blame you."

"Oh no—you wouldn't, would you?" says Tar, looking terrified.

"No, of course not… well, at least not yet. I'll let you settle in first. Trust me, my nickname isn't Teflon for nothing."

"Teflon… why Teflon?"

"Because nothing sticks!"

Eventually, it sinks in, and he smiles. I get the feeling he's not the sharpest knife in the drawer, but I'll give him some latitude for now because he seems like a good kid.

We work through the pre-departure checklist while Jock and Tom head up to the deck to pick up the anchor. Rob joins us on the bridge to take his position at the helm because Thrush always switches to manual steering coming into port.

The engineer calls up from the engine room and advises us we've got full use of the engines. Thrush gives the order to Jock to heave up the anchor. The yacht becomes underway and slowly heads towards the marina.

I give Tar a nudge.

"Any minute now, Tar, he'll pick up the binoculars to see if our place at the berth is clear."

THE CREW

"I don't think we should be doing this, you know," Tar says nervously as Thrush moves over to the port side and picks up the binoculars.

Thrush speaks to the port authority on the VHF radio and confirms the berth, lifting the binoculars to his eyes for a better view. With a smirk, I whisper in Rob's ear that the eagle has landed. Rob is watching the instruments, so he hasn't had a chance to look at Thrush yet.

Thrush puts the binoculars down and walks towards Rob to give the order for the next alteration of course. It has worked perfectly.

He looks like he's just done ten rounds with Mike Tyson. Both eyes are circled with big, round black marks. I can't help feeling very proud of myself, and I have a quiet chuckle.

In the meantime, Thrush is giving helm orders. We have to acknowledge orders verbally by saying, 'Roger.' The only problem is, Thrush mumbles, and it's bloody hard to hear him. Rob and I have asked him a hundred times to speak up, but he never does.

Thrush gives Rob a helm order of five degrees to starboard, and Rob can just about hear him. Then Rob spots his panda eyes and nearly bursts out laughing, but disguises it as a cough. Rob and I try not to make any eye contact because that would really set us both off. Thrush is oblivious and walks out onto the bridge wing, giving another helm order—but we can't hear what he says.

Eventually, I lose my patience with Thrush's almost inaudible orders, and I think, *Enough is enough.*

'Fuck it! I've had enough of this. Nobody acknowledge his orders until he does as we ask and speaks up so we can hear him properly.'

Rob is thinking along the same lines and nods his head. 'Right, sounds like a plan. It's not as if we haven't asked him before.'

Thrush mutters something inaudible, and deliberately, there is no response from Rob or me. A few seconds go by, and again he mumbles something. Still, no response. After the third time, he comes steaming back into the wheelhouse, his face twisted with anger.

'For God's sake, people,' he says furiously. 'Will somebody ROGER ME!!'

Rob and I look at each other, and the sight of this human, panda-eyed goon, with his fly open, screaming for somebody to 'roger' him is too much to bear. We immediately collapse into fits of hysterical laughter. After we just about manage to stop laughing, we explain—*again*—that we couldn't hear his orders. He finally takes the hint and speaks up. He berths the yacht without a hitch but orders Rob and me to his cabin for another bollocking.

'I've got the sneakiest feeling we're in for a toasting again, mate,' says Rob.

'Yeah, I know, but it was worth it. Anyway, fuck him, we've asked him a million times, but the prick doesn't listen. Just let me do the talking.'

Five minutes pass, and Zecky comes to the bridge to tell us that Thrush wants us in his cabin—now.

'Come on then,' I tell Rob. 'Let's face the music.'

We walk into his cabin, where he's sitting at his desk, fuming with anger. His face is red with rage, and his eyes are even redder from trying to rub the polish off.

'Close the door, NOW!' he shouts, stabbing the table with his index finger.

Rob and I step inside and do as we're told.

'WHO DID IT?!' Thrush shouts.

I decide to play the idiot and look confused. 'Who did what, Captain?'

'Don't take me for a bloody fool! You know what!'

'Sorry, Captain, I don't have a clue what you're talking about.'

'Who put black shoe polish on the binoculars?!'

'Shoe polish… around the binoculars?'

THE CREW

'YES! Shoe polish!'

'I've got no idea, Captain.'

'Don't lie to me. Just admit it. You did it, didn't you?!'

'I beg your pardon, but are you insinuating that I'm guilty? Based on what?'

'I want a full apology from you this instant, or I'm onto the office about this. And I guarantee you'll get a written warning.'

'On what grounds? Your opinion? I'm afraid you'll need to do better than that, Captain. If you have any proof, then I'd be glad to see it.'

He stands up and points his finger at me. 'In fact, forget the office—I'm giving you a warning right now.'

'Right, I've had enough of these accusations. I'm going to prove to you that it wasn't me.' I take the phone and dial a friend's number.

'What are you doing?' demands Thrush.

'Clearing my name.'

Even Rob has a confused look on his face. The phone rings a few times, and I put it on loudspeaker so we can all hear. After a few moments, my friend Zak answers.

'Hi, Zak, it's me.'

'Now then, bitch… how's it going?'

'So-so, mate… sorry to bother you again.'

'You're OK, mate, I'm just on the crapper teasing out a monster turd. Feels like I'm trying to pass a brick!!'

Rob and I start to chuckle but try our best to remain composed.

'That's delightful, Zak, but listen. I haven't time to talk at the moment. I'm in a bit of a situation. Could you just tell me what you found on your new binoculars when they got delivered to your yacht last week?'

'Binoculars? Oh yeah, the eyepieces had boot polish on them. Some guy in the factory must have been a practical joker.'

'Thanks, mate. I've got to go now, but I'll speak to you soon.'

'OK, mate, catch you later.'

'Cheers.'

I switch off the phone and go over to Thrush, looking him in the eye.

'I believe you owe me an apology, Captain,' I tell him with a very serious face.

'I'm not apologising for anything.'

'Right, I've had my lot of this. I'm calling the office now, and I'm going to tell them exactly what has happened and get them to make you apologise. I've even got a witness. If you want to go through that, then that's your choice.'

I pick up the phone and start to dial the office.

Thrush grabs the phone furiously. He turns his back on me and mumbles, 'Oh, very well then… I apologise.'

'I'm sorry, what did you say?'

Again, he mumbles his apology.

'Well, turn around and look me in the eye when you say it, so at least I know you mean it.'

I know I'm pushing it, but I'm having too much fun. Thrush slowly turns around, makes eye contact with me for a split second, and apologises again—very quietly. It obviously kills him to say it.

'What about him?' I say, pointing at Rob.

'I didn't blame him!' says Thrush, sounding exasperated.

'No, but you would've done if I hadn't proved to you it wasn't us.'

'No, I wouldn't.'

'Yes, you would.'

'I wouldn't!'

'Well, why did you bring him in here then?'

THE CREW

Thrush is now going purple with frustration.

'OK… OK, I apologise to you as well, Robert.'

'That's OK, Captain. Everyone makes mistakes,' says Rob.

'Right then, we're all square,' I say, opening the door to leave. 'But I won't forget this in a hurry, Captain. Anyway, we've got work to do, so we'd better get on.'

He's very frustrated now, so he turns his back on us and looks out of the window to stew in his own embarrassment.

'Yes, OK… carry on.'

Rob and I walk out and close the door behind us. I look over my shoulder at Rob as we quickly walk down the alleyway, and he's already looking at me with a big grin on his face. We don't say a word until we're out of earshot.

'What a fucking goon!' I whoop.

Rob starts shaking his head in disbelief.

'Fuck me, boss, you've got some front. They don't call you Teflon for nothing, do they? But who was the guy on the phone?'

'Just a mate who owed me a favour. I told him what I was going to do half an hour before. Although why he felt the need to tell me about his turd at that particular moment, I'll never know!'

Chapter 12
Priapism

The sun is just setting, and the marina is starting to bustle with people and crew strolling along the quay.

"Have you seen the amount of booze up on the barbecue deck?" I say to Tom.

"Quite a bit, is there?"

"I'm amazed the yacht's still floating, mate! The boss'll be down in about an hour. I've just been told he'll have about twelve to fifteen guests. Thrush says he sounds as if he's pissed."

"If I wasn't so tired, I'd look forward to it," Tom says, rubbing his eyes.

"I wonder who's coming with him. When we dropped him off, there were only about seven blokes."

"I bet you he brings some chicks on board."

"Nah, he wouldn't risk losing all his millions."

"Yes, he would! He's pissed, and we all know what he's like after a few. The wife's away out of town, I think. When the cat's away, and all that."

Zecks walks onto the quay to have a word with us. "Hey, you two, how's it going?"

"Not too bad—how's your good self?"

"I've been rushing around like a blue-arsed fly trying to get everything sorted for his lordship tonight. Chef's sweating his knackers off in the galley, making his favourite nibbles. I think he'll be more interested in the bubbly, though, to be honest."

"That doesn't surprise me. He's been at it all afternoon in the clubhouse and hotel after his round of golf. I bet he's in a right state. Where do you want me to take them when they arrive?"

"Just bring them up to the barbecue deck where the food and booze is. Oh, and by the way, here are his epilepsy pills. Make sure he gets a couple down him, because he's prone to fits when he's pissed, as you well know."

"Fucking hell, yeah, I do. Remember last year when I got called out of bed by Jock? His written report was fantastic."

"What happened?" asks Tom curiously.

"Last year, we were cruising the Amalfi Coast with the boss, and we were anchored just offshore. The boss wanted a Jacuzzi underneath the stars, on his own, and it was getting into the early hours, so he told everyone to go to bed and that he'd see them all in the morning.

"Anyway, Jock gives it an hour and hopes the boss has gone to bed so he can tidy the top deck and clean the area ready for his morning dip. As he walks up to the Jacuzzi, he finds the boss lying down, half-naked and semi-conscious on the deck."

"Was he pissed?"

"He'd had a few, but it was mainly due to a fit. He was OK in the end because we got him off the yacht to the nearest hospital pretty quickly."

"So what happened?"

"Well, I had to get Jock to write a full report on the incident for the office, but as you know, he's not the most educated bloke in the world, and he doesn't really know about report etiquette. He's huffing and puffing about having to write it, so I just told him not to worry about it and not try to be clever. I told him to just put it in his own words and, at the end, add a 'lessons learned' statement to help prevent the incident from being repeated."

"So what did he put?"

"I'll tell you exactly what he put. Because it was so funny, I memorised it so I could tell the boys. The really funny thing was, he wasn't even trying to be funny—he just took what I told him literally. I'll try my best vocal impression of Jock, so this is what he wrote, and I quote:

"I went for a lie-down on my bed for an hour and watched Sex and the City *whilst the boss was having a soak in the tub. I thought, when the boss buggers off to bed, I'd clean the Jacuzzi area there and then 'cos I was a bit knackered and fancied a good kip and a lie-in. Anyway, I walk up to the top deck and find the boss face down, arse up on the deck, shaking and looking like a starfish. I thought he was taking the piss, so I started to laugh a bit. After a minute or two, I figured something was up, so I bent over and saw his face. I saw foam coming out of his mouth. My initial impression was: fuck me... the cunt's got RABIES!! Then I realised he wasn't arsing around, so I went off to get my boss, who was around Robbie's cabin having a livener. Turns out the silly sod was having a fit because he hadn't taken his epilepsy tablets. Lesson learned—make sure the boss takes his pills before he starts breakdancing!"*

"That was his report before I doctored it. I emailed it to everyone I knew because he'd taken my instructions so literally—but with fantastic results. I don't like to remind him of it because he gets a bit embarrassed."

Zecky jumps in: "That's bloody hilarious! I can totally believe Jock did that. Do you remember that really posh dinner we had in Monaco last year? He made what I thought was a belching noise, so I turned around and asked him if he'd just burped."

"Oh yeah, I remember."

"He said of course he hadn't burped—he'd just lifted his leg to let out some gas! It didn't even register with him that farting is probably worse than belching. I tell you, the boy's a savage. Anyway, boys, I've got things to be getting on with, so make sure he gets his pills, and I'll see you later, OK?"

"No problem, Zecks, and if there's any of the good grub left, can you send some our way? A bit of fresh lobster would go down nicely."

THE CREW

"Yeah, of course I will, sweetheart. There should be loads left because I've got a feeling they'll only be interested in booze tonight. By the way, where's Tarquin?"

"Oh, he's around somewhere."

"Do his mummy and daddy know he's playing sailor?"

"I know he's a bit wet behind the gills, but he seems a good kid. He's just got very limited life experience, but all that's going to change after a few weeks living aboard here with us. His parents won't recognise him when he gets back—I know mine didn't. I take it you don't have any romantic intentions towards the young lad, then, Zecks?"

"I doubt if he even knows what it's for yet."

An hour or so passes, and the Captain receives a phone call telling him Mr Thomas and his guests are on the way. The hotel limo drops them off, and it's a very merry bunch who get out. Jock and I are the first to meet and greet as we open the car doors for them.

"Hello, Jock! How are you?" asks the boss, as he puts his arm around Jock's shoulders.

"Never better, sir. How was the golfing?"

"It was OK, but not as good as the drinks in the clubhouse afterwards. One of the girl caddies fell over and hurt herself on the green."

"Really? Where?" asks Jock.

"Between the first and second hole."

"Well, that doesn't leave much room for a bandage, does it?"

The boss and his friends find this hilarious and all slap him on the back.

Tom meets them at the top of the passerelle and invites them to follow him up to the barbecue deck, where the food and drink are laid out. They're only up there for a few seconds when the boss puts on some lively music, and they fire straight into the nosh and booze.

His friends are a good mix. They're around his age, and most of them are businessmen, dressed in slacks and shirts—apart from two in their late twenties, who have obviously flown out with their fathers for the ride. They sit on the side of the yacht, overlooking the quay, drinking cocktails and loving the attention they're getting from gawpers down below. The boss seems to be having a great time with his mates, swapping stories and quaffing champagne.

Then, one of the boss's friends turns the music down so he can be heard making a little speech.

"OK, chaps, I just want to say a few words before we all get too ratted. I haven't seen you lot in a good few years, and it's been fantastic so far. It's great to see you all again—it takes me right back to when we were kids, hanging out together. Turning 60 makes you think about your life and what you've done with it, and you realise you just have to take each day as it comes and live every day like it's your last. I think we're pretty much on track for that tonight!

"I've had a great life so far, and I reckon I've got a few more years left on the clock—though I probably won't think that tomorrow morning. Anyway, I'm getting sick of my own voice now, so all that's left to say is… thank you, from the bottom of my heart, for turning up and taking the time out to meet up."

Mr Thomas presents him with a gift-wrapped magnum of vintage champagne and a gold-engraved personalised goblet.

"Bloody hell, cheers, you big softy," says the birthday boy. "I wasn't expecting anything except your company."

"Well, we've got another surprise for you—well, for all of us," announces the boss. "We've got a group of fine young ladies arriving soon for a bit of recreation while we're all away from home."

"I take it what happens on tour stays on tour?" shouts one of the guests.

"Never was a truer word spoken," says the boss, tapping the side of his nose. A big grin crosses his face as he thrusts his fist in the air before turning the music back up and yelling, "Let's 'av' it, then!"

THE CREW

"When the cat's away, the mice will play, eh?" Jock says to me.

"Looks like it. I had a feeling this was gonna happen. But the boss is taking a big fucking risk—never know who might be strolling along the quayside with a camera. Can't believe he wants to stay alongside. I'll go and have a quiet word with him."

I take a walk over to the boss, who's standing alone, eating a massive tiger prawn and smoked salmon, washing it down with champagne.

"All right?" he says. "How's it going?"

"I'm OK, sir. You having a good time?"

"Champion! Thanks for producing the goods tonight."

"No problem. Just doing my job, you know that. I see you've got the hiccups there."

"Yep, too much bubbly. Still, if you can't get pissed with your mates on a day like this, when can you, eh?"

"Exactly."

"Try a bit of this—it's Loch Carnan smoked salmon, best you can get, I reckon."

He hands me a chunk of salmon on a plate and tells me to taste it.

"I get it sent over from the Hebrides once a month. Delicious, eh?"

I shouldn't really be eating on duty, but since he's offered, I play along. I squeeze some lemon juice over the salmon and nod my approval. He winks and hands me a flute of Cristal champagne. The boss is great like that—it's the little things he does that make a big difference. And it only encourages the crew to go that extra yard for him. Last year, we had a really busy season and made him a good bit of money. To show his appreciation, he popped aboard and gave me $4,000 in cash to take the crew "for a drink" for a job well done. The crew don't mind going that extra mile for someone like him.

I wait for the right moment—just as the boss takes another bite of salmon—before dropping the question as delicately as I can.

"Sorry to bother you like this, sir, but I couldn't help overhearing one of the guests saying we're expecting more company."

"Yep, that's right."

He holds my eye contact for a few seconds, but as he doesn't elaborate, I have to prompt him.

"Do they have any, erm… special needs for the visit?"

"Not tonight," he says with a twinkle in his eye, "but one of them will need a padded seat for their arse tomorrow morning after I've had my wicked way."

He's made himself perfectly clear now, so I get to the nitty-gritty.

"OK! I'll keep my voice down, sir," I say, leaning in closer. "I'm pretty sure I know what you mean."

He slaps me on the arm.

"Good man! Glad we understand each other."

"How long will they be staying, do you think?"

"Just a few hours."

I hate to ask this, but I have to look out for his best interests. His missus won't be too chuffed if he goes home with a dose of something nasty.

"I take it you're sorted for condoms, sir? Safety first and all that."

"Ah, yes… I've got a padded headboard at the ready, so at least she won't get a headache." I can't help but laugh at his attitude—he's clearly playing with fire. "And don't worry about the condoms, my old mate. I've already got some stashed in my back pocket. Just make sure there's plenty of air freshener around in my room."

"Air freshener? Why air freshener?"

"For the smell of burning rubber!" he laughs.

"Have we been on the Spanish Fly, sir?" I joke.

"No, but at my age, you need all the help you can get. I tried some Viagra the other week, and I haven't had a hard-on like that since I was in my twenties. You could have hung your coat on it!"

"Sir, just be careful not to take too much. Apparently, it's not too good for your ticker, and you don't want to end up in a situation like the one I found myself in."

"Why? What happened?"

"Well, when Viagra first came out, I was curious about its effects, so I bought some. It was around the time I was on leave from working at sea, and most nights I was out on the town, drinking. After a while, the booze takes its toll, and sometimes I'd get brewer's droop—if I was lucky enough to pull."

"We've all been there at some time in our lives, mate."

"I didn't want to miss out on a top night with the boys either, but at the end of the night, I wanted to be up to my nuts in guts. That was the dilemma—stay fairly sober and perform in the sack but not have a really funny evening, or get pissed up with the boys and have a corker of a night."

"So which one did you choose?"

"I was a bit crazy in those days, sir, so I didn't choose one or the other—I chose both. I didn't want to miss out on a really funny night or a great shag, so I popped some Viagra twenty minutes before jumping into the sack."

"Did it work?"

"Erm, yeah… a little too well. Even though I was hammered!"

"Why? What happened?"

"I was really sensitive to it, and I got a boner like a totem pole. I must have taken too much because I got priapism."

"Priapism?"

"When you get an erection, but it won't go down!"

"Well, that sounds fucking perfect! I can't imagine anything better than having a fucking great hard-on for an hour or two."

"Try nineteen hours."

The boss almost chokes on his tiger prawn. "NINETEEN FUCKING HOURS? I bet she was sore afterwards!"

"Well, it certainly put a smile on her face and a grimace of pain on mine, sir."

"How did you… you know… deflate it, then?"

"About half a dozen ejaculations, cold showers, and half a bottle of Jack Daniels."

"Fuck me, mate—that's priceless! I always knew there was some reason I hired you!"

"That wasn't the worst of it, though, sir. It was bad enough having a dick that looked like it had been through a mincing machine, but I almost lost my job because of it."

"Your job? Why?"

"Because I was supposed to go to work in the morning, but I didn't make it out of the house because my stiffy wouldn't go down. I couldn't very well turn up at work doing a wigwam impression, now could I?"

"That's one of the funniest things I've heard, mate. I can't imagine what your boss thought when you told him. What did he say?"

"He almost sacked me! He said I sounded pissed, and I told him I was—and why I was—but he found it hard to believe the story, as you can imagine."

"So how did you prove it to him—or shouldn't I ask?"

"Well, all I could think of at the time was to produce photographic evidence, so I sent him three photos on my phone. One was of the naked girl in bed, one of the packet of Viagra, and one of my stiffy."

THE CREW

The boss is now laughing so hard it looks like he might choke at any second. "Did he believe you, then?"

"Well, he said he wasn't a hundred per cent convinced, but he thought it was such an original story he'd let me off. So remember, sir—take it easy on them tonight."

Mr Thomas finally catches his breath while wiping tears from his eyes. "I'll bear that in mind. Right, I'm off to join the party. I'll catch you later, Bonk-on Billy!"

"OK, sir, and by the way, here are your epilepsy pills. Don't forget to take them—we don't want you having another fit and starting to break-dance again, do we?"

Chapter 13
Escort the Escorts

'What was the boss laughing about just then?' Jock asks me.

'I was telling him the story of my Viagra experience—warned him to take it easy on them after what happened to me.'

'Everyone seems to be enjoying themselves, by the look of things.'

'Yeah, it won't be long before the old boy starts busting some moves before disappearing somewhere quiet for a knee-trembler.'

'Are we going to bet on how long it takes him to go for it, then?'

I jump at the chance to place a bet with Jock, whose record of unsuccessful wagers is exceeded only by the number of verbal warnings and work reprimands he's received.

'Yeah, OK, you're on, sunshine!'

'Fifty euros says he'll disappear with her within the hour. Let's make it interesting—let's say a hundred.'

'It's your money you're throwing away, Jock, but if you want to make it a hundred, so be it. That's more beer vouchers for me. So, you reckon an hour?'

'Yep.'

'No way, mate,' I say, shaking my head. 'He's got guests here. He'll want to make sure they feel welcome and enjoy himself with them.'

'Yeah, I know, but they're here for a reason. Since it's his yacht and he's hosting, my guess is he'll lead by example and kick things off, so to speak.'

Jock watches the boss intently, trying to gauge what's going through his mind.

'I still reckon he'll have a laugh for a couple of hours first before "releasing the meat",' I say confidently.

THE CREW

'OK, whatever. Just don't go spending your winnings yet, because my pocket's going to be bulging tonight, my old china.'

'Bollocks, I can feel it in my bones—I'm onto a winner here. Let's face it, your betting history is pretty shoddy, isn't it?'

'That's all going to change tonight, matey.'

'All right, let's make it interesting. You know that hot chilli sauce in the mess room?'

'Yeah, I fucking love it.'

'Up your nose?'

'Eh?'

'Whoever loses has to snort half a capful up each nostril.'

Jock's smile falters. 'Are you serious?' he asks nervously.

'Yeah.'

'That stuff really hurts. When I went to sea for the first time and crossed the Equator, the crew held a crossing-the-line ceremony for first-timers. I was just a kid, and they got me shit-faced, tied me face-down on the bar table, covered me in oil, and stuck chicken feathers all over me. Then the rotten bastards poured a whole bottle of chilli sauce down the crack of my arse.'

'I bet that hurt,' I say, grimacing.

'I screamed the fucking house down. There's a photo somewhere of a young, naked, screaming kid running up the alleyway looking like a plucked chicken.'

'So, Jock, the question is: are you a man or a mouse?' I tease, knowing full well that Jock never backs down from a bet—especially when a hundred euros is at stake.

'Nah, I'll do it, because it won't be me sniffing it, pal.'

'All right then, bud. It's a bet! Now, back to business.'

We glance over at one of the boss's guests, who's trying unsuccessfully to worm his way into a girl's knickers. It's obvious she's having none of it. He's boring as hell, keeps readjusting his tie, and pulls his sports jacket over his sweaty shirt in a futile attempt to conceal the rolls of fat spilling over his belt.

The girl catches our eye, silently pleading for help. I give her a wink and tell Jock to get her away from the sofa and into the party crowd when he sees me drop the tray.

I grab a food tray with some nibbles and approach the bloke, offering him some before 'accidentally' dumping the tray and its contents onto his lap.

'Jesus Christ!' he shouts. 'What the hell are you doing?'

'I'm very sorry, sir. The tray just slipped out of my hand.'

'You shouldn't be so bloody clumsy.'

'All I can do is apologise, sir. Let me escort you to the men's room—we'll get you cleaned up. There's a hand dryer in there; your shirt should be dry in a few minutes.'

Muttering under his breath, he makes his apologies to the long-suffering girl and follows me to the men's room. The moment we're out of sight, Jock swoops in and rescues her.

'We saw you were in trouble, so we thought we'd help you out,' he tells her. 'Hope you don't mind.'

'Mind? You both deserve a medal.'

'I'll take you over to another group so it looks like you're mingling.'

'Thanks for that. I owe you one.'

'No problem.'

Jock leads her to the dancefloor, where she starts dancing with a few of her 'associates'. The men watch as they dance, whispering amongst themselves. The women, thick as thieves, are clearly doing their job—

strategising, no doubt, to rid the girl of 'Mr Blobby' and ensuring she has backup in case another boring arsehole tries his luck.

A few of the more pissed-up guests down their drinks and stagger to the centre of the floor, where the girls immediately get to work, grinding on them and stroking their egos. It's hilarious to watch.

The boss unsteadily gets out of his seat and eagerly jumps into the party, busting his moves—there's leg-strutting and arm-pointing all over the place. He's grinning from ear to ear as a couple of girls join him, his pissed-up eyes locked onto the ample cleavage of the girl in front of him.

Jock and I share a smile as Mr Blobby comes back out, noticing that his girl is no longer there. He spots her across the floor and shuffles over, beginning to dance within her group. I use the term "dancing" loosely. By the way he's moving, he could be having a seizure. He's invented a new dance that's somewhere between body-popping and punk-pogo.

I glance at my watch and see there's about ten minutes left until Jock's hour is up and he loses the bet. I point at him to get his attention, then motion to my watch, followed by a cutting gesture across my throat before pointing back to him. Jock understands straight away what I mean, and he starts to look fidgety, glancing over at the boss. Another ten minutes, and he's lost the bet!

After about twenty minutes, the guests—apart from the energetic younger lads—begin to filter off the dancefloor and flop down on the sofas. More drinks are consumed, and a few guests are starting to look pretty cosy with some of the girls. One of them is sat opposite where Jock is standing, wearing a very, very short skirt. He leans over to me, cupping his hand to block out the music.

'If there are three types of mini skirt—mini, micro, and "don't bend over"—then that's definitely the third,' he jokes.

'I know, mate, but don't be so bloody obvious. You're not the most subtle guy.'

'I can't help it. With all this skirt around, I feel like a dog with two dicks.'

'Jock, you always feel like a dog with two dicks. You need to calm down, my old son. You'll wear yourself out the way you live the fast life.'

'Live fast, die young, and leave a good-looking corpse. Anyway, you can talk.'

'Well, you certainly walk the walk, Jock, I'll give you that. I don't know how you stay in shape. You live on bar snacks, smoke like a chimney, and drink like a fish. You must have internal organs as tough as tyres.'

'Genetically gifted, me, boss,' he boasts, flexing his arm.

After about half an hour, the flirting between the guests and the escorts escalates to another level. The two young lads are smooching with girls on the dancefloor, their hands straying all over their bodies. A few of the older men have taken this as the green light, and all over the back end of the yacht, couples are having fun. The boss is sat with his mate, whose birthday it is, while two of the girls dance and laugh in front of them. The men's facial expressions have shifted from cheeky grins and smiles to concentrated, carnal lust. The birthday boy leans over to the boss and says something to him, and the boss nods in agreement. Moments later, he and the boss take the girls by the hand and head toward the boss's cabin on the next deck. That's probably why Mr Thomas chose the sofa nearest the door to the lounge, so as not to draw attention when they succumbed to their desires.

All is well so far, so Jock and I leave Zecks and her crew to attend to the other guests. We brief Zecks on who's gone where, who's with whom, and who's drinking what, then Jock and I join Rob and Tom in the crew room for some supper. Zecky's come up trumps tonight—she's laid on lobster, champagne, tiger prawns, and rare duck that the crew love, not to mention cake, so everyone's happy.

'How's it all going up there, boys?' Tom asks as we sit down at the feast.

'Everything you'd expect, mate. There'll be a few sore heads tomorrow.'

Jock joins us at the table. 'Not to mention a few sore cocks if they keep heading the way they're going.'

All is quiet in the mess room as we take a well-earned break, tucking into the food and catching up on a bit of TV, until the ship's mobile suddenly rings loudly.

'Who the hell is that at this hour?' I think to myself. I wave over to Rob, who's at the end of the table. 'Get the phone, mate.'

'Hello... Rob speaking.'

The voice at the other end is difficult to hear due to the poor reception inside the steel yacht, but Rob can just about make out a quiet, well-spoken female voice.

'Hello, Robert, this is Mrs Thomas speaking.'

Rob's face drops like someone's just told him he's got an hour to live. He stops chewing his food, looks at me with terror in his eyes, and mouths: 'IT'S THE BOSS'S MISSUS!!' Jock and I look at each other in disbelief.

'WHAT?'

We can hear the voice on the phone repeating, "Hello? Hello? Robert, are you there?"

"Stall her, for fuck's sake!" Jock whispers urgently.

Rob clears his throat. "Errr... hello, Mrs. Thomas. How can I help?" He jabs his finger toward the crew room door, signaling Jock to close it and muffle the sound of the music.

"Yes, this is Mrs. Thomas. I've just been to see a show with some friends, and we're not far from the port. Rather than going back to the hotel, I thought it would be easier to stay the night aboard."

Rob takes a deep gulp and runs a frantic hand through his hair before responding. "You're coming down... tonight?!"

"Yes, me and a friend. We'll be going straight to bed, so no need to wake Zecky."

"Do you need picking up, Mrs. Thomas?"

"No, no… we're only about twenty minutes away. I'm just calling to find out what berth you're on so the driver can pull up to the passerelle."

"We're at Berth 13, Mrs. Thomas."

"Okay… I'll see you in or around twenty minutes, then, Robert."

Before Rob can say anything else, the line goes dead.

He turns to Jock and me, his face as white as a sheet. "She's coming down."

"When?" we ask in unison.

"NOW!"

"NOW? You're fucking shitting me!" I yell, leaping to my feet.

"RIGHT NOW?" Jock cries.

Rob looks exasperated. "Yes, Jock—right fucking now! I think we established that in Act One!"

"How long do we have? And who's with her?" I ask.

"Twenty minutes—her and a friend."

I take a deep breath. "Right, everybody calm down and do exactly as I say because we need to pull out all the stops to get the boss out of this one. Do you know what will happen if she comes aboard and finds all these escorts here?"

Jock rocks from side to side, blinking manically. "OH FUCK! THIS IS REEEALLY BAD!"

**"No shit, Sherlock. Right, Jock, this is where your 'direct' personality will, for once, pay off. I don't care how you do it, but get the escorts to the forward deck—quick sharp. And by quick sharp, I mean like YESTERDAY. I'll turn off the lights up there so it's in near darkness.

"The plan is to get the girls off the yacht by lowering them into the boat and sneaking them out through the harbor. You'll drop them off at another pier around the corner. We can't risk them being seen stepping off the yacht onto an illuminated quay and then strolling up to the gate. If Mrs. T bumps into them, she'll put two and two together, and we're all royally up shit creek without a paddle. For all we know, she's deliberately checking up on him.

"Tell the girls we've had a bomb threat—whatever it takes. Just get them moving!"**

"Don't worry, boss. I'll have them up on the forward deck faster than you can say 'fuck me sideways,'" Jock grins before dashing off.

Tom and Rob fire up the forward boat crane, swinging the small vessel out, ready for Jock and the girls. I radio Zecky, briefing her on the situation.

"Zecks, you need to get your crew moving. Change the bedsheets in any rooms that have been used, and if anyone asks, only the boss's male friends were on board tonight. Got it?"

"Got it."

"Good. Stand by the passerelle and keep watch for Mrs. T's car. The second you see it, radio me."

"Every second counts, Zecks. Your girls need to move like their lives depend on it."

"I hear you. I'm on it."

"One more thing—when you get to the passerelle, use the remote control to lift it clear of the quay. That way, she won't be able to board immediately. I'll send an engineer down to make it look like there's a problem. That should buy us a few valuable minutes. When the boat's clear, I'll give two short whistles over the radio. That's your cue to signal the engineer to lower the passerelle and let her on."

"Cool."

I snort. "Cool isn't the word I'd use, Zecks—more like pressure-cooker meltdown hot. But yeah, let's roll with that."

I take a deep breath. The worst part is still ahead—I have to break into the boss's room and drag him out. Last time he was seen, he and his mate were heading in there with two of the escorts.

"Rather you than me, matey!" Zecks laughs.

I'm not relishing what's next. God only knows what I'm about to walk in on. Hopefully, it won't be as bad as Jock's little hotel escapade a few nights ago. That one would take some beating.

I sprint down the alleyway towards the boss's room, heart pounding. From the opposite end, Jock comes tearing toward me, gripping the arms of two very nervous-looking girls. He, on the other hand, is grinning like a madman.

"I WAS BORN FOR THIS!" he shouts as he barrels past.

I skid to a halt in front of the boss's door. Music thumps from inside. I rest my hand on the door handle, take a deep breath, and steel myself. Then, I knock rapidly and push inside.

The dimly lit room is bathed in candlelight, with just a small corner lamp keeping the ambience intimate. The music is loud and ballsy. The boss and his mate are sprawled in plush armchairs, drinking Scotch and watching the two girls grinding on them. The girls are down to black lace stockings and suspenders, teasing away to the beat.

I don't want to interrupt. I really, really don't. But I have no choice.

The sudden flood of light from the alleyway spills into the room, making them all squint.

"Sir, I need a word," I call out.

The boss barely glances at me. "What? Now?" he asks, astonished.

"I'm kind of in the middle of something here."

"Afraid so, sir. It's urgent."

"Oh, I'm sure it can wait till morning. Close the door on your way out, mate."

Normally, I'd never push the boundaries with the boss. But tonight, I have no choice. There's no time.

I stride across the room, pushing past the two girls, and stand directly over him.

Then, I drop the bombshell.

"Sir, we've got a bit of a crisis on our hands. Your wife is expected in the next ten to fifteen minutes—maybe even sooner. I've got a plan, but there's no time to explain. We need to move all the girls to the front deck, right this second."

His face drops in terror, his eyes widening so much I think his eyeballs might pop out. He's already breathing faster with panic as he leaps out of his chair and rushes to the sound system's volume control. He quickly turns it right down and switches on the overhead halogen lights.

"GET THE FUCK OUT, NOW!" he shouts, pointing the girls towards the door. I tell them to grab their clothes, then take them by the arms and push them through.

Jock is sprinting down the alleyway towards me when the radio in his pocket crackles.

"A car is at the gate at the end of the wharf. If it's her, she'll be here in a few minutes," Zecky reports breathlessly.

"Calm down, Zecky. Just stick to the game plan and keep the passerelle up so she can't board. I think we'll only need another three or four minutes. Tom, are you there? How's it going up forward with the boat?"

"There are two more girls to get in, and then I think we're good to launch."

"Cool. The boss's wife will be at the passerelle any minute, so when you launch, use minimal engine power so she won't hear it. She won't be able to see the forward end of the yacht because of the other yachts rafted alongside us. As long as she can't get up the passerelle, we're home free."

"Gotcha!"

Jock ushers the two half-naked girls up the alleyway, but instead of watching where he's going, he's too busy ogling their bouncing tits. A moment later, he vanishes over the top of a flight of stairs at the end of the alleyway, followed by a loud crash as he slams into the fire door at the bottom. Seconds later, he's back up, giggling, and carries on as if nothing happened.

I make a mad dash to the lounge area and do a quick sweep. A stray handbag and a lipstick are left on the table—I grab them and hand them to the stewardess to throw in the boat. The boss's mates are still gathered by the bar, looking bewildered, so I quickly brief them and tell them to sit down and act normal.

I radio Rob. "Are you missing any girls?"

"The last one's just getting in, boss."

"OK. Once she's in, lower the boat, take them round the corner to the quay, and drop them off. Tell them to wait in the bar across the road—I'll send a taxi to take them wherever they need to go."

"Cool."

Moments later, I hear the boat being launched and head back to calm the boss.

"Right, sir, the girls are off, your mates have been briefed, and there's no evidence left lying around. Your wife won't suspect a thing—unless you're flustered and acting weird. Now, take off your shirt and give it to me."

"My shirt? Why?"

"Lipstick on the collar—and you smell like a bloody perfume factory."

"Oh, right! Shit!"

"The main things are taken care of, but it's the details that will sink the ship, so to speak. Jump in the shower and scrub yourself from head to toe. If she asks where you are, I'll tell her you're freshening up after golf. As far as she's concerned, all you've done today is play a round and come back for drinks with the boys, OK? I'll see you on the aft deck in ten minutes—I've delayed her long enough, I need to let her on."

"Christ, if you must," he mutters, still looking flustered.

"Oh, and sir—make it a cold shower. Looks like you need cooling down."

I leave the room and dump his shirt in the crew waste bin. A couple of sharp whistles down the radio signal the all-clear, and I walk aft to meet Mrs Thomas. Jock catches up with me halfway, grinning.

"What a tangled web we weave, eh, boss?"

"It's not over yet, mate. Hope for the best, plan for the worst."

As we arrive at the back of the yacht, Mrs Thomas is just stepping aboard with her friend. Zecky stalls her, handing them cooling lemon flannels fresh from the fridge and engaging her in a chat about the opera. Every time she moves towards the accommodation, he asks another question, buying time.

Ten minutes pass. Suddenly, the boss strolls down the stairs looking as cool as a cucumber.

"Hello, dear! I wasn't expecting you."

"The opera was closer to here than driving back home, so I thought we'd stay the night," she says. "How was your evening?"

"Oh, quiet. Just a few drinks with friends after a game of golf," he replies smoothly, leading her to the lounge.

Chapter 14
Initiation by Fire

It is 11 a.m. the following day, and all the tidying up from the night before is done. The guests have been fed and watered and sent on their way, happy enough. A good time was had by all, even when she turned up. She only stayed with her friend for half an hour before going to bed, leaving the boss and the boys to get drunk and relive old times. It is the most excitement they have had in years.

Mr Thomas and his wife are up early, and all seems to be well. They are in the Jacuzzi, soaking up the morning sun, and both look happy. The boss is looking a little worse for wear, but he is sipping one of Zecky's miracle working Bloody Marys with an aspirin, so he will be fine soon enough. Rob is on the quay polishing the Bentley, and the chauffeur is having a fried breakfast in the crew room before taking Mr Thomas and his wife back to Monaco in about an hour.

"Bloody hell. That was a close one last night," Tom says, shaking his head.

"Yeah, I know, mate, but it is over with. Part and parcel of the job, I am afraid. I am glad Tar was tucked up safe and sound in his stinker though. I cannot imagine he would have handled the pressure all that well, being a first timer and all."

"He would have probably shit his pants, eh?" Jock chuckles.

"Well, who could blame him? We almost did, and we have been doing this job for years."

"You are not wrong there. The adrenaline was surging, and I could not stop giggling," Jock says.

"I noticed, mate. What was that all about? Was that nervous laughter?"

"I do not know, really. Every time I get nervous, I just seem to giggle. I guess it is my fucked up way of dealing with pressure. It has dropped me in the shit a million times."

"How so?"

"See this scar on the back of my head?"

"Yep."

"That was my old man. He came back one night after the pub and his dinner was not cooked and waiting for him. One thing led to another, as it usually did when he was pissed, and he started battering Mum. He hated people laughing at him, so all I could think of to get him away from her was to giggle at his drunken attempt to knock her head off. Every time he hit her, I was hurting inside, but he was a big guy and I was only a nipper, so I had no chance of taking him on."

"Bloody hell, Jock. You have never told me this."

"Yeah, well... anyway, I started laughing at him, and he turned his attention to me instead of Mum."

"So you got a pounding?"

"Yeah, one of many, but the pain was nothing compared to Mum getting punched."

I cannot help but give the big guy a hug and a punch on the shoulder. "So many people take you the wrong way, mate. If only they knew what makes you tick instead of just seeing the public image. There are not many people who would do that, especially at that age. I know you fuck up and give me some headaches with your antics, but you are a good egg. People just need to look a little deeper where you are concerned."

"I do not care, mate. The people that matter do not mind, and the people that mind do not matter."

"Wise words, and you are right."

I have always known Jock was a good one. When I look into his eyes, I see no hidden agenda, just pureness. That is very rare in this world. There is an ancient pearl of wisdom that says, "The nail that stands out gets battered," and that is Jock in every sense. He stands out because he is different. If you had lived the life he has, would you not be? He is as basic as they come, but he has a pure heart and an endearing, coltish nature.

I go down to the crew room for some breakfast and brief the Captain on what happened last night. He had already gone to bed when it all kicked off, and I did not have time to wake him. He would have been half asleep and clueless anyway. That is one of the things that annoys everyone about this goon. He gets uptight and annoyed about tiny, insignificant things, then disappears when the boss comes aboard. If he was half the Captain he thought he was, he would be on deck with his crew getting stuck in. To be fair, though, the crew are glad he is not. If any of us have to speak to him twice a day, it is twice too many.

The quickest way to make an absolute fortune would be to buy Thrush for what he is worth and sell him for what he thinks he is worth. His inability to think outside the box is pretty entertaining. If something is not written down in the rule book, he is fucked. God help us if he ever had to think on his feet and make a spur of the moment decision. The job would go to rat shit.

After the boss has had his Jacuzzi and is feeling human again, he comes looking for me.

"Hey, mate. I have got to thank you for saving my bacon last night," he says, putting an arm around my shoulders. "That was quick thinking, and you earned every dollar of that huge salary I pay you."

"It is not nearly big enough, boss," I joke. "I felt every one of my thirty five years during last night's little escape and evasion exercise."

"Oh, come on now. A young lad like you can handle it."

"It is not the age, boss. It is the mileage, and last night you put another fifty thousand miles on my clock," I say, gasping for effect.

"I must admit I was shitting bricks myself for a minute there. I honestly thought I was done for. My arse was twitching more than a rabbit when a ferret gets put down its warren."

"Well, that makes two of us, sir. All I kept thinking was half of your millions going up in smoke in the divorce court. You'd need a lawyer who not only knew the law inside out but also knew the judge. That could have been the most expensive shag in history!"

"All's well that ends well, thanks to you and your crew, so here's a little something to say thank you." The boss hands me a large envelope full of cash. "I trust you'll spread the wealth, mate. Make sure everyone gets their fair share and make bloody sure they don't mention anything to anyone else about last night."

"Our lips are sealed—guaranteed. You don't have to do this, though," I say, holding out the envelope.

"No, really… fill your boots. You all deserve it."

"Second thoughts—yes, we fucking do. I think we deserve a pint or ten. Based on the fact that we probably saved you millions in the divorce court, I don't feel too bad about accepting a little extra this time. I'll need the extra cash for a new ticker if you keep this up!"

The boss laughs, and I can see he is happy to make the bonus payment. "Another thing I'd like to do for you all is let you have the use of the Wally Power for the weekend when you aren't chartering. Just bring it back in one piece—that's all I ask."

I can barely believe my ears. Personal use of a Wally yacht! Now that is a gift. He uses it as a weekend boat sometimes because it's more compact and great for getting into the smaller berths and jetties. To me, she encompasses everything a power yacht should be. In my eyes, they are without a doubt one of the sexiest modern power yachts you can lay your hands on. His is 118 feet long and made of reflective metal from bow to stern. She has all the comforts of home on the interior but also has some serious grunt. Three main engines kick out 5,600 horsepower each. She is the ultimate as far as I'm concerned, and if I had the money, no question—this is the yacht I'd buy. With a futuristic design, she's like something out of *Star Wars*. Having a free weekend in one of these is on a par with a go-kart driver being let loose with a Formula 1 car.

An hour later, I gather all the crew on the aft deck to see the boss and his wife off. Jock takes the luggage to the Bentley, then opens the door and gently helps Mrs Thomas in. She likes the fuss, but the boss is the opposite—he can't be doing with "all that bollocks." We wave them off, and as soon as they're gone, we start the yacht's main engines and let go from the quay. Once we're out of the harbour, we set a south-easterly course for Porto Cervo in Sardinia to meet up again with the Russian guests.

It's about 150 miles to the Bonifacio Strait—the stretch of water between Corsica and Sardinia. It will take the yacht around fourteen hours to get there at cruising speed. We could make it more quickly if we went at full speed, but for every extra knot or two, you burn an extra third in fuel. For that, it's hardly worth the expense.

Tar is on duty in the wheelhouse for the crossing. It's getting a bit bumpy out on the ocean, and the yacht is pitching and rolling in the swell. Tar arrives at the wheelhouse ten minutes before the watch, ready for Tom to hand over to us. Jock also turns up, holding a sandwich the size of a doorstep.

"Right then, Tar," I say, "first things first—make us all a coffee. I'm still half-asleep."

"OK, how do you take it?"

"Up the arse," shouts Jock from the other side of the bridge.

"Very funny, wise guy. Sharp as a razor. Tar, I like mine NATO standard, mate."

"Erm... I'm not sure what that means exactly."

"Milk and two sugars. Jock likes his like he likes his women—hot, black, wet, and sweet."

"You know it makes sense," says Jock.

Tom begins handing over the watch—including the course, speed, and traffic situation—and Tar listens intently. There's usually a handover sheet with about twenty different checks to make and pass on to the relieving officer. However, Tom's handover usually consists of the latest joke he's heard, what stupid fucking questions Thrush has been asking him, and what the latest football scores are. Today's handover from Tom consists of the following:

- Who has the best tits—Carmen Electra or Lucy Pinder? (two minutes)
- Why is belly button fluff always blue? (thirty seconds)
- What should Tarquin's punishment be if he doesn't memorise certain collision regulation rules? (three minutes)
- How easy it would be to hijack a private yacht and nick the cash from the safe whilst at sea (ten minutes)
- What's the point of eating sweetcorn if it comes out the same way it goes in? (thirty seconds)

After discussing these five relevant and important issues, Tom decides to leave us all in peace. Jock, Tar, and I are alone, and we discuss what Tar's punishment will be if he doesn't remember his test on the collision regulations.

"It's like this, Tar," we tell him. "If you're going up for your oral examination soon, you're going to have to learn the collision regulations thoroughly, as well as a million other things. Some regulations you'll have to learn verbatim. One thing is guaranteed, mate—if you fuck up on the collision regulations or buoyage in front of the Marine and Coastguard Agency examiner, your arse is grass. Some things you can screw up and he'll let you get away with it, but those two are critical because you can run the ship aground if you don't know them."

"How many rules are there, then?" asks Tar.

"There are thirty-eight rules and four annexes, so there's a lot to learn. You've not only got to know what they actually say, but also how to use them. There's no time like the present, so since you're up here as look-out, you might as well learn Rule 6. That's the look-out rule. It's probably the shortest rule of the lot, but it's an important one. You've got twenty minutes to memorise it, or you'll be punished by Jock here."

"Punished?"

"Of course. When I first went to sea, we lost privileges if we couldn't remember rules come question time. That usually meant stopping our beer allowance for a few days. I'm not going to do that to you because you look like you need a beer to loosen up a bit. However, Jock and I had a curry earlier, so I think farting on your head would be sufficient for a fuck-up."

"What do you reckon, Jock?"

"Couldn't agree more, but it has to be bare arse cheeks to face," says Jock.

"Well, that goes without saying—is there any other way?"

"That's agreed, then."

"What about if he fucks up on a really important rule? I reckon he gets the metre-long wooden ruler across his arse."

"I concur. That's sorted, then. Right, Tar—Rule 6, verbatim, twenty minutes, and the clock starts now."

Jock and I go out on the bridge wing for a cigarette and have a giggle at Tar trying to memorise the words to the rule. "Initiation by fire, eh, Jock?" I say. "To be fair, though, if he can keep his head and remember everything with the thought of what we're going to do to him, he'll breeze the exam. It's better than stopping the beer tap because you need one after a hard day's work."

"You're right not stopping his beer, boss—that's a bit too cruel."

"I wouldn't dream of it. Anyway, if I was going to stop anyone's, it would be yours, sunshine. That way I might get some peace and quiet."

After twenty minutes or so, Jock stands in front of Tar and starts loosening his trousers with a big grin on his face.

"What time are we on, Jock?" I shout from the bridge wing.

Jock hums the *Countdown* clock tune as he unzips himself. "Doooo doo da do, doooo doo da do, da da da… do do do do DO DO DO DOOOOO!"

THE CREW

"Time's up, Tar. Let's have it," I say, clapping my hands as Tar looks on nervously.

"Oh, come on, this isn't fair. How do you expect me to learn it under this sort of pressure?"

"This is nothing compared to what you'll feel in the exam room. Now let's have it. What part of the collision regulations is it, and what section?"

"Erm… Part B, the Steering and Sailing Rules."

"Good start! What section is it?"

"Erm… Section 1."

"So far, so good, mate. You might have to zip yourself up again, Jock. Right, crunch time… and I want the rule verbatim. Any mistakes and I let Jock's performing rectum loose on you!"

"Oh, bloody hell! Errrr, right… 'Every vessel shall at all times maintain a lookout by sight and hearing, as well as all available means appropriate to the prevailing circumstances and conditions, so as to make a full… a full… appraisal… erm… so… so as to make a full appraisal of… a full appraisal.' Oh, shit!"

Jock starts laughing loudly and drops his trousers to his ankles.

"Oh, look, there's no need for this," says Tar, quickly moving away from Jock.

Jock shuffles after him in hot pursuit. "You can run, but you can't hide, Tar. The rusty tea towel holder is puckered and ready."

He manages to manoeuvre Tar into the corner of the wheelhouse between the radar and the radio station. Backing into him, arse first, he grabs the back of his head before shoving it tight against his hairy cheeks.

"I believe the ending you were looking for, Tarquin Worthington-Smythe, was 'and a full appraisal of the situation and of the risk of collision,'" he says loudly before letting out an almighty fart in Tar's face. Even from several metres away, it sounds loud.

A long groan comes from Tar just as Thrush appears around the corner to check on everything.

"WHAT THE HELL IS GOING ON HERE?!" he bawls, palms outstretched.

"Just training the cadet, Captain," Jock explains without missing a beat.

The Captain takes another look at Tar, whose face is pressed against Jock's hairy arse. He doesn't quite know how to deal with this, so he rolls his eyes and walks back out. Jock's face goes crimson with the straining, then he lets rip with another almighty fart. As he does, his expression changes from smug to serious, as if he has just been caught off guard. He thinks for a moment, then nods his head and goes for number three.

"What were you thinking just then, Jock?" I ask.

"Thought I'd followed through there for a second," he says, laughing.

"Well, be careful, because he doesn't need any more freckles, mate."

"Noooo, I don't!" snuffles Tar.

"All right, Jock, let him go. That's the first lesson out of the way."

Jock releases Tar while sniffing the air. "Fuck me, that was a ripe one!"

"Judging from Tar's watery eyes, he doesn't doubt it, mate. Not to worry, Tar, you'll get your own back soon enough. Jock lost a bet last night, and he has to inhale some chilli after the watch."

The navigation watch passes fairly quickly, and I send Tar down to the engine room for some false errands, such as *rubber nails, glass hammers, golden nuggets,* and *long stands,* much to everyone's amusement.

A thick fog rolls in for an hour or two, reducing visibility to less than twenty metres. I start a close watch on the radars, slow down, and complete all the usual wheelhouse checks for blind pilotage in poor visibility. This is crucial because, with no clear sight of other ships, the risk of collision increases significantly. The safe navigation of the vessel has to rely entirely on radar, which becomes our eyes.

We don't tell this to Tar, though, because there is far too much fun to be had.

We send him up to the bow of the yacht, the furthest forward he can go, and equip him with a VHF radio, a catapult, and a bucket full of pebbles. He is told to fire each pebble in front of the yacht at regular intervals. If he hears a clang or anything that sounds like a pebble hitting a ship, he should run like hell and radio us immediately so we can quickly alter course.

It is an absolute joy to watch as he fires each pebble into the thick fog with his catapult. Every so often, his mind plays tricks on him, and we see him leaping to his feet and sprinting as fast as his little legs can carry him down the deck with a look of pure terror on his face.

Chapter 15
He Speaks the Language Like A Native

It has been a long and painful few hours for Tar in the rough weather of the crossing to Sardinia. The movement of the ship, combined with Jock's foul-smelling farts and the fear of crashing into another vessel in the fog, has really unsettled him. Being thrown in at the deep end, I believe it is called.

'You all right, bollocks? You look like shit,' says Jock, offering his unique brand of empathy in the only way he knows how.

'No, I'm not feeling too well,' murmurs Tar.

'You'll be fine, buddy. Just stay in the fresh air and focus on the horizon.'

'How's that supposed to help?'

'I don't know… it just does. Try eating something as well. Buttery toast works.'

'You're just saying that because you want me to be sick.'

'For once, little mate, I don't—because I'm fucked if I'm going to clean it up!'

'Nothing to do with not wanting to see me in discomfort, then?'

'Fuck no—that would be hilarious!'

'Errr… I actually think I might feel better if I was sick,' he says, clutching his stomach. 'My dinner feels like a lead weight, but I can't seem to make myself throw up.'

'Fair enough, matey. Wait there, I'll be back in a minute.'

Jock disappears and returns to the wheelhouse with a jar of cockles in vinegar, warmed up in the microwave. He keeps it hidden until they are back on deck.

'Right then, Tar. Tilt your head back and empty this into your mouth. It won't hurt you.'

THE CREW

Tar feels so awful that he does as he is told, pouring the small jar's warm, vinegary contents into his mouth. The yacht pitches and rolls with the waves. Jock waits, but there is little reaction. Tar chews and swallows the first mouthful with surprising ease.

'Are these cockles?' he asks.

'Yeah.'

'I don't see how they're supposed to make me sick, because I actually like cockles.'

'Trust me, mate, they will.'

Tar tilts his head back and finishes the rest of the jar, then hands it to Jock. There is one left, so Jock picks it out with his fingers, holding it up close to Tar, who is still chewing.

'Cockles, eh? Looks and tastes like a skanky old whore's clitoris, doesn't it?'

Tar stops chewing. He stares at the wobbling, warm cockle between Jock's fingers—then instantly retches over the side of the yacht.

'Too easy!' Jock says, turning on his heel and heading back inside, giggling.

'Oh Christ, Jock! What have you done now?'

'Chill, mate, it was for his own good. He said he'd feel better if he puked. He gave me the green light to do my worst.'

'Well, you'll be the one cleaning it off the side of the yacht if it dries before we reach port, so be warned. How's he doing anyway?'

'I've seen him look better.'

'I think he's had enough for one day. Send him for a lie-down.'

Jock heads outside and tells Tar to get some rest, which he gratefully accepts. As the yacht moves out of the fog and into open water and sunshine, Thrush joins us in the wheelhouse. I do not think he ever really knows what to expect when walking into a room with Jock in it. Fortunately, this time Jock is being professional, watching the radar, scanning the sea with binoculars, and reporting vessel positions to me as he should.

Thrush joins him, but not before checking the binocular eyepieces for boot polish. After five minutes of silence, he fails to find anything to moan about and mutters something instead.

'I want you to slow down next to that fishing boat ahead and ask the skipper if we can buy some fresh fish from him,' he says.

'OK. What fish are you after?'

'Some mackerel, octopus, or tuna would be nice. We might have a barbecue over the next couple of days.'

Jock and I exchange glances. We cannot believe our ears—he is actually thinking about the crew for once.

'OK, I'll ask when we get closer.'

After ten minutes, the yacht comes to a stop 100 metres off the fishing boat. I try to contact them on the VHF radio.

'Fishing vessel Porcupine, fishing vessel Porcupine, this is the yacht off your starboard bow on Channel 16. Over.'

A minute passes before a response comes—but it is in Spanish. I attempt to communicate in my very poor Spanish, but it is no use. I switch to English, but they do not understand me.

'I don't suppose you speak Spanish, do you, Captain?'

'Unfortunately not. I only speak French.'

'Neither do I. I guess that's that, then.'

'Why did you learn French instead of Spanish?' asks Jock.

'I thought it sounded smoother than Spanish.'

After a moment's contemplation, Jock sets the binoculars down on the table.

'I'll speak to them for you,' he says.

THE CREW

The Captain turns towards him. 'You speak Spanish?' he asks, his tone dripping with condescension.

'Yeah, no problem,' says Jock. 'Me? I speak Spanish like a native.'

There is a brief pause before Thrush asks Jock to speak to the person who answered the VHF on the fishing vessel.

'Tell him that your captain would like to speak to his captain because we would like to purchase some fresh fish. I'll turn up the speaker volume on deck so they can hear you over the machinery.'

Jock takes the radio handset, clears his throat, and lifts the microphone to his mouth. I am already anticipating what will come out of it. I do not have to wait long.

'HELLOA, HELLOA! MY CAPITANO WANTA SPEAKY TO YOUR CAPITANO... PRONTO... PRONTO... FOR FRESH FISHY... OKAYYYY?!'

'Oh, for God's sake,' groans Thrush, putting his hand over his eyes.

'Errr, Jock, when you said you spoke Spanish like a native, did you mean a Native American?' I ask.

The Spanish fishermen look utterly confused. I call Zecky to the wheelhouse and explain what we need. She takes the handset and gets an instant response. She seems to be haggling over the price of fresh tuna, and true to form, she refuses to be ripped off. She can negotiate with the best of them—even salty old fishermen.

After a few moments, she leaves the wheelhouse and steps onto the foredeck. She haggles some more before shouting something across to the fishermen. To my surprise, they all applaud and cheer. Moments later, she calls the wheelhouse.

'Are you there?' she says through the radio.

'Yeah—what is it, Zecks?' I answer.

'Do me a favour and put the music CD on. Choose track six and play it through the loudspeakers.'

'Why?'

'Just trust me. To get a bit, you've got to give a bit. The dirty old sods will give us two big tuna and some swordfish steaks for a pole dance.'

'A fucking pole dance?! Which dirty old bugger wants that?'

'The old guy with the grey beard mending the net on deck. They've probably been at sea a while by the looks of it—bless 'em!'

'Are you sure, Zecks? You don't have to do that, mate. We only need some fish.'

'Do you know how much this would cost on the market? It's a good deal, believe me. Anyway, I want some sushi tonight, and I plan on teasing Jock, so it's as much for me as anyone else!'

By now, the entire crew of the fishing boat has gathered on the foredeck under the blazing sun. The music starts, and Zecks climbs up, holding onto the foremast, bumping and grinding against it. The fishermen go wild, and their wolf whistles nearly drown out the sound of the music. As she starts peeling off her clothes, the cheering intensifies.

Jock watches, astounded. 'Bloody hell! Makes me love her even more,' he mutters.

After a few minutes, the music stops, and she puts her T-shirt back on. A moment later, one of the fishermen tosses over a couple of large plastic bags filled with fresh tuna and swordfish.

'Looks like we'll have a feast tonight, boys,' she tells us through the handset.

Zecky is great to have around when you are ashore in foreign ports, whether you fancy a beer or want to haggle in the market. Last time we were in Turkey, I spotted a black leather jacket I liked, but the price was ridiculous. Zecky told me to wait in the bar opposite the stall and get some beers in. She then approached the stallholder, looking gorgeous with freshly applied make-up, neatly brushed hair, and a slightly lower neckline than usual.

THE CREW

After ten minutes of flirting, she talked the price down from $230 to $130. The guy thought he was taking her out for drinks that night, but we sailed a couple of hours later.

Zecky also had a good money-making routine whenever we berthed in a Turkish port and a big cruise ship was in town. Some of these ships carried thousands of passengers, all eager to buy souvenirs. If they had stopped in Egypt, they wanted wooden camels or pharaoh ornaments. If it was Greece, they wanted Greek god statues. In Turkey, it was rugs—some of which cost a fortune.

Zecky's cut was ten to twenty per cent of each sale. She would confidently approach American tourists and ask if they were interested in buying a rug. If they hesitated for even a second, she handed them the business card of one of the many shops on the front, with her name on it. By the end of the day, she would have made hundreds of dollars in commission.

She also bought navigation charts of the Mediterranean, worked out the cruise ship routes, and marked their voyages, leg by leg, with distances and fancy notations. She rolled them up, tied a ribbon around them, and sold them to the punters.

You have to hand it to her—she is a smart entrepreneur. She could sell sand to the Arabs and talk her way into the best deals. Or, in this case, charm some salty old fishermen into parting with expensive fresh fish by wiggling her arse.

Chapter 16
All You Need Is a Good Ashtray

As we wave goodbye to the cheering Spanish fishermen, Zecky looks up to the wheelhouse, licks her finger, and makes a downward motion in the air to signify that she has one up on Jock. These two seem to have an unwritten competition over who can acquire things that benefit the crew without paying for them. At the moment, they are evenly matched, but it is all just for fun.

Jock's last freebie was some extra fuel when he was refuelling the yacht's tenders, which were used to tow guests for waterskiing. He urinated in a sample of fuel and took it back to the fuelling station, demanding that the boats be refilled for free.

The vendor did not argue because Thrush regularly refuels the yacht there, and he is in on a little scam. Thrush gets a receipt for a full tank of diesel, but the vendor does not actually fill the tank, while still charging the full amount. On a big motor yacht with large engines, this can be substantial. For argument's sake, let's say it costs £10,000, though it could be much more. However, with only £7,000 worth of fuel actually supplied to the yacht, Thrush and the vendor split the £3,000 difference between them. The crew, of course, never see any of this. It all goes towards keeping 'Puppy' and Olga in Gucci.

As a result, the crew have to come up with their own ways to supplement their wages. It is hardly a crime; it is just the way things work in the charter world. Everyone has a scam—it is only the amounts that differ.

Zecky will only use certain suppliers for food and beverages, ones that offer a 'kickback' of around five per cent, though it can be much more. I only use suppliers for deck equipment who do the same. Sometimes, a yacht pulls into a port where it needs to drop anchor. The Mediterranean ports get very busy, and there is not much space on the quay. Because of this, yachts and powerboats save space by reversing into the berth rather than berthing lengthways, which takes up more of the premium space. Instead, they back into the quay so that only the stern is against it.

To stabilise the yacht, ropes are secured at the stern, while anchors are dropped at the bow. The problem is that when multiple yachts drop anchor in a confined area, their chains overlap. This can cause difficulties when one yacht wants to leave, as pulling up its anchor may drag up others.

Because of this, divers have to assist just before departure. They dive to the seabed with bags that they attach to the anchor chain, then fill them with air to lift the chain off the bottom. This allows the crew to manoeuvre the anchor around the others. As a result, it does not matter if a yacht is berthed before or after others—it can leave at any time, provided divers are available. The availability of divers can vary greatly, and the best service always goes to the yacht that offers the biggest tip.

The crew will tell the captain they had to tip fifty euros, but in reality, they only gave thirty, pocketing the difference. The same happens when arriving or departing a port. The port staff handle the ropes as they are thrown ashore. On paper, they receive the same fifty-euro tip, but if they are even slightly late, they may not be tipped at all. That means another fifty euros in someone's pocket. One thing is for sure— they are never late again, so it works both ways.

I hand over the navigation watch to my relief and head below deck to freshen up and get some dinner. I am halfway through my shower when I hear paper rustling, followed by a cheeky fart. I pull back the shower curtain to find Jock sitting on the toilet, trousers around his ankles, with a chicken leg in one hand and my FHM magazine in the other.

'All right, matey?' Jock says, taking a bite of his chicken and turning a page.

'Jock! What the fuck are you doing taking a crap in my cabin?'

'It was a bit touch and go, mate, and Tar has locked the door to our cabin.'

'Christ, could you not have waited five minutes?'

'Not really, mate. The tortoise head was running for daylight, so to speak.'

'I'll see you in the crew room for dinner, you bloody reprobate,' I shout, as I towel off, get changed, and leave the cabin.

'Yeah, all right, mate. Make me a brew while you are in there, would you?'

I walk down the alleyway shaking my head. First, he takes a crap in my cabin, and now he wants me to make him a brew. Unbelievable.

As I enter the crew room, I find the table laid out with food and wine. Chef has cooked up a feast, including some of Zecky's freshly caught fish. There is nothing quite like eating fish that was swimming in the ocean only an hour ago. The fish you buy at home can be days or even weeks old.

The chef, Mr Kerr, is a decent cook but full of shit. He trained in restaurants on the Côte d'Azur, so he knows his craft, but he is a pompous pain in the arse who looks down his nose at anyone unfamiliar with fine food and wine. He is a small, dumpy man, very well spoken, and looks like a cross between Colonel Sanders and Chief Wiggum from *The Simpsons*.

Jock nicknamed him 'Wan' because of his surname, and for some reason, Kerr liked it. One of the crew once told him it stood for 'Nourishment With Attitude', rearranged as 'WAN', so he thought it was a compliment. In reality, Jock simply meant 'WAN-KER'. It is not rocket science, but Kerr never caught on. Thrush and Kerr get on well, as you would expect. They spend their time stroking each other's egos, and it is laughable to listen to.

Chef is also one of those irritating people who ask themselves questions and then answer them aloud for everyone to hear. Tom once asked him if he was going to make homemade burgers for a barbecue.

Chef immediately stopped what he was doing, arched his back, and stroked his chin before answering.

'Will I be making burgers for the barbecue? Let's see now. Am I a classically trained chef? YES, I AM! Have I learned my trade in the best French hotels and restaurants? MOST CERTAINLY! Will I insult my culinary talents by making burgers? NOT A CHANCE!'

Tom decided to answer him back in the same style, just to take the piss.

'Am I going to tell Jock on his birthday that he cannot have a simple burger? I DO NOT THINK SO! Will there be a forfeit if you do not make burgers? YES, THERE WILL! Am I carrying a fire extinguisher? YES, I AM! Will I be inserting the flexible pipe up your big fat arse and pulling the trigger if you do not? OF COURSE, I WILL!'

Jock takes no prisoners when it comes to Chef. When Kerr joined the yacht from working ashore, he wanted to convince the crew that he was a master wine connoisseur. He droned on about different grapes for what felt like an eternity, until Jock had had enough.

At the next mealtime, Jock steered the conversation towards wine after Chef presented a supposedly fine bottle of Bordeaux. It was an expensive brand, but the original contents had been drunk the night before at a party. Jock had retrieved the empty bottle, refilled it with cheap cooking wine, and put it in front of Chef to see how much he really knew.

Chef picked up the glass, took a sip, and smacked his lips. 'Ah, yes... a classic red Bordeaux. I can taste blackcurrant and plum. Fruity yet classically metallic, with a round, full finish. This is clearly not a cheap wine.'

'How much would you say it costs?' Jock asked.

'Oh... this brand is rather expensive, and you can taste the quality.'

'You can tell a good wine from a bad one, can you?'

'Of course—it is as easy as one, two, three.'

'Well, that is your cooking wine, you bullshit merchant!'

* * * *

The yacht alters course so the swell waves are astern of us. This settles the yacht's movement, making it a bit more comfortable. Tar and Jock join me in the crew room, and the boy is looking a little better, bless him.

"You feeling stronger then, Tar?" I ask.

"A little, yes."

"Well, you've got a bit of colour back in your face now, mate. Anyway, you can get your own back on Jock shortly because, if you remember, he still has to snort the chilli sauce for losing the bet."

Tar raises a smile and takes a seat. Zecky makes him a coffee and gives him a hug. He has obviously brought out her maternal side.

"Don't you worry, Tar, you'll soon get used to it. Your body just thinks it's normal after a while, and you won't even notice the yacht's movement."

"That feels like a million miles away at the moment," Tar says. "I'm going to stock up on all sorts of drugs when I get into port. If anyone needs anything, just let me know."

At that moment, Jock walks in and catches the end of the conversation. He sits down next to me and stares at Tar, unable to believe what he has just heard. After a few moments, he shrugs his shoulders, reaches into his pocket, and slams fifty euros down on the table.

"Fuck me, Tar, I wouldn't have thought you were the type, but I admire your honesty. Get me as many bags of weed as you can with that, and none of that weak shit either. If I'm going to get high, I want to be in fucking orbit. Know what I mean?"

Tar looks confused. "Weed? No, I think you've... I can't get you any weed."

THE CREW

"Well, just get us some E's, then. Mitsubishi's, if you can find them."

"I think you've caught the tail-end of the conversation, Jock. I wasn't offering to buy drugs."

"I just bloody well heard you!"

"Not weed or E's! I meant sea sickness tablets, for God's sake!"

"Sea sickness tablets? Why? Do you chop coke up with them or something? I fucking hate it when dealers do that. Oh, hang on a minute... do you stick them up your arse like a suppository? I've heard about this."

"No, no, you've got it all wrong."

"Have you tried sniffing vodka, Tar? That's a bit rushy but a lot of fun!"

Zecky has to explain to Jock that Tar had been talking about getting some tablets for his sea sickness.

"Oh, for fuck's sake, Tar, forget all that shit. All you need is a good ashtray and a full packet of Marlboro."

"Honestly, Jock, you're certifiable," says Zecky, shaking her head.

"Oh, thanks very much."

"That means you're a nutter, mate," I tell him, bursting his bubble.

Jock shrugs his shoulders like he has heard it a million times before.

"I blame the parents," says Zecky with a mock sigh.

"Come on then, Jock, you owe me a forfeit, my old mate," I say. "Chilli sauce, remember?"

"Oh, I don't know, mate... it's pretty hot."

"You should have thought about that before you made the bet, buddy. Anyway, if you can snort vodka, as you've so delicately told us, then this should be a breeze for you."

"Yeah, come on, Jock. You've given Tar enough shit already, so it's payback time for him... and he gets to choose the chilli sauce."

Tar can't help but raise a faint smile. You can see he would enjoy getting his own back on Jock, but he is wondering if there will be repercussions.

"What do you reckon then, Tar? The sweet but sticky chilli sauce or the Tabasco?"

"Well, that's a tricky one. The sticky one would be harder to get down and would leave more residue, so he'd be coughing it up for a while. The Tabasco, on the other hand, is a lot hotter, so that would be more painful."

"You're between a rock and a hard place, really, aren't you?" I say, slapping Jock on the back.

"Fuckers," says Jock, holding the two sauces out in front of him and inspecting them.

"You see, mate, every time you think of betting, you'll remember this pain," I tell him. "Neuro-Linguistic Programming, I think it's called. When you snort it, we're all going to shout, 'DO NOT BET!' and hopefully, it will be etched into your subconscious forever."

"Which sauce then, Tar?"

"The Tabasco, I think."

"Tabasco it is then. Right, on the count of three. One... two... three!"

As we anticipate, Jock does not back down from a challenge. He holds the bottle to his right nostril while pinching the other, then tips his head back and inhales sharply.

"DOOOOOOOO NOT BET!" we all shout at him.

He puts the bottle down on the table and maintains his composure for a few seconds. Then the pain hits, and no doubt it feels like he has just shoved molten metal up his nose. His face turns bright red, and his eyes bulge. Suddenly, he jumps to his feet and lets out an almighty scream before leaping over the table to the cold water tap.

"AAAAHHHH!! FUCKING HELL, I'm on FIRE!!" yells Jock, jumping up and down on the spot and throwing water on his face.

I grab Tar's hand and shake it while gesturing over at Jock. "And that's how we learn, Tar. That's how we learn!"

I do not know if Jock will learn, though. I know of three fairly nasty cases of gonorrhoea Jock has had, but it does not stop him screwing around. My guess is that this will be no different.

After ten minutes of torture, Jock gradually recovers. Rob, sitting in the corner with Sally the stewardess, is pondering Jock's state of mind.

"That boy is troubled," he mutters, pouring himself a large Jack Daniels and Coke. He pours Sally one and asks if anyone else is indulging.

Everybody is, and I know what is happening here. They are all having a few stiff drinks to make sure they sleep long enough in the uncomfortable sea conditions. If they do not get any sleep, they will feel like zombies the next day and be in no state to look after the guests.

Tar takes a sip of the Jack Daniels, but it is clear he does not usually drink. He nearly chokes, and some of it comes back up out of his nose.

"My God, that tastes horrible!" he says, holding his nose.

"You see, and you think I'm enjoying myself every time I drink a bottle of it," Rob jokes. "The first gulp is always the hardest, buddy. Besides, you'll sleep like a baby after a couple of these."

"I think after a couple of these, I won't ever wake up," Tar replies, looking at the glass.

"Rob's measures are a bit on the liberal side," I tell him.

"A bit on the liberal side? You could fuel a jet car with it," adds Sally, who is also struggling to get it down.

'Like I said, Tar, have a few of these and push your lifejacket under one side of your mattress. Then sleep in the "V" between it and the bulkhead,' says Rob, making a V shape with his hands. 'It'll stop you rolling around when the yacht rolls and pitches.'

'What's a bulkhead?'

'It's nautical talk for a wall. A bulkhead is a wall, the deck is the floor, and the deckhead is the ceiling.'

'And the dickhead lives between them all in the captain's cabin, right?'

'You're catching on, Tar, I'll give you that,' Zecky grins.

'There are millions of jargon phrases and words in the nautical world, Tar,' adds Rob reassuringly. 'So don't worry, you won't learn them all at once.'

'There can't be that many, can there?' asks Tar naively.

'You're kidding, aren't you, mate? If you think about it, hundreds of everyday phrases come from working at sea. It's one of the oldest industries.'

'Like what?'

'Well, you name it,' I say. 'Let's put it this way—I'll pour us all a drink for every slang word or phrase that comes up in our conversation around this table.'

'All right, but it has to be in context.'

'No problem. Let's see… Jock's just been for a shit, right?'

'Yeah.'

'Admittedly in my bloody toilet,' I add, shaking my head at him.

'I was just keeping it warm for you, boss,' Jock grins.

'Well, the word "shit" comes from the sea… and I shit you not.'

'Really? How?'

'Years ago, almost all goods were transported by ship, and this was before commercial fertilisers were invented. Shipments of manure were common. It was shipped dry because, in dry form, it weighed a lot less than when wet. Once seawater hit it, not only did it become heavier, but fermentation began. A by-product of that is methane gas, which is explosive.

'Since the manure was stored below deck in bundles, you can imagine what happened. Methane built up, and the first time someone went below at night with a naked flame… BANG! Ships blew up like this loads of times before someone finally asked, "What the fuck is going on?" After that, the bundles of manure were stamped with the instruction "Ship High In Transit," meaning sailors had to stow it high enough off the lower decks so seawater wouldn't reach the cargo and start the methane process. That's how we got the term "S.H.I.T."'

'I wish we could stow your bowels high in transit,' says Tar to Jock.

'I know. It's like a rat's crawled up your arse and died sometimes,' adds Sally.

'I must admit, they can be fairly fragrant,' says Jock, knocking back his drink.

We have a few more drinks, and everyone starts throwing out phrases.

'Wanker?' suggests Jock.

'Don't know that one, but I bet it's slang for thrush,' says Tar.

Now that Tar's had a few drinks, he's becoming quite funny.

'Down the hatch then, Tar,' I say, filling everyone's glasses. 'That's a drinking expression that comes from sea-going procedures. Cargo was lowered into the hatch.'

'Neck it and pour another, then, Tar,' says Jock.

'Oh… I don't know if I can drink this all in one just yet,' he says wearily.

'Honestly, Tar, you'd better toe the line with this drinking game… There's another one.'

'What?'

'"Toe the line" means to conform to rules. It comes from when a ship's crew was lined up to receive their pay. Each sailor stepped forward to a line marked on the deck and gave his name.'

'This is too easy. We'll be as pissed as rats at this rate.'

'What do you mean, "will be"?' says Tar, already feeling the effects.

'Now, now, Tar—you can't wimp out now, or you'll show the boys your true colours,' says Rob.

Tar looks at Jock in anticipation. Jock smiles and nods slowly.

'I'm afraid so, buddy. "True colours" comes from naval etiquette. While false colours or flags could be used when approaching an enemy ship, true colours had to be flown once battle began.'

Less than an hour later, everyone around the table is pissed—especially Tar. He's hugging Zecky, and she's hugging him back in a motherly, protective way. His head is firmly planted on the side of her left breast.

'You feeling better now, Tar?' she asks.

'Never bloody better,' he burbles.

Jock is staring at them, deep in thought. He taps my leg under the table to get my attention, then whispers, 'Do you reckon if I act all vulnerable, she'll let me rest my head on her tits?!'

Chapter 17
Don't You Just Love the Smell of Puppies?

The next morning, Thrush makes a loudspeaker announcement throughout the yacht, half an hour before we reach the port limits. A few groggy people gather on deck, suffering the effects of three bottles of Jack Daniel's from the night before. Tar is sitting on the open deck next to Jock, looking worse for wear. Jock, on the other hand, is as fresh as a daisy. He has done the decent thing this morning, getting Tar some Alka-Seltzer, a strong coffee (of the non-special kind), and some toast.

The girls are on deck, helping the boys prepare the rubber fenders and ropes for docking. The fenders are large, inflatable rubber types covered in towelling material to prevent scratches and bumps as the yacht backs into a berth. The quay is packed with yachts, and at first glance, it looks like we will need a shoehorn to fit into the allocated space. There should be just enough room for the width of the yacht and the fenders to back in. Although Thrush is a dickhead of the highest order, he is skilled at manoeuvring the yacht. It is a shame he does not have the same ability when it comes to managing people.

After breakfast and a couple of cigarettes, the crew start to feel human again. Some are in the water, scrubbing algae growth from the hull. They are usually assisted by the resident grey mullet, or 'shit-gobblers'—fish known as the dustbins of the sea. Some people catch and eat them in the Black Sea and Caspian Sea, among other places, but the thought of eating something that has just been sucking on sewage is rather off-putting.

I once worked on a ship in Croatia that was moored in a harbour for several months. Because it did not move, algae built up on the hull, fed by a sewage overflow a short distance away. Every day at 10am and 4pm, the overflow would release waste and debris, and the grey mullet would swarm in, all guns blazing. Hundreds of them would gather in the dirty water, swimming between prophylactics and sanitary towels, chomping on floating turds. Then, a small boat would arrive carrying a couple of fishermen wearing long, thick rubber gloves. They would cast a net, scoop up the fish, and sell them at the local market.

I reckon those fish are grey for a reason. You would look grey and pale too if you ate the filth they do. Nobody on the yacht eats grey mullet anymore.

Zecky is on the aft deck, helping Jock with the fenders, and they are having a banter about the benefits of being male versus female. Jock asks her to name some reasons why it is better to be a woman.

'Well, Jock, if this yacht sinks while we are at sea, us girls would get off first, for a start,' she says, ticking off her reasons on her fingers. 'We can pretend to cry to get out of speeding fines, we do not look like a frog in a blender when dancing, we can hug our friends without people thinking we are gay, and if we sleep with someone and do not call the next day, we are not the devil.'

'Is that all?' Jock asks, raising an eyebrow. 'I thought you were going to convince me.'

'I have only just started, sunshine. Free dinners, free drinks…'

'I can get free drinks.'

'Only when you know the barman. What else? Taxis stop for us, men die earlier, gay waiters do not make us uncomfortable, we never regret piercing our ears, we have an excuse to be a total bitch once a month, and we are more cultured.'

'I am cultured.'

'You are cultured? My arse! The first time we visited Venice, you said you did not think much of it and that we should come back when it was not flooded, for Christ's sake!'

'No one told me most of it was supposed to be underwater!'

'If you were cultured, my boy, you would not need to be told. And what about that time after the last charter when we all ate at that French restaurant?'

THE CREW

'What about it?'

'We all ordered that wonderful chicken dish—suprême de volaille à l'estragon. When you were asked why you were not ordering it, you said you did not like that foreign Mexican crap.'

'Well, how was I supposed to know it was not Mexican? I do not speak the lingo!'

'Did the French music, French décor, French wine, French menu, and the restaurant's name—Café de Paris—not give you any indication?'

'Must have been having an off day.'

'To top it off, when you finally realised it was a French restaurant, you asked the waiter if he had frog's legs.'

'They serve frog's legs in France!'

'Yes, I am well aware of that, Jock, but when he said he did, you asked him to hop into the kitchen and get you a burger and chips.'

'Yeah… well, that was a joke, wasn't it?'

'Ha! Maybe the frog's legs thing was, but you still ordered burger and chips in a top-quality French restaurant. I bet the Michelin-star chef was pulling his bloody hair out!'

'Anyway, why is it better to be a man, then?'

'Loads of reasons.'

'Go on, then, convince me,' she says, smiling.

'We can go to water parks wearing white T-shirts, and chocolate is not the meaning of existence for us.'

'Well, it is not for me.'

'Yeah, right! I'm amazed you don't piss around your chocolate drawer to mark your territory!'

'Go on then, name some more.'

'Hairdressers don't rob us blind, two pairs of shoes are enough, underwear costs less than ten quid for a three-pack, and we don't have to stop and think for a few minutes before tightening a bolt! Oh, and by the way, Zecks, my new nickname for you is Spanner because you make my nuts tighten.'

'Anything else?'

'Fucking loads. Our telephone calls are over in thirty seconds, we can open jars, we can do our nails with a pocket knife, Christmas shopping for ten relatives begins on 24 December and lasts forty-five minutes… and we know stuff about engines.'

'Finished?'

'Nope. We can easily pee in public, which infuriates every woman because, secretly, you'd like a cock.'

'Secretly we'd like a cock?!'

'Of course you would.'

'For what reason?'

'For that reason.'

'Admittedly, it would be easier to pee in public, but that's it. As for needing a cock, we can buy a vibrator at Ann Summers that will outperform most of your gender.'

'Well, feel free to put me to the test, my darling.'

'Nice try, sunshine.'

'Anyway, that vibrator comment was below the belt. That's every man's fear.'

'We know! That's why, whenever we buy one, it has to be just the right size. Not too big to upset your fragile egos, and God help us if we bought a black one. You'd be thinking we have a thing for coloured men.'

'Well, it's a touchy subject. How would you feel if we went out and bought a synthetic pussy? Could you imagine us disappearing off to the toilet during a boring meeting to service ourselves with a plastic girl?'

'Ha, not really, no.'

'Anyway, a vibrator can't mow the lawn and get a round of drinks in, can it?'

'Well, if it could, you'd be extinct. OK, we both have some valid points, but back to your comment about us secretly wanting a cock.'

'Yeah, what about it?'

Zecky slowly walks over to Jock, lifts the top of her shorts, places her hand on the back of his head and tilts his head down. 'I have one of these, and because I have one of these, I can have as many cocks as I wish.' She then gently slaps his cheek and struts off to the other side of the boat to man the fender as we begin backing into the berth.

Thrush berths us successfully, and we get ready to pick up the guests again. They've been staying at one of the top hotels in Porto Cervo on Sardinia's exclusive Smeralda Coast and have asked to be collected at noon. They want to go waterskiing and perhaps do a little diving before partying at the Billionaire Nightclub, a haunt of the rich and famous, tycoons and celebrities.

The Smeralda, or Emerald, Coast is one of Sardinia's main claims to fame. An idyllic resort on the northeast of the island, it has secluded little bays and coves lapped by a crystal-clear, emerald-green sea. Prince Karim Aga Khan IV visited in the 1950s and established a resort. However, it is not a resort in the usual sense of the word; its natural beauty is fully protected, and there are no high-rise buildings.

As well as the main harbour in Porto Cervo, the larger bays are full of beautiful mega-yachts. It's entertaining to watch the yachts battle for an anchorage, with all the owners vying to impress. The helicopters are polished on the flight decks, and everything is pristine. It's a game of who has the biggest dick with their floating penis extensions. If someone orders a new yacht to outsize the largest yacht in the world, you can guarantee that someone else will place an order for an even bigger one the moment it is launched. It's a case of, "You've got a nine-inch dick, but I've got a ten-inch."

Noon approaches faster than we anticipate, and we are a little behind with the cleaning and polishing. Because of this, and the fact that Rob is still hungover, I leave him and Tom to work in the fresh air. Jock and I will escort the chauffeurs and drive out to the Hotel Cala Di Volpe to pick up the guests.

Silvio is the chauffeur in my limo. He's a great Italian guy whose family has lived in Sardinia for centuries. He likes to drive at this time of year in case he meets someone famous. He has photos and autographs of many of the rich and famous, and the car's glovebox is full of them. If you need anything in Sardinia, Silvio is your man. He knows people everywhere on the island.

As I get in the limo, I'm welcomed with a friendly shoulder punch.

'Well, fuck me if it isn't the Italian Stallion,' I say, greeting him with a reciprocal punch.

'Eh, mate, ya big clown! You not Captain yet, ya waster?!'

'Working on it, mate, working on it,' I respond in equally jovial fashion. 'Hope you're going to keep your eyes on the fucking road this time, buggerlugs.'

I'm very fond of Silvio, and he feels the same about me, but I hate driving with him when we are having a conversation. Silvio is typically Italian—he likes to get up close and personal when he talks to you. He holds eye contact intensely and gestures expressively with his hands and arms to emphasise his points. However, this is not always ideal when navigating the busy, winding roads of Sardinia at the height of summer. Taking your eyes off the road for even a second is asking for trouble.

There is a well-known joke that sums it up perfectly: How do you stop an Italian man from talking? Tie his hands behind his back. If you have ever worked with Italians, you will know how true this is. You have to love them, though—they are passionate people. Just look at the cars they build, their architecture, and their fashion.

THE CREW

Silvio has just arrived from Bosa, a picturesque town on the island's west coast beside the River Temo, famous for its Malvasia wine. Knowing how much I love it, he hands me a bottle, along with another from the island's renowned Sella e Mosca vineyard. Sardinian red wines, made from local grapes, are fantastic.

After exchanging pleasantries, we set off for the hotel. Silvio immediately launches into his usual non-stop barrage of questions. I try my best not to engage or make eye contact, but it is no use. The more he talks, the more animated he becomes. I realise that the only way to get us both to the hotel safely is to keep talking myself, leaving him no chance to get into full stride. I continue chatting until we arrive at the hotel, safely followed by Jock in the second limo.

The Hotel Cala di Volpe sits on a stunning stretch of coastline, dotted with unusual rock formations that enhance the area's beauty. The scent of oleander, laurel, and juniper drifts on the ocean breeze. The coast is lined with secluded inlets of clear, warm water—perfect for swimming, snorkelling, and scuba diving. Built in the 1960s by the renowned architect Jacques Couëlle, an honorary member of the Académie des Beaux-Arts of the Institut de France, the hotel's exterior was designed to resemble a traditional Mediterranean fishing village. White stucco walls, interconnecting terracotta rooftops, turrets, and terraces give it a charming, rustic feel. Inside, archways and columns support beamed wooden ceilings, complemented by locally crafted woven textiles, wood carvings, and intricate tilework. It is one of the most glamorous resort destinations for celebrities, royalty, and the international elite.

Jock and I walk up to reception, where we are met by the concierge. If this man cannot get you what you want, nobody can. He deals with high-profile guests all day long. I ask him to let Mr Big know we have arrived, and as we wait, we stand in the hall observing the guests. There are no football shirts in this hotel—everyone is dressed stylishly and immaculately.

After a minute, the concierge informs us that the guests are out waterskiing. We thank him and stroll through the gardens to the hotel's private beach jetty, but Mr Big is still out on the water.

'That's good, mate,' says Jock. 'I'm dying for a piss, so I'll just go drain the main vein while you wait for them.'

'OK, but don't be long in case they come back early.'

'Sorted.' Jock disappears while I look around for somewhere to sit out of the sun. I spot a large table in the shade where an elegant, middle-aged woman is sitting. She wears a wide-brimmed hat, designer sunglasses, a sarong, and a bikini top. I approach her politely.

'Would you mind if I sit here?'

'Certainly,' she replies. 'It's much cooler here in the shade.'

'It sure is—it must be over ninety degrees in the sun today.'

'I'm Sarah.'

'Pleased to meet you, Sarah. Are you having a nice holiday?'

'Wonderful, thank you. This hotel and island are beautiful—I'll definitely be coming back.'

'It's lovely, isn't it? Are you here alone?'

'Oh no, I'm here with my two girls.'

'I see. Do you mean your daughters?'

'In a funny kind of way, yes.'

'Where are they today?'

'Underneath the table, next to your feet.'

I lean down and lift the tablecloth to find two small dachshund puppies.

'Their legs are a bit short,' I joke.

'They reach the ground, don't they?' she laughs.

'Good point. I love them at this age. Don't you just adore that puppy smell?'

'Yes, it's delightful, isn't it?'

'Mind if I have a sniff? It's been years, and it would take me back to when I got my own puppy.'

'Of course, go ahead.'

'They don't bite, do they?'

'They will probably lick you to death, but that's about it.'

I scoop up the tiny puppies, one in each hand, and lift them to my nose.

'Ahhhh, I'd never get sick of that puppy smell,' I say, laughing as I place them back under the table.

Sarah and I continue chatting for a few minutes until Jock returns and sits down.

'This is Sarah, Jock. I've just smelled her puppies.'

Jock stares at Sarah, looking astonished. 'Really?!'

'Yeah, it was great.'

Sarah starts to rise from her chair. 'Feel free to smell them yourself. Many people have—they're irresistible.'

Jock shrugs, looking slightly bewildered. 'Oh, what the hell,' he grins. He leans over the table, cups both of her ample breasts in his hands, and buries his face between them, inhaling deeply.

Sarah and I look on, flabbergasted and speechless.

'Not bad, not bad at all,' Jock says, nodding at her and giving each breast a final squeeze before sitting back down.

Chapter 18
Cruel to Be Kind… Or So He Thinks!

Although she is initially shocked and taken aback by Jock sniffing her breasts, Sarah eventually sees the funny side of it. I imagine it is not every day that a complete stranger manhandles and sniffs her fun bags. Still, that is Jock for you—two plus two equals five.

Jock and I eventually leave Sarah and her adorable puppies (both sets) in peace and head off for a smoke.

'For fuck's sake, Jock, what were you thinking?' I ask, struggling to contain my laughter.

'You told me you'd just sniffed her puppies,' Jock replies.

'Well, that's true, but didn't it occur to you that I might have meant actual puppies rather than her tits?'

'I didn't see them until she jumped up and they came running out from under the table.'

'Fair enough. I'm just going to nip to the toilet, then we'll head back to reception and find out what's going on with the guests. Where are they?'

'What?'

'The toilets. You've just come back, haven't you?'

'Er… yeah, but you don't want to go in there yet.'

'Why not?'

'It was a bit fragrant when I left.'

'Upset stomach, have we, mate?'

'Yeah… something like that.'

'It's been a few minutes—it should be fine now. Anyway, I'm bursting, so where is it?'

Jock shakes his head and reluctantly leads me to the toilets. As we approach, a man walks out wearing a disgusted expression.

'Right, wait here, Jock. I'm just going to drop my load, then we'll get going.'

'Er… yeah, all right.'

I step into one of the cubicles and am immediately met with a sight to behold. The toilet bowl looks as though a mud bomb has exploded inside it, and the stench makes me gasp for breath.

'Ohhhh, for fuck's sake!'

'Sorry, mate,' says Jock.

'I take it this was your cubicle, then, you dirty bastard?'

'Yep, I'm afraid so.'

'Don't you ever flush? That's fucking disgusting!'

'I tried, but the water wouldn't wash away the bits stuck to the side of the pan.'

'I'm amazed any of it made it into the water at all! It looks like you shoved a stick of dynamite up your arse and it went off the moment you sat down! Bloody hell, some of it isn't even inside the toilet bowl!' I say, jabbing a finger at the porcelain.

'Well, I got caught short. It was already on the way, if you know what I mean.'

'Caught short? What the hell have you been eating—hand grenades?!'

'No, I've been taking salts for the upset stomach.'

'Salts? You've been doing fucking somersaults in there, by the look of it!'

'Well, I was hovering a bit. I don't like sitting on public toilets… germs and all that.'

'Jock, I've seen you pick up polystyrene food containers with half-eaten cheeseburgers from a bin outside a kebab shop before now!'

'When?'

'Last time we were in the UK. We were out on the piss in Harrogate, remember?'

'Oh yeah, but I saw the girl buy it fresh. She only took one bite before throwing it away. Waste not, want not.'

'That's hardly the point, mate. And for fuck's sake, what's with the colour?'

'The colour?'

'Yeah, the colour. Are you a bloody amphibian or something?'

'What are you on about?' Jock looks genuinely confused.

'Your shit—I'm talking about the colour of your shit!'

Jock holds out his hands, looking even more perplexed. He sticks his head back into the cubicle, glances down at the porcelain, then turns back to me.

'I can't see anything wrong with the colour,' he says, shaking his head.

'Are you seriously telling me you think that colour is normal?'

'Yeah, looks all right to me.'

'It's fucking GREEN!'

Jock peers back into the toilet and mutters under his breath. 'I thought everyone's shit was green.'

'No, mate, it's usually brown—sometimes tan—but never green. I'd go see a doctor if I were you. Anyway, sort it out while I use another cubicle, because you can't leave it like that. It's enough to turn anyone's stomach.'

Back at reception, the concierge informs us that Mr Big and his guests will be down for their limos in fifteen minutes.

When they arrive, the guests are accompanied by bellboys scurrying around, hauling their luggage like seagulls circling a trawler in search of a tasty morsel. As we approach, Silvio is running a cloth over the limo's paintwork. The cars are already spotless, but it adds an extra touch of professionalism—an impression of perfection and pride in our work.

Mr Big sits in the back with the blonde and the brunette, while I am in the front with Silvio. The others take the other limo. We head back to the yacht, and the journey is fairly uneventful, except for the fact that Silvio cannot stop looking in the rear-view mirror to get an eyeful of the ladies. At least it keeps him quiet while he is driving, but his eyes are on anything but the road.

The girls are dressed in shorts and bikini tops that leave little to the imagination. They are professionals, and no doubt Mr Big has paid a hefty fee for their services. He is clearly more interested in cosmetic appeal than emotional connection. The girls are just doing a job—boosting his ego.

In the quietness of the drive back to the yacht, I have a rare moment of clarity. I watch the two girls in the back via the mirror and find myself longing for an honest, pure relationship again. I think back to my younger, wilder days of promiscuity, as well as the times when I was in loving relationships. I reflect on how people change and grow with age and maturity. The things I desired as a late teenager and as a man in his twenties no longer matter to me now.

I remember the superficial relationships I had back then and how none of them made me truly happy, even though they were fun at the time. As I look out at a field, I see dozens of shallow holes in the ground but only one deep water well. In my present state of mind, I take this as an omen. You can drill a hundred shallow, dry holes and never reach anything worthwhile, or you can persevere and dig one deep well to uncover sparkling, life-preserving water. Looking back on my past relationships, I realise that being in a committed, monogamous relationship gave me more freedom and fulfilment than any of the fleeting encounters I had experienced. From that moment on, whenever I saw Mr Big and his escorts, I no longer envied him—I pitied him.

Five minutes from the yacht, I telephone Zecky to let her know we will be arriving shortly. As the limos pull up, Rob and Tom are standing by the passerelle, ready to help the guests aboard and take their luggage. Zecky is also waiting with her signature ice-cold, lemon-scented face towels.

As the guests are welcomed aboard, Mr Big and his bouncers head to the top deck overlooking the quay for a cold beer and, no doubt, a line of coke. The two girls disappear below, likely to take a shower and apply their war paint.

As they strut along the teak deck towards the aft accommodation door, Rob turns to Tom.

"It must be a nice job being a pro. All you have to worry about is keeping your body in shape and your make-up fresh. I might give it a go—it looks like a piece of cake to me," he jokes.

"Not with your ever-growing beer belly, sunshine," Tom replies. "I know what you mean, though. I bet they get paid a bloody fortune."

"All they have to do is suck up to the client, then lie on their backs and suck on something else. It's easy money! What do you reckon, Tom? Shall we become ladies of disrepute?"

"You wouldn't catch me sucking someone's dick for all the tea in China."

"Well, you wouldn't have to, you clown. You'd be a male pro."

"I already am, with the shit I have to do for the guests just to get a tip!"

"I don't think spending an extra couple of hours taking the guests waterskiing is quite the same as taking a shafting up the shitter, mate."

"Well, you've got a point there, I suppose."

"Hang on a minute—what if you were hired by a six-foot, eighteen-stone lush with loads of money? Let's say she wanted you to ravish her, but she had a body like a sack of potatoes?"

"You'd have to ravish her in segments. Big, flabby segments."

"Ha! Seriously, though, you're a professional, so you have a job to do. How would you get the job done to her satisfaction?"

"I suppose you'd think of the cash, close your eyes, and pretend it was Pamela Anderson."

"That would take a lot of imagination! You'd be humping away on an eighteen-stone mass of blubber. It would be like shagging a walrus. With all the will in the world, you'd have a tough time pretending it was Pamela Anderson."

"I don't think you'd even manage to shag a six-foot, eighteen-stone woman, Tom. You're only ten stone and five foot seven. You'd disappear in a fat fold somewhere. She'd envelop you like a Venus flytrap."

"Death by lard, eh? What a way to go. Imagine that on your tombstone: *Here lies Thomas. Loved by all, except for the lard-arse that shagged and smothered him to death.*"

"How would your parents tell your mates? They'd have to lie to save face."

"They'd probably say you died while rescuing a drowning child or something. Anything but *Here lies blah blah blah, died while shagging a porker*."

"What position do you reckon fat birds shag in, then?"

Rob and Tom fall silent for a moment as they ponder the question. Then Rob comes up with an answer.

"Well, if she was shagging you, you little short-arse, there's no way she could squirm around on top, not at eighteen stone."

"Imagine the view I'd get from underneath. I'd have her arse cheeks covering my legs and her belly rolls on my chest."

"At least it'd keep you warm, mate. Like a penguin covering its egg in the Antarctic."

"Her big flabby tits would be bouncing like basketballs on top of her belly, and because she's looking down at me, she'd have more chins than a Chinese telephone directory."

"All right then, we'd have to rule out the 'her on top' position. The weight would probably cut off the circulation to your cock, which means a serious case of Mr Floppy. That's no good when she's just paid a small fortune to hire you."

"What about her underneath and me on top, then?"

"There are two problems there, mate."

"What's that?"

"You'd have to be hung like the proverbial rutting rhino to get anywhere near her fanny because you'd be lying on a blubber mountain. You'd have to shag her off the horizontal, with her lying on a table and you standing up, holding her massive thighs in the air."

"Plus, if I was on top, I'd end up burning my bare arse on the lightbulb, eh?"

"Christ, this is a real dilemma."

"Doggy it is, then?"

"It would have to be, wouldn't it? You'd just have to part the huge arse cheeks before going for gold."

"It'd be a bit like parting the Red Sea."

"Do you reckon if I slapped her arse hard enough, the pressure wave would travel up her fat and clout her on the back of the head?"

"I don't know, mate, but it's theoretically possible."

"I wonder... I wonder how much fat birds can shit."

"Ah, for fuck's sake, let's not get onto that, mate!"

"Loads, I reckon. They must eat their fair share of pies to put on the poundage."

"Well, they don't get that size by eating salads, do they?"

"I used to know a fat chick once. She blamed her size on big bones."

"Ah, that old chestnut. Did she also blame incredibly heavy shoes whenever she stepped on the scales?"

"Yeah, and the scales always read heavier because they were *partially broken*."

"Or the other classic: 'I'm this size because I have a hormone problem'."

"A hormone problem that makes her a greedy fucker."

"I'll have a family bucket of fried chicken and fries, a chocolate milkshake, and… let's see… better throw in a chicken wrap…"

"Because she obviously missed breakfast!"

"A large popcorn chicken… and a DIET COKE!"

"I know, mate. You feel like shouting at them, don't you?"

"THE DIET COKE IS NOT GOING TO STOP YOU POUNDING THE 10,000 CALORIES YOU'VE JUST STUFFED DOWN YOUR CAKEHOLE FROM SETTLING ON YOUR ARSE!!"

"Ha! I can't even think about how much they would shit after that. Imagine someone that size trying to squeeze out the last twenty-four hours' worth of fry-ups and desserts. How would they get their arse on the seat?"

"I guess they'd throw one flabby arse cheek over one side of the toilet, then throw the other over the other side."

"I wonder if some big girls ever cover up the air gaps between the toilet seat. It'd be a nightmare if that happened and they pulled the chain on an aeroplane with a big vacuum suction."

"Oh shit, yeah – it would cause an air seal, then a vacuum in the toilet bowl, and suck them inside out."

"At least they'd be thinner when they got off."

"You would be if your bowels and intestines were sucked out and flushed around the U-bend."

"Eurgh! That's it, mate – time out, time out! You deserve a red card for that one."

"Right, come on, let's stop this conversation right here. It's turning my bloody stomach. Let's get the luggage down to the ladies."

"Where are they again?"

"Master bedroom."

"What, both of them with Mr Big again?"

"Yeah."

"Dirty bastard."

Tom and Rob fetch the guests' bags from the limo and carry them down to the master bedroom. Rob knocks on the door and waits for an answer before entering.

"Come in!" a voice calls out.

Tom and Rob shuffle inside, struggling with the heavy bags. One of the girls is lying on the bed watching TV, while the other is rubbing oil into her superbly toned, bikini-clad body, preparing for sunbathing.

The oiled-up brunette smiles and asks them to put the suitcases on the bed so she can sort out the clothes that need washing. The boys stand about a metre from the bed as she stands in front of them. She bends over, taking out the clothes and explaining which need to be hand-washed, which can go in the machine, and at what temperature.

However, when an oiled-up, bikini-clad, high-class hooker with the body of a supermodel is bent over right in front of you, it's pretty difficult to focus on what she's saying.

After a minute or so, she turns around and hands each of them a set of clothes.

"Thank you, boys. We'll see you later," she says with a wink.

THE CREW

The blonde on the bed giggles, clearly amused by their inability to multitask. Tom and Rob mumble their thanks, walk out, and close the door behind them.

"Did you remember anything she just said to us in there?" Rob asks.

"Not a fucking word, mate. My brain was on other things."

"You're not alone. I think we'll have to start carrying a Dictaphone every time we talk to those two, just so we can play it back afterwards."

They drop the clothes off with Zecky at the laundry, explaining the situation. She laughs and tells them she'll handle it. They then head back up to the outside deck to talk to me and Jock.

"I take it the pick-up was uneventful, then?" Rob asks.

"Depends how you look at it," I say, nodding towards Jock.

Tom and Rob start laughing, already anticipating another Jock story. They aren't disappointed when I tell them about the toilet and breast-sniffing incidents.

"They're strange dogs, dachshunds, aren't they, Jock? I guess they're small and easy to miss," Rob says, trying to make Jock feel a little better.

"Weird-shaped little fuckers, aren't they?" Jock agrees.

"Yeah, they are," Rob says. "I think it's a bit cruel that breeders make them that way. They must suffer from back problems when they get older. And I bet their dicks get filthy because they're so close to the ground. They must get all sorts of infections."

"Sounds a bit like me. I wish I had a ten-inch cock instead of this fucking massive thing," Jock says, grinning.

"Ha! You should have a licence for that, mate," Rob replies.

"You wouldn't be the first to say that. Anyway, I think it's bloody cruel what they do to dachshunds. If I could get my hands on the bastards, I'd grab them by their necks and ankles and stretch them—

just like they do to their puppies. How long do you reckon they have to pull them before they're the right length?"

"Eh?"

"Pull them—the puppies—to make them longer… how long?"

"Ha! Nice one… you almost got me there, mate."

I turn to Jock, who is looking at me with another confused expression.

"Oh, for fuck's sake, Jock!" I groan, holding my head in my hands.

"What?"

"They don't hold them by their necks and ankles and pull them! They breed from the ones with longer backs over generations to create the breed's look."

"Oh, right. Well, I'm glad about that, because I don't like to see animals suffering," Jock says.

"Good on you, Jock. Neither do I. Whenever I run over something on the road, I have to stop and make sure it's dead—or put it out of its misery."

"Me too, mate. I remember when a couple moved in next door to me, about a week before I moved out of my flat in Glasgow. They had this poor, skinny dog."

"How skinny was it?"

"Skinny, mate. It had big, long legs, a tiny stomach, and a long, slender head. They had two other little dogs—looked like terriers. They used to take them all out in the field behind us every day, and they'd come back with rabbits."

"Sounds like the guy was a poacher."

"Anyway, I used to shout at him from my window, telling him to bloody well feed the skinny one up, but it never got any fatter. On the night I moved out, I went into his yard and put the poor little sod out of its misery."

THE CREW

"You killed his dog?!"

"Yeah—well, more like put it out of its misery. I couldn't bear to see it looking so skinny. It obviously never got fed. I could get my hands around its waist, for God's sake! I'd see the poor little bugger running after rabbits in the field, so it must have been starving. It was the best thing to do for it, I reckon."

"How did you 'put it out of its misery', so to speak?"

"Shovel to the back of its head. It didn't feel a thing."

"Jock, do you know what breed of dog it was?"

"Er, yeah… I remember its owner went mad at me and shouted back that it was a 'whuffet' or something and that they were supposed to be skinny. Lying bastard. I reckon he just couldn't be arsed to feed it."

"Jock, are you sure he didn't say 'whippet', mate?"

Jock snaps his fingers in front of my face.

"Yep! That's it… whippet. I remember now—the poor little fucker could run like lightning."

Rob, Tom, and I all cup our heads in our hands and let out a long groan.

"Jock, I hate to have to tell you this, mate, but you slaughtered a perfectly healthy hound. A whippet is like a miniature greyhound—they're used for racing or chasing hares and rabbits. They're meant to be lean, you nobber!"

"So you're saying I…"

"I'm afraid so, mate."

"Fuck!"

Chapter 19
Swine Rodeo

Poor old Jock disappeared below deck to the crew room with his tail between his legs, you might say, after I pointed out the error of his canine execution.

"His heart was in the right place, I guess, and it's a mistake any of us could make," says Rob.

"Er… no, it isn't!" laughs Tom.

"No, I guess you're right, mate. There aren't many people who would make that mistake and go to such drastic measures."

"Jock wouldn't hurt a fly intentionally, though. He obviously thought he was doing the right thing in the grand scheme of things."

"I'm sure Hitler thought the same back in Germany during the war," says Zecky, walking up the deck behind the boys.

"How's tricks, Zecks?" I say.

"Could be better. I've just been babysitting Jock down below. He's coming to terms with his canine slaughter. And I've just noticed there are jizz stains on two of the girls' garments you gave me. Looks like my afternoon will be taken up with a pair of Marigolds, some stain remover, and a bowl of hot water."

"Errrr! Russian jizz, eh? I bet that's a bastard to get off. Does it smell of vodka and pelmeni?"

"Firstly, I'm not going to sniff this jizz in a million years, and secondly, what the hell is pelmeni?"

"It's a national dish of Russia – meat covered in dough."

"Or, in this case, clothes covered in man dough," says Rob, laughing.

"Whatever's in his jizz, it's going to be a bloody nightmare to get out."

THE CREW

Tom suddenly puts on his finest and deepest Russian accent to mimic Mr Big. "Ahhhh, Miss Zecky... I was wondering if you 'av ridded my lover's clothes of my crusty Russian jizzzz?"

"That was quite a decent accent for you, Tom," I tell him. "Your portrayal of foreign languages is usually on a par with Jock's timekeeping—shit!"

"I bet you never thought in a thousand years, when you applied for this job, that one day you'd be in Porto Cervo, surrounded by mega-yachts, removing a dodgy millionaire's jizz off a dress," Rob says to Zecky.

"You're not wrong. And by the way, it's two dresses, each owned by a different girl. He's a naughty boy, is Mr Big. Maybe I should give the job to Tar," she giggles.

"Oh, don't you worry, Zecks. He's going to have enough on his plate for the rest of the trip without cleaning off jizz. Anyway, Jock has come up with a plan to loosen him up. He reckons what Tar needs is a few nights on the beer and a dirty shag," I tell Zecky, laughing.

"What?!"

"Jock has come to the conclusion that Tar needs to lose his cherry and get laid for the first time," says Rob.

"Has he now? Who's the lucky girl going to be, or shouldn't I ask?"

"We don't know yet, but it's in the pipeline, so to speak."

"Don't you think you should let it happen naturally?"

We all look at each other and shake our heads with an expression that suggests Zecky is trying to kill our fun.

"Naahh!" comes the unanimous reply.

"Well, be nice and make it special for him, because he'll remember it for the rest of his life."

Jock is clearly over his extermination sadness, as he bounds up behind Zecky to join the conversation. "I don't remember my first time, so that's a load of bollocks," he says, giving her a friendly swipe on the bottom with the back of his hand.

"Hey, you! Don't touch what you can't afford," she says.

"You don't remember what you had for breakfast a few hours ago, Jock. Then again, that's what decades of alcohol abuse does to your memory," I tell him.

"There is definitely a price to pay for such frivolities," he laughs.

"Jock, I'm fucking amazed you can walk and talk at the same time, based on what he's just said," says Rob.

"Cheeky bastard! It's true, though—my short-term memory is fucked. I can't remember anything."

"How long have you had this problem?"

"What problem?" jokes Jock.

Tom has a puzzled look on his face. "I'm a bit surprised, though, even for you. How the hell don't you remember the very first time you had sex? You don't just forget that. I remember my first time like it was yesterday."

"Go on then. Where were you?" says Jock.

"It was a full moon party in Thailand."

"How old were you?"

"Seventeen."

"What was her name?"

"Fuck knows."

Everyone bursts out laughing.

"You see? Even you don't remember, so I'm not on my own," laughs Jock.

"Hang on a minute. The salient point here is, I was in the moonlight on a beach in Thailand, stoned off my lord. I was seventeen and she was around twenty-one. She was from France, about five feet six, with shoulder-length curly hair and great tits. We did it lying on the sand, and she was on top. I got sand down the crack of my arse and lasted about two minutes with all the excitement of the first time. The fact that I don't remember her name doesn't really count for anything. It's the vibe, the surroundings, and the cosmetics that you mainly remember."

"All right, fair point, mate," Jock concedes.

'What about you, Rob?' asks Tom.

'It was a small goat at a farm in Wales. Her name was

Flopsy and we shared a wonderful moment together.' Zecky splutters over her coffee.

'It was idyllic,' Rob goes on. 'It was by the river when our eyes met. I coyly took a wander over and asked her if she'd like to have a drink with me at the trough. She said yes, then after a wonderful afternoon I asked her for dinner in the next field where we dined on a hedge… it was just magical!'

'I always knew you were part Welsh. Really, do you remember everything, though?' asks Jock.

'Sure! Just imagine trying to find lingerie that would fit her woolly behind properly.'

'Ha! Come on mate, seriously, your first girl I mean.' 'Yeah, I do actually. My parents were away on a night out. I was fifteen and I got abused by the babysitter who was called Claudia. She kind of violated me, really.'

Zecky puts her arm around Rob to comfort him. 'Oh

Rob, that's awful. Poor you, that must have been horrible.'

'Horrible my arse! It was fucking brilliant. For months afterwards I used to tell my folks I was scared to be left alone in the house when they went out. They took pity on me and they'd get Claudia round to baby-sit. I was milking them of sympathy while the babysitter was milking me… literally. It was the best time of my fucking life!'

Zecky has a good laugh before offering her perception on the differences between the sexes. 'What are you like? This is the difference between men and women, you see. We want romance and a connection and you lot just want a wet hole and a beer.'

'Well, yeah, but not necessarily in that order,' adds Tom, joking.

'Listen, Zecks,' says Jock with a serious face. 'Tom doesn't speak for all of us. Sometimes we like a cuddle and a bit of tender loving care as much as women do. Sometimes I like to lie down and talk for a while to connect, then lay her down on a bed covered in fresh rose petals with some gentle soothing music in the background.'

There is a long pause before Rob breaks the silence.

'That's actually a load of crap really, isn't it, Jock?'

'Yep, it's all about a good deep dicking for me!'

'Thought so.'

'Got any more jokes, have we, Jock?' asks Zecky, looking fairly underwhelmed.

'I know a great joke about women.'

'No Jock. Not that one – it's a bit offensive,' I warn him.

'No, go on, Jock. I'm a big girl – I can take it.'

'All right, what's the function of a woman?'

'Go on.'

'To be a life support system for a pussy.'

Even Zecky finds this funny. She can't very well tell him off, considering she told him earlier that men would be extinct if vibrators could get a round of drinks in.

'That's charming, Jock,' says Zecky, 'but I still can't believe that you truly can't remember who you first had sex with, out of all the girls you've been with.'

'Look, if you eat a tin of beans you don't know which one makes you fart, do you?'

Everyone has a good laugh at this before I steer the conversation back to the job and matters in hand: 'Anyway, Zecks, what do the guests want to do today?'

'The girls are being taken into Porto Cervo so they can to get some clothes for the Billionaire Nightclub tonight.' 'That'll cost him,' I say, raising my eyebrows.

'You're telling me!! It's all designer labels over there. You'll have to pop up to the Captain and get some money out of the safe. Mr Big told me on the phone this morning that he wants another thirty thousand in cash.'

'How the other half live, eh?'

'It's small change to him.'

'Let's hope he tips as much as he spends. If he does, it's going to be one hell of an end-of-charter-party.'

'What does he want to do himself?'

'Are you ready for this?'

'Go on then.'

"He wants to go horse riding, and two of you are to go with him because his bodyguards will be with the girls. To be fair, I think he's sick of the sight of the guards and just wants a bit of freedom and a couple of fresh faces."

"That's a tricky one. Can anyone ride a horse?" I ask, looking around at the boys.

At that moment, Tar joins us and catches the tail end of the conversation. "Did you say, 'Can anyone ride a horse?'"

"Yeah."

"Well, I can."

"That figures. Well-off family living in the country—he's bound to have owned a horse or two at some point," sniggers Rob.

"What was he or she called, then?"

"She was a black thoroughbred called Ebony. I had her for about five years until she was stolen."

"I take it you didn't get her back, then?"

"No. She's probably in a barn somewhere being used for breeding."

"All right then, Tar, you can go since you can ride. Who else has ridden?"

I look at Rob and Tom, but they shake their heads.

"I've ridden a horse a few times," says Jock.

"I'm not talking about those festering old donkeys you see on the beaches at British seaside resorts, mate."

"Yeah, I know."

"When have you ever ridden a horse?"

"Well, it was a while ago, but it was back home."

"Jock, you're not having me on, are you? If I'm going to send you with Tar, you'd better know what the score is, because no doubt the client will be hiring some decent nags and trotting through the countryside."

"Yeah, no problem."

"I don't know if I believe you, Jock, but you've never lied to me yet. So if you shake my hand on it, I'll let you go."

Jock shrugs and puts his hand out for me to shake.

"All right, mate. I've not got a particularly good feeling about this, but you've shaken on it, so that's that."

"What time do you want them ready, Zecks?" I ask her.

"Three p.m. at the passerelle."

THE CREW

"Right then, that's sorted. I'm going to see Thrush and get some money out of the safe for the girls to waste in town, all right? You two had better crack on with cleaning the boat and give the jet skis a good look-over," I tell Rob and Tom.

Rob, Zecky, Tom, and I move off the deck to carry on with our chores, leaving Tar and Jock behind. As Tar starts to walk away, Jock holds his arm to stop him and quietly asks him to wait until they're alone.

"Right, Tar, you're going to have to give me a few pointers on how to drive a horse, mate."

"What? You just told everyone you've ridden before."

"Well, my knowledge of riding a horse stems about as far as going backwards and forwards on a rocking horse at my granddad's house as a kid. That and jumping on the backs of big pigs at my mate's farm."

"Rocking horses? Pigs?!"

"Yeah. When I was a kid, my mate used to run into the pigpen on a farm with his cap gun to scare the pigs. They'd shit themselves and bolt for the exit. I used to hang onto a wooden beam over the doorway, and when they passed under me, I'd let go, drop onto their backs, and hold onto their ears."

"You rode pigs and used their ears as reins?!"

"Yeah, but only the big strong ones."

"You're kidding?"

"No, mate. My record back then was twenty-five seconds before it flipped me off!"

"I very much doubt they enjoyed the experience."

"Big Samson didn't. You had to run like hell and jump over the fence before he caught up with you. He was a big boy!"

"I'm not surprised. I think I'd want revenge if someone jumped on my back and held onto my ears. So your total riding experience to date basically consists of a metal rocking horse—"

"It was a wooden one, actually."

"Sorry, a wooden rocking horse and a few pissed-off porkers?"

"Basically, yeah... that's about it."

"You'll bloody kill yourself on a real horse, especially if it gallops. It'll probably be a twitchy thoroughbred, so you'll need your wits about you."

"My granddad said never work with kids and never trust anything that's bigger and dumber than yourself. I'll be doing both this afternoon, so you're going to have to give me the basics if you don't want me to kill myself."

Tar looks more than a little flustered and nervous at the task ahead of him. "Jock, riding a horse is not the same as riding a bike. It's complex, and each horse is different. It can take ages to get the basics, but to get proficient at it can take years. And we're bloody leaving in an hour!"

"You'd better get cracking then, matey."

"Oh Jesus... where do I start?"

"Look, all you need to tell me is how you start it."

"Start it? It's not an engine, Jock."

"You know what I mean—start, stop, turn. The rest I'll figure out as I go along. If it doesn't do as I tell it, I'll give it a bollocking."

"A bollocking... oh Jeeeesus!" says Tar, rubbing his forehead and looking worried.

"Relax, little man—everything will be cool."

"Jock, you shook hands on it to say you've ridden before."

"Well, he didn't specify what type of horse, so technically I didn't lie. I've always wanted to have a go on a real one.

"Anyway, how hard can it be?"

Chapter 20
Live Fast, Die Young and Leave A Good Looking Corpse

Jock and Target changed into something suitable for horse riding, and Jock seemed to be getting into the spirit of things. He had put on his tight jeans and had 'borrowed' Rob's leather cowboy boots and Zecky's kangaroo-skin cowboy hat, which she usually wore at the beach. It was even funnier because he wasn't taking the piss—he was finally living his dream of becoming a cowboy, even if just for the afternoon. All he needed now was a pistol, a spittoon, and maybe a few tomahawk-wielding Native Americans to shoot at, and he would be right there in the Wild West. Everyone knew he was a massive fan of John Wayne, and he had all of his films in his cabin.

Eager as a beaver, Jock was the first to turn up at the passerelle, followed by Thrush and Tar. Thrush was his usual solemn self, with not a hint of humour in sight. The man couldn't cheer up a laughing hyena if his life depended on it.

"Here is some money from the slush fund," Thrush said, staring at Jock intently. "I expect receipts for everything you spend, and none of it is to go on alcohol. Is that understood?"

"Yep, no problem," Jock replied, lifting his hat.

"Tarquin, I want you to stay with him at all times. I expect the best from both of you this afternoon. This is an unusual circumstance, and it's not often that a guest of his stature goes on an excursion away from the yacht without their bodyguards."

"This doesn't usually happen often, then?" Tar enquired.

"No, and especially not with a guest like this," Thrush replied.

"What do you mean, if you don't mind me asking?"

Thrush, as always, tried to answer in his usual over-diplomatic and non-committal way. "Let's just say that perhaps his wealth hasn't come from the more normal or legitimate avenues."

Tar was starting to look a little worried.

"I think what he's trying to say is that his cash has probably been made illegally, and he's pissed a few people off along the way," Jock explained.

"I didn't say that, young man, so don't put words into my mouth," Thrush said.

"Well, that's exactly what you meant. You're trying to say he's a dodgy fucker."

"Still, you put words into my mouth."

Tar now looked even more concerned. "My God, I've just had a terrible thought. We could be in danger. If he's made his fortune through illegal means and upset a lot of people, we could get caught up in a vendetta."

Without offering any reassurance or attempting to pacify Tar, Thrush turned and walked back inside. It was bloody typical of him, but this was all new to Tar. Life was new to Tar. He was now working aboard a mega-yacht, in an alien environment, far from home, and completely out of his comfort zone. He wouldn't be human if he didn't feel at least a little apprehensive.

Tar was being overdramatic, much to Jock's amusement, but he played along for sheer entertainment value. It was becoming clear that Tar could be a complete drama queen at times.

"Jock, I could be in trouble here."

"Why's that, little man? Have you pissed your pants again?"

"Mr Big might have a price on his head for crossing some enemy back in Russia," Tar said, frowning.

Jock was now thoroughly enjoying Tar's flustered state. "You might be right. Are you prepared to take a bullet for the man?" he asked with a straight face.

"No, I'm not! Of course not," Tar said, his eyes widening.

"Ah, you see—you'll take tips off the guests, but you won't put your arse on the line for them when the going gets tough, eh?"

Tar's voice climbed even higher. "Jock, there's a world of difference between doing a few extra hours for the guests' benefit and taking a bullet for one of them."

"Would you take a bullet for £5,000?" Jock asked.

"No."

"£10,000?"

"No, I bloody wouldn't."

"£15,000?"

"Jock, the point I'm trying to make is that you can't spend it if you're dead as a dodo."

"Fair point, little man. As long as you're prepared to get caught in the crossfire and back me up, that's all I can ask of you, I suppose."

Tar stared at Jock's poker face, unsure if he was serious. Just then, Zecky stuck her head through the porthole and told Jock their ride was about to pull up at the yacht and that Mr Big would be on his way down in a minute or two.

"No problem, gorgeous, I'll be ready with the door," Jock replied. "It doesn't look like we'll have a chance to go over the riding basics now, Tar, because we're leaving."

"Brilliant... that's just brilliant. Now I might have to deal with you breaking your neck and possibly getting caught in a revenge killing," Tar muttered, flustered.

Jock took a coin out of his pocket and placed it in Tar's chest pocket.

"Here you are."

"What's that for?"

"It's for you to go out and buy some testicles," Jock said, struggling to hold back a fit of giggles.

"It's not funny, Jock. This could all be very real. Is it beyond the realm of possibility? I ask you that."

"I think you should've seen Zecky for some Imodium before you came out, Tar."

"Imodium? Why?"

"Because it's the only thing that'll stop you from shitting yourself."

"Very funny, Jock. Honestly, you should be on the stage," Tar said sarcastically.

"Well, personally, I've always thought that. I reckon I've got hidden talent."

"Well, I hope you find it one day."

"Ha! You cheeky little sod. Anyway, quiet now—Mr Big is walking towards us. If you see any red laser lights from rifle scopes passing over me, let me know, OK?"

The limo driver parked at the foot of the passerelle and opened the door as Mr Big, Jock, and Tar walked down. Mr Big sat in the front while Tar and Jock sat together in the back. The driver spoke fluent Russian, which was unusual for this area. He and Mr Big started having a conversation, leaving Tar and Jock to talk quietly amongst themselves in the rear.

Tar finally gave Jock a few very basic pointers on riding a horse.

"I don't know what you were bloody worried about, Tar. All of that seems fair enough. It's not exactly rocket science, is it?"

"Hang on a minute, Jock—that was just some of the very basic theory. The practice is much more difficult. And to top it all off, you never know what the horse will do. They all have minds of their own."

THE CREW

At the stables, they were met by a Corsican woman named Maria, who showed them the eight available horses and provided them with a map of various routes and distances. The horses were all large, muscular beasts in perfect condition. Her staff must have spent hours each day grooming and caring for them, and it showed. She introduced each horse by name and described their different personalities.

Mr Big is clearly impressed by a beautiful grey thoroughbred stallion named Sirius. Maria explains that he is a feisty one who loves to gallop. He is also the alpha male of the group, and the other horses are happy to follow him. Sirius instinctively knows he is about to go out; he becomes agitated and starts kicking the door in excitement. One of the stable hands leads Sirius into the courtyard, where Mr Big prepares to saddle up and get acquainted with him. Mr Big clearly has extensive experience with horses. Perhaps he made his fortune smuggling drugs over the Ural Mountains on horseback or something equally outrageous. Whatever his past may be, it shows—he runs his hands over the horse, instantly calming him down.

Next, Tar and Jock choose their horses. Maria asks about their riding experience to determine which horse suits each of them best. Tar has the most experience, and he talks for about five minutes about the rosettes he has won and his equestrian friends, much to Jock's boredom. Jock just wants to get out and live the cowboy dream, so when Maria asks about his experience, he simply points at Tar and says, "Same." Mr Big is already on his horse, ready and waiting while Jock and Tar finish saddling up.

"You get on first, buddy, so I can see how you mount," Jock tells Tar quietly.

The horse seems to dwarf Tar, and once he is on, he looks like an action figure perched on a Shire horse—completely out of proportion. Now it is Jock's turn. With his back to Mr Big, he strokes the horse's nose and whispers that if the horse does not hurt him, he will not hurt it. It seems like a fair deal. Following Tar's lead, he runs his hands along the horse's neck and back, then places his foot in the stirrup and climbs up. So far, so good. Maria wishes them well, then turns and leaves them to it.

"Okay, gentlemen, just try to keep up and follow me," says Mr Big. With a click of his heels, Sirius begins to walk out of the courtyard and down one of the bridle paths into a clearing in the woods. Jock mirrors the movements of those ahead of him, and everything seems to be going smoothly. Tar glances over his shoulder and says, "Jock, if you don't want your horse to run fast, just make a bet on it in your head."

"How's that going to help?" Jock whispers back.

"Well, judging by your track record, betting on a horse slows it down," Tar replies, unable to resist a bit of teasing.

Jock, however, is unfazed. Dressed as a cowboy, riding a horse—or at least sitting on one—with the sun on his back, he is living the dream. A big smile spreads across his face as he pulls a cigar from his chest pocket and sticks it in the corner of his mouth. The aroma is rich and inviting. Tar catches a whiff of it, turns around, and sees "John Wayne Jock" fully in his element.

"He's got to be kidding," Tar mutters to himself.

After about half an hour of gentle trotting, they reach an open field. Sirius starts to get restless, snorting and stamping his hooves as if he knows this is where he can burn off some pent-up energy. Mr Big stops and tells the boys he is going for a gallop and will meet them at the ranch, which Maria suggested would be a good place to stop for lunch. Then, with a flick of the reins, Sirius takes off as though he has been eating amphetamines rather than hay. It is mesmerising to watch—the horse's muscles tighten, and he accelerates from a standstill, galloping down the field before disappearing behind a wooden fence at the bottom of the meadow.

Now, all is still except for the breeze rustling through the trees and the gentle sway of meadow flowers under the hot sun. Jock has a thousand-yard stare, his face a picture of concentration as he gazes at the distant fence. Tar knows exactly what is going through his mind.

THE CREW

"Don't even think about it, Jock. You've only walked on that horse so far—galloping and jumping fences is way beyond your skill level."

Jock does not respond. He is lost in the moment.

"Jock, are you listening to me?" Tar repeats.

After a long silence and quiet contemplation, Jock finally speaks. What he says is unexpectedly profound—a moment of rare clarity.

"I've just had an omen," he says. "Have you ever noticed how beautiful the landscape looks when you're standing at the edge of a cliff? Look at this place—it's stunning."

"An omen? About what?"

"About how to live life. I'm going to gallop down this meadow and leap over that fence." Jock points towards it.

"No way, Jock. You'll kill yourself. It's far too dangerous, especially with your limited experience. And how do you know the horse will even try to jump it?"

"Faith. All you need is a little faith and belief—just like in life. Anyway, Tar, you came to sea to work, didn't you?"

"What's that got to do with anything?"

"Well, you had no prior experience, and working at sea is one of the most dangerous jobs in the world," Jock points out.

"That's completely different. I'm working with people I trust—people who know what they're doing."

"You've only known us a short time, so how can you be sure you can trust us?"

"I just feel it."

"Well, I feel that I can trust this horse completely."

"Jock, I still think you should play it safe and go around the fence. Jumping it is too risky."

"Fuck the safe option, Tar. Life is a risk every single day. Nothing worthwhile ever comes from playing it safe. Life is only truly satisfying when lived at the extremes. Sometimes, ships go out to sea in terrible weather, but that's never stopped them from leaving the harbour. Don't settle for mediocrity and safety just because it's easy. You'd be amazed at the feeling you get when you dare to be the person you've always wanted to be. When you put yourself in a position where you could lose everything, your true nature shines through. Be that fearless, intrepid spirit who strives to conquer. Live without fear—because fear is the only thing holding you, and everyone else, back. Denying your natural instincts and emotions is denying your true self. And the realisation of your true self is the ultimate purpose in life."

Tar is stunned. He struggles to think of something logical to change Jock's mind, but nothing comes. Everything Jock has just said is true. A life lived in fear is no life at all. Without contrast, nothing has meaning. Sometimes, you do need risk and extremes to remind you who you are—to feel truly alive.

Tar takes a deep breath and looks back at Jock over his shoulder.

"I must be going out of my mind, but I've just had déjà vu of this exact space and time. You on that horse, those words, and this view," says Tar.

"I'll see you on the other side of the fence, Tar."

"Hang on, Jock, I'm not jumping that."

"Yeah, you are."

"I'm not—no way!"

"Okay, but you'll have to live with yourself, looking in the mirror every day, knowing you could have been the person you've always wanted to be but backed down at the challenge. Anyway, you've jumped obstacles on a horse before, and I haven't, so you have the advantage."

"Obstacles that were a couple of feet high, that's all. It's hard to see from here, but that fence looks about six feet. We don't even know if the horses will jump. If they stop at the last moment, we'll be off."

"Faith, remember?" Jock tells Tar, looking him in the eyes.

No further words are spoken as Jock and a terrified Tarquin sit on the backs of their horses. After a brief period of contemplation, Jock runs his palm gently between the horse's ears and down the side of its neck. The horse snorts loudly and stamps its hoof, as if it knows what is about to happen. Jock cracks his reins and digs his heels in. His horse momentarily rears up before bursting into a gallop down the field towards the fence.

Jock's posture is wrong, and he looks unsteady as he struggles to keep his balance on the animal. He seems like he could fall off at any moment. As Jock and the horse race towards the fence, Tar claps his hands over his mouth.

"Shit… shit… shit… he's going to kill himself!" he mutters.

Moments later, he sees Jock's horse rise as it launches over the fence. Somehow, Jock remains loosely on its back as it takes off, but at the peak of the jump, there is a clear gap between them. The horse lands cleanly on the other side, and Jock can be seen lying flat along its back, his arms wrapped around its neck. After a moment, he slowly sits upright. Whether he is processing what he has just done or silently thanking a higher power for not breaking his neck is unclear.

Tar squints, struggling to make out Jock and the horse in the distance, but he is sure he can see a cloud of cigar smoke around his friend's head. Jock shouts something, but Tar can't hear him. He watches Jock gesturing wildly, and the message is obvious.

Tar battles with himself, willing his body to move, but fear keeps him frozen. The instinct for self-preservation overrides his deep desire to step out of his comfort zone. He is just about to turn away, ready to admit defeat, when Jock's words echo loudly in his mind as if spoken right beside him.

"Fuck it!" he yells, digging his heels into the horse's flanks.

Startled by the intensity of Tar's outburst, the horse is already moving. Fearful but fully alive, Tarquin shifts his weight onto his legs, balancing himself as he nears the fence. He sees Jock on the other side, urging him on with wild gestures. Fighting the natural impulse to shut his eyes, he keeps them open as the horse leaps.

The jump is graceful. The horse clears the fence effortlessly, helped by the light weight it carries. It lands with a heavy thud, kicking up a small cloud of dust. Jock is already yelling at the top of his lungs, thrilled that Tar had the guts to do it.

They leap off their horses and run toward each other, celebrating their triumph. Jumping in the air, shouting with excitement, they embrace.

"You took your bloody time!" Jock says, thumping Tar on the back. "I thought I was going to get arrested for loitering."

"It took me a while to pluck up the courage, I'll admit that," says Tar.

"Well, you did it, mate, and that's what counts."

"I did. I still can't quite believe it."

"I can't either. I thought you were going to chicken out on me!"

"Well… the thought did cross my mind a couple of times."

"Alright, Tar, enough hugging. If any women are watching, they'll think I'm taken, and we can't have that now, can we, little man?" Jock grins, clamping his teeth around his cigar.

"That was bloody amazing!" Tar shouts, unable to contain his excitement.

"It was one hell of a jump, mate. Let's put it this way—it was a lot smoother than mine."

"It did look like you separated from the horse at one point. I thought you were going to go one way, and the horse the other!"

"That makes two of us. I was hanging on for dear life! You ever seen those crazy motorbike riders on TV? They go full throttle up a ramp, leave the bike in mid-air to do tricks, then get back on before landing? Well, that was me—except my bike was that horse. I didn't mean to leave it!"

"Crikey, I bet that was terrifying."

"Terrifying? I nearly shit myself halfway down the meadow, even before the jump!"

"Maybe we should have taken some of that Imodium you mentioned."

"I tell you, mate, this fence-jumping lark is the best laxative I've ever had."

"What went through your mind when you were in the air?" Tar asks.

"Errr… 'You're fucked, Jock!'"

"Hah! No, really—what were you thinking?"

"Just… live. Live to tell the tale."

"Yeah, same here. I've never wanted to live as much as I did in that split second. I felt so alive—I can't even explain it."

"It's called adrenaline. Now tell me, what do you think is worth more, now that you've done it—a life of mediocrity or just a few seconds of what you've just experienced?"

"I don't think you even need to ask," says Tar. "I've had at least a little horse-riding experience, even if not at that level. But you had none! Seriously, Jock, you could have died today."

"Yep, but look at it this way, little man. As I've always said—I'd have lived fast, died young, but left a bloody good-looking corpse."

"Well, there is that."

"By the way, Tar, you can give me back that coin I put in your pocket."

"Why?"

"Because you no longer need to buy yourself a pair of balls."

Chapter 21
Inspiration Comes in Many Forms

After their fence-leaping celebrations, Jock and Tar catch up with Mr Big and Sirius at the meeting place along the track. They have a light lunch, and then Mr Big insists on introducing them to the merits of Stoli vodka—in large quantities. This spontaneous drinking session lasts much of the afternoon and, after some initial language difficulties, turns out to be great fun for all involved. They spend a long time giggling hysterically at Sirius trying to mount Tar's horse. After a few more vodkas, Jock even teaches Mr Big to moonwalk and demonstrates how to create a circumcised erect penis by carefully folding a beer towel in the right places. According to Jock, it is essential knowledge.

However, the afternoon of vodka drinking affects Tar more than the others. It becomes clear that he has had enough when Jock has to carry him over his shoulder and manhandle him onto his horse.

Back at the yacht, in very good spirits—vodka, to be precise—they are greeted at the passerelle by Zecky and Thrush. As Zecky opens the limo door to offer Mr Big a cool face towel, she is met by a cloud of acrid cigar smoke. Jock and Mr Big are on either side of Tar in the back seat, propping him up while puffing on huge cigars.

Jock gets out and helps the still-giggling, blind-drunk Tar. Mr Big climbs out the other side with a big grin and slaps Jock on the back as he passes him at the foot of the passerelle. He clearly does not want to talk to Thrush, whose face is turning crimson with anger at the state of Tar. Instead, he walks straight past him and heads up the outside stairs to the sun deck, where the girls are in the Jacuzzi.

'What the hell have you two been doing?' thunders Thrush.

'Looking after our guest,' replies Jock.

'I expressly told you not to drink alcohol!'

'That's not quite what you said,' Jock says, shaking his head.

THE CREW

'Don't you tell me what I did and didn't say, young man.'

'Well, you never said that.'

'Yes, I did! I told you that I wanted your best this afternoon and not to spend any of the money I gave you on alcohol.'

'Hang on a minute,' says Jock, helping Tar sit down on a rope mooring bollard. He steadies him, ensuring he is in a position of temporary stable equilibrium, then watches him for a second before continuing his conversation with the wild-eyed Thrush.

'What you said and what you meant were two different things. I didn't spend any of the money on alcohol.' Jock pulls the cash from his pocket and hands it back to Thrush. 'Every last penny you gave me is there.'

'It's allll therrrre,' slurs Tar, still sitting on the bollard with his eyes closed in a drunken stupor. As he begins to wobble from side to side, Jock holds out an arm to steady him.

'You knew what I meant when I said that,' Thrush says, jabbing a finger into Jock's chest.

'First of all, Captain, you'd better get your finger out of my chest before I rip it off.'

'Don't you threaten me, young man.'

'I'm not threatening you, but if you keep jabbing me, I'll have to stop you. That's all I'm saying. Secondly, if you meant otherwise, you should have been more specific.'

'Don't you tell me how I should or shouldn't talk to you, young man.'

'Look, we were just looking after the guest, as you told us to.'

'Yes, but not by getting blind drunk, you idiot!'

'To be honest, Captain, I know I've had a few, but I'm not drunk. I've still got all my faculties. Fair enough, Tar is a bit worse for wear, but the guest insisted. We couldn't let him drink on his own, could we?'

'Why not? You were on duty, for God's sake.'

'Well, he insisted, and it's bad form and rude to refuse a drink when offered. Have you ever drunk alone while everyone else stayed sober? It wouldn't have been much fun for him, so that's why we joined in.'

'Look, don't lecture me about drinking. I used to drink.'

'Well, you should have kept it up, because you look fucking miserable!'

'Miiiisssserable,' mutters the still-giggling Tar.

'How dare you speak to me like that! I can assure you this will be taken further. As for you, Tarquin, I expected much better from someone who has only been aboard a short time.'

There is no response from the swaying Tar. Thrush pushes his shoulder to grab his attention, but instead, he knocks him off balance. Tar nose-dives like a Stuka into the teak deck, somehow landing in a position of pure comic perfection—his left cheek flat against the deck, arms by his sides, knees tucked under his chest, and arse sticking in the air. If he tried a million times, he would never be able to replicate it.

'Oh, for God's sake, look at the state of you—that's pathetic!' Thrush winces.

Thrush is thinking 'pathetic', while Jock is thinking 'priceless'. Jock secretly wants to rush to his cabin and grab his video camera. This is prime YouTube material.

'What have you got to say for yourself?' Thrush shouts at Tar.

There are a few seconds of silence as Tar's befuddled brain processes the question. Then, at last, he drawls an entirely inappropriate response.

'Fuuuucking gooood afternooooon,' he slurs, before vomiting green bile over Thrush's Italian leather shoes.

* * * *

Tar is taken straight to bed and spends the rest of the day in his bunk, sleeping it off. Jock, on the other hand, has a couple of coffees and is fine after an hour or so. He decides to keep a low profile and disappears down to the forward store to carry out an inventory. Mr Big has a Jacuzzi with the girls, then sleeps for a few hours to recuperate. Feeling a little shabby and hungover when he wakes, he decides to powder his nose with some more coke to refresh himself. As Zecky brings him a constant flow of strong filter coffee, she catches him doing two lines off the top of the glass table.

"Christ, it looks like he's been using the table for baking, judging by the amount of white powder," Zecky tells Rob on her return.

The limo arrives just before nine o'clock to take the guests to a party at Billionaire's Nightclub, leaving only the crew aboard the yacht. Even Thrush manages to get ashore for a few hours to do whatever it is that Thrush does. Nobody knows what he gets up to. He doesn't drink or go down to the beach, and he's too bloody tight to pay for a decent meal. Jock thinks he goes cottaging or something equally sneaky. Rumour has it he's suffering from cabin fever and just needs a break. Not surprising, really. Before leaving, he tells me and Zecky that the ship will depart Porto Cervo at nine o'clock in the morning, heading for Ibiza, where the guests will eventually disembark.

Once the guests leave for the nightclub, I lift the passerelle and raise it to a forty-five-degree angle. The end is about seven feet off the quay, so nobody can board without using their personal remote controls to lower it to ankle level. A buzzer will sound in the crew room to warn us if it's being lowered, so we can relax.

I invite everyone to gather in the crew room, break open a case of beer, and go over the sailing plans. We also want to hear Jock's story about his afternoon with Mr Big. Judging by what I've heard so far, it wasn't exactly a normal day. Tar's vomiting has cleared most of the alcohol from his system, but Zecky is drip-feeding him water to make sure he's all right for the morning. He looks like shit, but that's to be expected—he's not used to it.

Everyone is seated around the communal table, waiting for Jock to finish showering. After about five minutes, he walks in with a beer in his hand. No change there, then.

"All right, Jock, take a seat and tell us something we don't know," I say.

Jock climbs over the seats and sits between Tar and me. He takes a swig of his Heineken and thinks for a moment.

"For some reason, I've been having really dirty dreams lately about Cherie Blair. It's bloody weird because I don't even fancy her!"

The crew erupts with laughter while Jock sits there looking deadpan and bemused. Once I regain my composure, I put a hand on his shoulder.

"No, mate—I'm talking about today. What happened with Mr Big?"

"Oh right, yeah, got you. Thought you were talking about something else."

"Clearly."

"Just the usual, really. Drove to the stables, leapt a fence, had an omen, watched Tar get wankered, saw his horse get reamed by Sirius, and taught Mr Big how to moonwalk. Just a run-of-the-mill day," he laughs.

"How did you get on with riding a strange horse?" asks Zecky.

Tar relives the moment. "Well, I wouldn't call it riding, really. It was more of a partially controlled free-fall. You know when you skydive? You wouldn't call that flying, would you?"

"Well, yeah, he's got a point," says Jock. "I just about managed to stay on while it was galloping and when he leapt the fence."

"You leapt a fence?" asks Tom, incredulous.

"Yeah."

"How big?"

"Not that big."

"I beg to differ, Jock," says Tar.

"How big was it, Tar—truthfully?" asks Zecky.

"About as high as him, maybe taller."

"Are you mad?" asks Rob.

"I think we all know the answer to that one," says Tom.

"You could have killed yourself."

"Tar and I have already had this conversation, mate. Besides, I've seen enough John Wayne movies to know the basics."

"All except turning and stopping," laughs Tar.

"You told me you could ride, Jock," I say, looking pained.

"Yeah, I can. I was just getting used to a different horse," Jock replies, squeezing Tar's leg under the table as a silent prompt to keep quiet.

"How the hell did you get Mr Big to moonwalk?"

"You'd be amazed what vodka shots make people do. He was pretty good, actually."

I point at Jock and Tar. "I've got to tell you two—you might be in some shit after today."

"How so?" asks Tar, innocently.

"How so?! You came back blitzed and puked on Thrush's shoes, for a start."

"Fair point," says Jock.

"I did what?! Noooo!" Tar looks genuinely astounded.

"You don't remember?"

"I remember getting on the back of the horse, but everything after that is a blur. What did Thrush say?"

"He was pretty pissed off, and I'd guess you'll find out tomorrow. Plus, you were both hammered while looking after the guest," I say, biting my lip.

"He bloody loved it, though, mate, and it was his idea," Jock protests.

"Well, the only way you're getting out of this is if Mr Big tells Thrush he insisted on it."

"Look, I've taught him my cock trick with the beer towel. He loved it! I reckon I'll have no problem getting him to say it was his doing. I think me and him have got a bit of a bond now."

"Hope for your sake you have, mate."

"What else did you get up to?" asks Zecky.

"The weirdest thing ever," says Jock. "Not sure if I believe it yet, but I reckon we should all get our laptops and bring them in here."

"Why?" asks Tom.

"It's a weird one. After a few vodkas, Mr Big's English got better, and he was easier to understand."

"That's weird, because it usually goes the other way when drinking," I say.

"Yeah, I know. But maybe he was relaxed and using a different part of his brain. I don't know. Anyway, he told me in pigeon English that he made his money back in Russia from music and buying clubs."

"We all thought he was dodgy."

"Well, he is. He initially made his money through the usual illegal ways."

"I thought as much. Anything specific?"

Jock smirks. "Well, he looked me dead in the eye, put his finger over one nostril, and sniffed through the other. Then he smiled at me and winked. Take from that what you will."

"Ohhhh, gotcha. No surprise there, then."

"Then he came out with the weirdest thing. He said he got his inspiration for everything by sitting in the dark with his earphones on at full volume, staring at his computer screen."

"His computer screen? Why? What's on the screen, and what's in the earphones?"

"He said I'd think he was crazy if he told me, but after I pressed him for a bit longer, he gave in."

"What was it, then?"

"He told me, but I couldn't understand it, so I asked him to write it down. He explained, in a roundabout way, that you could learn the secrets of the universe."

"The secrets of the universe?"

"Yeah, and everything about yourself. He said you need to have a couple of beers to relax, then put the screensaver on and listen to a particular song on repeat. Once you've listened to the track three or four times and let your eyes unfocus while staring at the screensaver, everything just comes to you. He reckons you get these powerful, random thoughts that surge into your mind like a juggernaut—a bit like a more visual form of meditation. He swears he owes all of his great ideas, knowledge, and even his money to this."

Everyone stares at Jock, silently trying to comprehend what he has just told us.

"Are you bullshitting us, mate?" I ask him.

"Nope. Swear on my mother's life, that's what he told me, and I know he was serious. I didn't detect a hint of bullshit. He was straight up."

"Well, for all your faults, you do have a fairly decent bullshit detector," says Tom.

"How come I don't remember any of this?" asks Tar.

"Because you were sat at the bottom of the steps, out of your box on vodka, watching Sirius trying to shag your old nag and wondering how his cock got to be that size."

"I wasn't staring at his cock!"

"Yeah, you were. Mr Big and I were laughing at you."

"All right, I'll admit I was in awe of it. It was massive!"

"You like a bit of cock, do you, Tar?" I ask, unable to resist a little leg-pulling.

"No! I'm just saying I've never seen a horse's... you know... that big before, that's all."

"That's probably why your nag was trying to get away from it, mate. If it was the size you say, you wouldn't really want that up your jacksy, would you?"

"I think we're getting off the point here," says Zecky.

"Yeah, we are. What was the bloody screensaver, and what was the track?"

"The track was called 'Govinda'," says Jock. "It's by a British band called Kula Shaker. It's on their album *K*."

"What does 'Govinda' mean?"

"Govinda is what the sages call Krishna," says Tar, suddenly confident. "He pervades all the worlds, giving them power."

"And who or what is Krishna?" asks Zecky.

"Krishna is a worshipped deity," explains Tar. "Many religious groups call him different names, but he is generally recognised as the Supreme Being."

"God?"

"Yes, if that's what you want to call it, but I prefer 'the higher power'. When you say 'God', it stirs up a lot of strange emotions and feelings in different religions."

"And how do you know so much about this, Tar?" asks Rob.

"I had to study religion at school."

"Oh, right."

"What was the screensaver, then?" I ask.

THE CREW

"It's in the Windows Media Player menu. You put the CD in or play the downloaded song from your hard drive until Windows Media Player pops up. Then you right-click the screen, hover over 'Battery' in the submenu, and select 'The World' screensaver. Well, you do in Windows XP, anyway."

"Then what?"

"Then you plug in your earphones, turn up the volume, watch the screen, and let the mysteries of the universe unfold in front of your eyes… apparently. You have to have a clear mind and be relaxed when you start, though."

Everyone takes a sip of their beers, and we sit in silence for a moment or two. Rob is the first to move. This is right up his street. He's quite deep and soulful at heart. Eventually, curiosity gets the better of him.

"Fuck it, I'm going to give it a go. Come on, you lot, grab your laptops and bring them in here. We'll turn the lights out and give it a try," he says.

Everyone fetches their computers, and Rob quickly downloads the song onto their hard drives. After fifteen minutes or so, we're all set.

"Right then," I tell them. "On the word 'go', play the song and put your earphones on. We'll listen to the track at least six times before we stop, turn the light back on, and take off our earphones. Now, is everyone sitting comfortably?"

"Yep," they all reply.

I switch off the light, shuffle back to my seat, put my earphones on, and give them the countdown. The room is silent except for the music in our ears and pitch black except for the faint, swirling coloured light emitting from the screens. Everyone sits there in the darkness, listening to the track again and again, staring blankly at the screensaver with unfocused eyes.

After the sixth play, everybody takes off their headphones. There is a short silence before Rob switches the light back on. We all glance at each other, looking spaced out and thoughtful.

"Oh my God! That was AMAZING!" says Zecky.

"Did you get any random thoughts spring into your mind?" asks Rob.

"Loads. I feel completely at peace with myself," she says, wiping a tear from her cheek.

"I know! I thought it was just a load of bullshit at first, but after the second or third play, I fell into a kind of trance and forgot where I was. It was the weirdest feeling. What about you, Tom?"

"The same, mate—except I saw my childhood. I feel really calm now."

"Is that all that came through? Just your childhood?"

"No, that was just one part. I feel like I'm wiser for some reason. Sounds crazy, I know, but I felt the presence of an immense, calm force all around us. I feel more spiritually aware."

"That's exactly what I was going to say—more aware of everything! It feels like I've taken a peek into the beyond, and all the answers are within my grasp," I tell them, not really knowing how this happened.

"Well, they say God speaks to us in many forms," says Zecky.

"Yeah, but come on! Through a bloody screensaver?" says Tom.

"What do you want? A burning bush?!"

"What about you, Jock? Did you feel anything?"

"I'm still tripping, to be honest. Feels like I've taken a tab of LSD. Apart from that, I felt pretty much the same as you lot. It was almost hypnotic, really. I feel different, for sure."

"Bloody hell, it's weird how we all felt the same things."

"You know what's really strange, though? You can get omens and pick up knowledge from everyday things. They speak a silent language that explains things to you," says Rob.

"For example?" asks Zecky.

"I went for a walk one day in the woods. I was just strolling along, thinking about where my life was going and what direction I should take with my job. I guess I just wanted a little inspiration from somewhere—and I got it."

"How so?" asks Rob.

"I just saw a tree. I watched how its trunk rises up, then how all the main branches come off it, then all the smaller branches and twigs branch off from those. That's when I realised—the different branches leading off the trunk represented certain jobs and life paths I could take. Some paths would only let me go so far before I hit a dead end. It's mad to think a simple tree could really help you out and put your mind on the right track."

Tar decides to share his experience. "Something similar happened to me. I saw a tumbleweed blowing down a dusty old street. I was worried about coming here because everything would be new to me. I guess I felt a little apprehensive since you lot are all more worldly-wise than me—you're older."

"So what did you get from the tumbleweed?" asks Zecky.

"As it rolled down the street, it got bigger and stronger as it picked things up. I saw it as an omen that I shouldn't worry about coming here."

"How so?"

"Because, like the tumbleweed, I'll grow from whatever I pick up as I cover new ground."

"That's really philosophical, Tar!" says Zecky, smiling at him.

"Well, I didn't consciously think of it. Like Rob said, it spoke a silent language to me. It's true—the simplest things can be the most helpful."

Jock nods in agreement. "Yeah, mate, I get them all the time as well."

"Really? What was your omen, then?"

"I remember shagging this bird doggy-style over the back of my sofa."

Everyone turns to Jock with confused looks on their faces.

"What thoughts did that inspire?"

MARC WILDER

"Well, I just remember looking down at her fat arse and thinking, 'Fuck meee, I'm going to have to tell her to go on a diet!'"

Chapter 22
We Are Us

The guests' night at the Billionaire's Nightclub was evidently a great success, as they didn't return to the yacht until nearly six in the morning. Zecky managed to get a couple of hours of sleep before the chauffeur called to say they were leaving the nightclub and would soon be back on board. She met them at the passerelle and brought them more drinks to round off their night. As expected, everyone was a little worse for wear.

Earlier, Thrush and his partner, Olga, had returned from an expensive meal ashore—one she had managed to extract from him. She later came down to the crew room for a drink, eager to tell everyone just how much the meal had cost and to brag about her new Gucci dress, which she had convinced Thrush to buy for her.

Tom couldn't hide his disdain. Leaning in, he whispered to Jock, 'That is some bloody woman, eh, mate? What a fucking gold-digger! How can Thrush not see what she's doing? If he lost his money, she'd be gone in a heartbeat.'

Jock smirked. 'It couldn't happen to a nicer guy. The silly sod deserves everything he gets. Rose-tinted spectacles, I think they call it.'

'I say "woman" in the loosest possible terms. She's more like a one-celled parasite living in his digestive tract, soaking up all the nutrients—bit like a tapeworm.'

Jock burst out laughing. 'Ha! Tapeworm! I think we've just found a new nickname for her.'

'I think we have, mate. Growing bigger and fatter with every mouthful.'

'Or every paycheque.'

In the end, the night proved to be quite the eye-opener for all of us. Thrush, as usual, didn't feel the need to socialise with the crew and went straight to bed when he stepped back on board. We were all grateful for that, but we still couldn't help but wonder—what was so wrong with coming in for one drink?

Olga, on the other hand, had a few more glasses of wine. Zecky and the other girls were polite but cautious. They watched what they said, more out of fear than anything else, because talking to Olga was, in a roundabout way, talking to Thrush. It was rare for her to join the crew for a drink, and that probably had everything to do with him.

However, last night was different. She was already a little drunk when she got back and carried on drinking in the crew room. The conversation soon turned to men and their little foibles—this was after she had spoken at length about her Gucci dress and how Zecky's new top wasn't designer.

Somewhere in the chitchat, she let slip that Thrush liked to be called "The Beast" in the throes of passion. Beautiful. It also came to light that they enjoyed dressing up. She wasn't quite drunk enough to reveal exactly what he wore, but there was a strong hint that leather was involved.

She eventually retired to bed after a couple of hours, and the rest of us stayed silent until we heard Thrush's cabin door close on the upper deck. Zecky crept up the stairway to double-check before darting back down to the crew room. Jock, Tom, Rob, and I all had huge grins on our faces as she came in and shut the door.

Jock couldn't contain himself. 'Fucking hell! "The Beast"—that's priceless! We're going to get some serious mileage out of this one.'

Rob burst out laughing. 'I feel like I've just won the bloody lottery or something. From now on, we have to slip the word "beast" into any conversation when he's around. And we can get away with it.'

The time for sailing came around far too quickly. Rob and I were up at seven to begin the usual cleaning routine. When we stepped onto the outside guest deck, we found Mr Big and his two girls crashed out on the sofa, still wearing last night's outfits. The ashtrays were full of

THE CREW

burnt joints, and a sizeable pile of coke still sat on the glass table. We decided it was best to leave them to it and postponed cleaning that area until later.

Then Thrush fired up the engines to leave port, and the rumbling and movement of the yacht woke everyone. The guests groggily dragged themselves inside and went straight to bed to catch up on sleep.

Once we were safely out at sea, I instructed Tar to assist Steve, the engineer, in fixing the navigation light on the forward mast. It turned out to be another complete piss-take.

I was on watch in the wheelhouse, navigating the yacht clear of traffic, when I noticed a very worried-looking Tar concentrating on a bucket full of water in front of him. He was sweating, fidgety, and visibly shaking. Floating in the bucket was a margarine tub, half-submerged and filled with white powder.

Steve had told Tar that, to fix the light, they needed to take some "white sparks" up to the bow. He had also warned him—under no circumstances was he to put the bucket down or let the margarine tub touch the sides. If it did, Steve had said, it might knock the crystal powder, setting off a very explosive chain reaction.

What he hadn't told him was that the white powder was just soap.

Steve had then disappeared from sight and joined me in the wheelhouse for a prime view of the show. We spent the next fifteen minutes rapidly altering course, making the yacht rock from side to side. Tar, panicked and desperate to keep his balance, began shouting at the top of his lungs.

Steve, hidden behind the radar, was in fits of laughter. I gestured through the thick wheelhouse window that I couldn't hear him, making Tar even more frantic as he swore like a true sailor.

The final straw came when I used the outdoor speakers to tell Tar that I was about to sound the ship's horn to warn a vessel ahead that I was altering course—and that he should cover his ears.

I know he has been told not to put the bucket down, so there is no way he can cover his ears at the same time. The ship's horn is immensely powerful and, in the right conditions, can be heard up to two or three miles away. Steve and I can barely control our laughter as the horn blasts out. It is a sight to behold—watching a terrified Tar hold up the bucket in front of him, prancing around like an Irish dancer while trying to shield his ears with his arms. This is not helped by yet another alteration.

After a while, Steve goes down to the foredeck to end his misery, and it appears that Tar has forgotten his manners and decorum.

'WHAT THE FUCK KEPT YOU?!' he squeals.

Even though he expects Tar to be alarmed, the lad's fury catches Steve slightly off guard.

'Oh, I had to take a phone call from the owner, mate. It couldn't wait.'

'I nearly dropped the fucking thing! He sounded the horn, and it's right above me. I thought my eardrums were going to explode!'

'Bastard, eh? OK, mate, you've done well. But the reason I ended the call was because I realised these are the wrong sparks. These are even more unstable than the ones I meant to bring.'

'More unstable?!'

'Yeah. Now hand me the bucket and be fucking careful. If you knock these sparks and they go off, we're done for. Don't even breathe on them.'

Tar slowly lifts the bucket with his tired arms and gingerly hands it to Steve. After a couple of seconds, Steve pretends he is about to sneeze. From what Tar has been told, this would clearly be fatal.

'Err… shit! Tar, get the… eeeeuuuur… I'm gonna snee…'

'WHAT? No, you can't!'

Tar now looks even more terrified, prancing around on the spot with bulging eyes.

'Ahhhh... Ahhhhhhhh... AAAAAAAHHHHHHH... CHOOOOOOOO!!'

Before the sneeze has even finished, Tar is already on the deck, curled into a ball with his hands on his head. Steve cannot help but look up to the wheelhouse. I now have tears rolling down my face.

After a few moments, Steve leans down and slaps Tar on the back.

'Come on, numb nuts, it's time for a coffee,' he tells him before dropping the bucket next to his head on the deck and disappearing off the foredeck.

It is not a very enjoyable day for Tar. After the bucket escapade, he spends an hour searching for some tartan paint, and then Jock asks him to get a bucket of seawater. However, this is not a joke. Jock had meant for him to open a fire hydrant on deck and get the seawater from there, but Tar thinks he is meant to fetch it from the sea. Dutifully, he finds himself a big bucket, ties a rope around the handle, then secures the rope around his wrist and throws it overboard.

The only problem is that the yacht is doing fifteen knots. When the bucket hits the water, the rope pulls tight and proceeds to drag the screaming Tar down the deck until Jock rushes to the rescue with a knife. By the time he reaches him, Tar is halfway over the side, gripping on with his knees and the inside of his arm. Jock cuts the rope, pulls the flustered Tar back onto the deck, and calms him down. After a couple of minutes, Tar is pacified—at which point Jock gives him a couple of slaps around the head **'for being a dopey cunt!'**

The rest of the voyage to Ibiza is spent taking the piss out of Thrush in subtle ways and watching Olga act very sheepishly around the dinner table. The crew doubt that she can remember much, given her low tolerance for wine, but it is fun to watch nevertheless. Even the usually stiff-upper-lipped chef sees the funny side of it and has to leave the room halfway through his main course to have a good giggle in the privacy of his cabin.

'This is one beast of a beef pie, chef! I wonder how many beasts it would take to make a hundred of these?' asks Rob, with a twinkle in his eye.

I walk in halfway through dinner after a workout and say that I have just beasted myself with the weights.

This is followed by Jock telling everyone around the dinner table that he felt like a sweaty beast working on deck in the hot sun. The ribbing continues for much of the day until everyone has had their mileage out of it.

* * * *

The voyage to Ibiza takes a day and a half, and we sail elegantly past the harbour breakwater shortly after 4 pm. Earlier, Zecky had told us that all the guests were going ashore into Ibiza Town for cocktails before heading to a very exclusive, private nightspot that doesn't appear in any guidebooks.

"If they don't advertise, how do they attract customers and make money?" asks Tar.

Zecky puts her arm around his shoulders and smiles at his naivety. "They obviously don't need to advertise, do they? Anything unique or niche is usually sold by word of mouth and personal recommendation. Some places have a cult following."

"Yes, I get that, but how many people would they be able to get through their doors to buy their product, so to speak, if they don't advertise?"

"Does it matter? If they have a niche market and a cult following, whatever they sell will be more expensive and sought after."

"Like what?"

"Well, you can go into a shop in most town centres and buy a cheap, mass-produced poster for your wall at home, but you can guarantee it's hanging on thousands of walls all over the world. It isn't exactly personal or exclusive, is it?"

THE CREW

"No."

"Or you could buy a Katherine Welsby oil painting of a landscape. Do you remember that really vibrant one I showed you the other day?"

"The one you said makes you feel like you've taken LSD when you look at it?"

"Me and everyone else, but yes, that's the one. They're really sought after. That would be painted personally by her for you, tailored to your colour scheme and exact specifications. When it's on your wall, you can rest assured there's no other painting like it in the world. It's exclusive. Apart from posting a few of her pictures on an art gallery website and a Facebook page, everything she sells is by word of mouth. Those who know, know. Do you get it?"

"Yes, I think so."

"Are you all set for a party tonight, then, Tar?"

"Party? What party?"

"Once the boys have cleaned the yacht, we're all going up the road for a bit of a knees-up. It's Saturday night, after all, and this is Ibiza in the summer."

"I thought we had to stay on board."

"Two people will, but it won't be us tonight, thankfully."

"When will the guests be back?"

"Not until tomorrow evening around six. Mr Big has a friend here, so they'll be staying at his place in the hills until then."

"That's a stroke of luck."

"Make the most of it because this doesn't usually happen on charter."

"Who's going, then?"

"The usual crowd. If you've never been to Ibiza, you're in for a treat. It's one of a kind."

As soon as the guests leave, the boys get straight to work washing down the yacht. It's amazing what the promise of a night out in Ibiza can do for motivation. The washing and leathering down take an impressive two hours, and by 7.30 pm, everyone is washed, changed, and ready to go.

The taxi arrives at the passerelle, and everyone piles in.

"Hola!" says the taxi driver with a welcoming smile.

"Hola! Café del Mar, por favor," says Zecky.

An overpowering mixture of aftershave and perfume fills the car.

"It smells like a bloody perfume factory in here," says Jock, winding the window down for some fresh air.

"Most of it's coming from you, Jock, so I wouldn't complain too much."

Jock puts his arm around Zecky and nudges up to her in the back seat.

"Well, I'm feeling lucky tonight, darling. I think this is our night," he whispers before biting her on the ear.

Zecky playfully slaps his face and elbows him in the ribs with enough force to make him wince. "Hey, you don't stand much chance anyway, but slobbering in my ear like a basset hound definitely won't help."

"Ah, playing hard to get again? Don't you want me to give you something you've never had before?"

"And what would that be, Jock? A micro penis or leprosy?"

Jock winks at Tar, who's sitting across from him in the taxi. After a few moments, he unzips his jeans, leans over, and slaps his dick onto Zecky's lap.

"Oh, Jesus, man! Put it away!" Zecky shrieks between giggles, trying to flick it off with her finger.

The taxi driver sees what's going on in the rear-view mirror and starts laughing.

THE CREW

"Sorry, mate. We can't take him anywhere," I tell him with a wink.

The driver says something in Spanish, and Zecky bursts out laughing.

"What did he say?" Tom asks.

"He said, 'Does he feed that thing live rats?'"

Everyone finds this hilarious, especially Jock, who turns to Zecky.

"Well, at least you don't have to worry about the micro penis thing. Looks like it's just leprosy I need to check for, then."

The taxi pulls up at Café del Mar, and everyone gets out and heads straight to the bar to order drinks. We then find a spot outside where we can slowly get drunk and watch the sunset. We sit together, telling stories, laughing, and joking as the sun sinks into the shimmering ocean like a molten orange orb. Holidaymakers and locals relax, absorbing the atmosphere, chilling on cushions, and enjoying the vibe. The music, which started as a murmur, grows louder and funkier as the sun disappears and the place comes to life.

"Well, Tar, how does it feel, mate?" Jock asks.

"Bloody fantastic! How could it be any better? I'm in Ibiza in summer, getting drunk with my new family. It doesn't get much better than this. I feel like I've grown really close to you all, even though it's only been a short time. I'd hate it if any of you had to leave the yacht."

"Well, little mate, you're going to have to get used to it, I'm afraid."

We all stop talking and stare at Jock. I put my pint down on the table. "What are you talking about, mate? Do you know something we don't?"

"I didn't want to tell you this, but I can't think of a better time, really. The vibe's good, and this will probably be the last time I'm ashore with you."

Tom leans forward over the table with a serious look on his face. "What's happened, mate?"

Jock clears his throat, then lights a cigarette. He sits back, takes a long drag, and finally answers. "I got sacked this morning," he says, raising his hands nonchalantly.

"What? Who? Why?" I splutter angrily.

"Who do you think? Thrush, that's who. He said he didn't like my attitude, and I guess coming back after a few drinks with Mr Big didn't help."

"Yeah, but come on!" says Rob. "You were only doing what the guest wanted you to do. Besides, he doesn't know anything else that you've done. We do, but he doesn't."

"Does that mean I'll be sacked as well?" asks Tar, looking worried.

"No, it doesn't, little mate," Jock reassures him. "He reckons you're too young to know any different, and since this is your first boat, he sees it as a learning experience for you. Anyway, I took the bollocking for you."

"It's either that, or he thinks he can bend you and mould you into what he wants," Rob adds.

"How can he sack you, anyway?" asks Tar. "Aren't there laws against this sort of thing?"

I shake my head. "Unfortunately for Jock, there aren't. The rules say that if the yacht is maintained under Section 8 of the Merchant Shipping Act 1995, a crew member like Jock can only take an unfair dismissal claim to the UK Employment Tribunal if certain criteria are met."

"Well, hasn't he met those criteria? He's worked here for months."

"It's a shit state of affairs, but no, he hasn't."

"So what you're saying is that Thrush can do virtually anything he likes in this situation?"

"As far as sacking is concerned, yes."

Jock tries to lighten the atmosphere. "Anyway, it's not the end of the world, and I'm fucked if it's going to spoil our night. Let's just forget about it. The guests are leaving tomorrow night, and he's given me a few days to sort something out. With a bit of luck, we'll get a good tip. There are loads of yachts and jobs around here at this time of year, so I'm not really arsed. Now, come on, let's have a laugh. Besides, there's no way I'm leaving this yacht before you lose your cherry, Tar. Jobs come and go, but deflowering a ripe virgin like you—that's something I'll remember forever!"

Everyone laughs, admiring Jock's total lack of self-pity. We all put on a brave face, but there's a definite sense of loss. It feels like we're losing both a big brother and a mischievous little one. For all his faults, Jock is the joker of the group, and his energy livens up any room. Everyone has time for him, and he's going to be deeply missed.

The crew drinks for hours, and before long, we're all drunk and back in high spirits. The place is bustling with holidaymakers—an eclectic mix of fashionable freaks, sexy street girls, local lads looking for easy prey, professional clubbers, and a fair share of chavs. The streets are a monument to hedonism. We hop from bar to bar, laughing at Jock's ingenious ways of getting rid of the bar touts trying to lure us in.

When approached, Jock sometimes uses reverse psychology. Instead of dodging them, he leaps up and hugs them tightly, crotch to crotch, running his hand down their back onto their arse. This is usually enough to send them running. Other times, he pretends he's about to vomit on them as they approach, which has the same effect. If they're short, he'll take a run at them, plant his hands on their shoulders, and leapfrog over them, treating them like obstacles in an assault course.

Around midnight, we find a bar with a great crowd, good music, and a lively vibe.

"See anything you like, then, Tar?" Jock asks.

"Not really," says Tar, looking around.

"What do you mean, not really? It's wall-to-wall here!" I say, pointing at the girls around the bar.

"It's true, Tar," says Rob. "This is definitely the place to pull. We just need to find someone your age, but I think the schools are closed at this time of night."

"I'm nervous because I'm not sure what to say," Tar admits, looking at Jock.

"Everybody is when they first approach someone, mate. Just feel the fear and go with it."

"You should just be yourself," Zecky tells him.

"Be yourself? Unless you're Jock, you mean!" Tom laughs.

"Well, yeah," she agrees.

"I don't really have much experience," Tar says hesitantly.

"Look, the journey of a thousand miles starts with a single step. Don't let the past dictate who you are—it should be part of who you become."

"I reckon you should just get over there with all guns blazing, Tar. Blaze a path for others to follow. Now, there must be someone you like the look of," Jock says, scanning the room.

Tar glances at a young blonde girl sitting with a friend. "Well, she's got a nice face," he says.

"Not a bad rack as well," Jock nods approvingly.

"Yes, she's very pretty."

"Right, mate, they're drinking bottles of Stella, so I'll take a couple over."

"No, Jock—not yet. I'm not ready…"

"Bullshit. Just wing it. You can't play the game of life with sweaty palms, mate. Remember—those who hesitate, masturbate!" Jock rubs his hands together. "If you waste all your time worrying about whether you'll pull, the bloody night will be over. You'll end up back at your cabin, wanking over a Playboy centrefold and sipping Horlicks. Action is what we need here, mate!"

THE CREW

No sooner has Jock finished his entertaining motivational speech than he orders a couple of beers and heads over to the girls. He hands them the drinks and lingers for five minutes or so before waving Tar over. Everything goes smoothly for about ten minutes until Tar asks one of the girls to join him at the bar for a drink. As she pushes her chair away and stands up, she turns out to be around six foot four. She smiles politely and tells Tar he's sweet, but she makes her excuses and leaves.

"Fucking hell! She was taller than me, mate. She didn't look that tall sitting down. You'd have needed a step ladder," Jock says, laughing.

"Oh well, plenty more fish in the sea," Tar replies, trying to stay positive.

"That's the spirit, mate. It's all about confidence," Jock encourages him. "Anyway, she'd have been no good for you at that height. Can you imagine getting down to business with her?"

"How do you mean?"

"Well, look, you're about five foot six, and she's six foot four. You'd never get away from her fanny if you were both naked!"

"How so?"

"Think about it, mate. When you're hugging her, your nose would be in it. When you're kissing her, your toes would be in it. And when you're shagging her, you'd have nobody to talk to!"

Jock's joke sends everyone into fits of laughter, and then we all hit the dance floor as the bass kicks in and the strobe lights flash. For the next hour or so, everyone is focused on nothing but drinking, dancing, and having fun.

Suddenly, a girl emerges from the dry ice surrounding the dance floor. Tar is bouncing around with Jock and Zecky in the middle of it all when she places a hand on his shoulder, drunkenly turning him to face her.

"You're fucking mine tonight," she declares, wrapping herself around him and shoving her tongue down his throat.

She looks about 18, roughly the same height as Tar but weighing around fifteen stone. She's Chinese, caked in make-up, and has a thick Liverpool accent. Dressed in tight spandex with a big sparkly silver belt around her waist that highlights her ample figure, she's the queen of chav city.

"Oh bloody hell! The poor kid hasn't got a chance!" Zecky shouts into Jock's ear.

"I know! Doesn't look like she'll be taking no for an answer."

The girl gets even more amorous, pushing Tar against the dark wall of the bar, her hands all over him. After a few minutes, she tells her friends she's leaving and that she's taking Tar back to her hotel room. Jock strolls over to check on him.

"You alright, kid?" Jock asks, grinning from ear to ear.

"She's mental, Jock!" Tar replies, looking astonished. "She's only known me for two minutes, and we're off to her room."

"She's a man-eater, mate! I think it's safe to say tonight's the night. She must love young lads. Besides, it doesn't look like you've got much of a choice."

"I know… and I don't really want to upset her."

"Don't forget, Tar, because she's Chinese, her fanny runs horizontal, not up and down like white girls. So when you shag her, you'll have to lay her down and go in from the side," Jock says, keeping a straight face.

"How do you mean?"

"You know… if you're looking from above, you'd look like a cross."

"Oh, right, I get you."

"She's a big girl, so if you can't find it among the rolls, just tell her to fart and give you a clue!"

Tar looks worried as the girl returns and pulls him towards the exit. He quickly whispers in Jock's ear, "Jock, will you come with me and wait outside so I can find my way back to the boat?"

"Nothing surer, mate. Go have a blast – I'll follow and wait outside."

Jock informs the group of the situation and says he feels a duty to look after Tar since it's his first time.

"Tar and I will see you back at the boat—well, if he's still alive. Catch you later," he says before disappearing into the night.

Jock follows the pair, keeping about twenty metres behind as the girl eagerly drags Tar through the bustling crowd and into her hotel. Tar keeps glancing over his shoulder to check if Jock is still there. She leads him inside and straight to her ground-floor room. Jock notes the room number before stepping outside and sitting by a tree near their balcony, close enough to hear what's going on.

As the balcony doors open, light spills out, and Jock quickly hides behind the tree. She's too drunk to notice. Grabbing a half-empty vodka bottle from the table, she takes a swig and forces Tar to do the same. Then she pushes him against the wall and unzips his fly. Jock decides it's best to turn away, though he can still hear Tar making a series of strange whimpering noises.

"Errr… wouldn't you like us to get to know each other first?" Tar asks, struggling to keep his voice steady.

"What the fuck for, lad?" she slurs in her thick Scouse accent before dragging him into the bedroom by his dick.

"Well… can I at least know your name?"

"Rita. It's Rita. Now shurrup—you're putting me off!" she snaps, stripping off and sprawling onto the bed.

Tar undresses nervously, surveying the tattooed, bobbing mass before him.

"Come on then, lad. What are you waiting for?" she taunts, beckoning him over with a finger.

He remembers Jock's advice and cautiously positions himself sideways, crotch to crotch, his body running across the bed. She blinks up at him, barely able to see past her ample chest, as he fumbles to find the right angle.

"What the fuck are you doing, lad?" Rita asks, bewildered.

Jock, unable to resist, peeks through the window. He has to summon every ounce of self-control not to laugh and give himself away.

Tar keeps trying, but his awkward attempts test Rita's patience. With an exasperated sigh, she throws him onto his back and mounts him with all the grace of a Rottweiler. She starts grinding against him while Tar stares blankly at the ceiling, her enormous boobs bouncing and slapping against him.

After only a couple of minutes, an almighty yelp escapes from Tar as he climaxes.

"For fuck's sake, lad! I've barely got started, and you've shot your muck already! What about me, like?!"

"Oh... sorry. I don't do this very often. I—"

"Never mind that, lad. Get down and eat me out," she demands, crawling up the bed and straddling his face with her thick thighs. "And for fuck's sake, hurry up—my boyfriend will be back soon."

Tar's eyes widen in horror.

"WHAT DID YOU SAY?!"

"My boyfriend... he'll be home soon."

"BOYFRIEND?! What the hell is this?!" Tar screeches, struggling frantically beneath her weight, his arms pinned helplessly by his sides.

"He screws around, and I'm not bothered. I just fancy a young white boy for a change," she says between thrusts.

When Tar hears this, it sends him over the edge.

"Ahhhh, I'd better go now... really... I'd better go now," he says, writhing like an eel.

THE CREW

Jock hears this and bursts out laughing, but his laughter is short-lived when he spots a coloured boy walking through the hotel gates. The boy pauses before entering, looks up at the balcony, and listens.

"Fuck," Jock mutters to himself.

The young lad's face twists with anger as he sprints towards the hotel entrance, shouting, "Dirty fucking bitch!"

Jock springs into action, climbing over the balcony and bounding into the room like a springbok.

"Who the fuck are you?" gasps Rita, not missing a thrust.

"Tar! Get the fuck out NOW!" Jock shouts, grabbing Tar's arm and yanking him from beneath her.

"No time to explain, mate—just run!" he says, clumsily shoving Tar out the window and over the balcony.

Tar stumbles away, his trousers still around his ankles. After a few strides, he has to stop to pull them up.

"Thanks for the rescue, Jock, but what's going on?"

"Boyfriend, mate—he's just rocked up. He'll be walking through that door any second, so run like fuck!"

No sooner has Jock spoken than Tar has his trousers up and is already overtaking him, sprinting through the hotel grounds. They keep running and laughing for a few hundred metres until they're safely among the crowds. Jock then takes Tar to a bar for a nightcap to calm him down before they head back to the yacht.

"Here you go, mate—get that down your screech," Jock says, thrusting a beer into his hand and offering him a bar stool. "So, stud, how was it?"

Tar gulps down the beer almost in one go, then turns to Jock with a big grin.

"I don't know what to say, really. It was scary, exciting, and bloody intimidating all at the same time."

"You didn't have much say in it, did you?"

"Not really. Shall I tell you what happened?"

"You don't have to—I heard everything and saw most of it."

Tar looks a little embarrassed now.

"You didn't see everything, did you?"

Jock winks and slaps him on the shoulder.

"You're all right, mate. I looked away at certain points."

There is a short silence before Jock smirks and asks, "So, big stud, how does it feel to finally lose your cherry? Was it everything you imagined?"

Tar can't help but laugh.

"It wasn't quite how I pictured losing my virginity or the type of girl I thought it would be with, but I guess I won't forget it in a hurry."

"Well, yeah, you definitely won't forget that. I must admit, when I saw her dragging you off, I didn't know whether to tell you to fight it or fuck it! She was some size, eh? I bet when she says it's Tuesday, it's fucking Tuesday!"

"I know. I didn't want to upset her, so I just went with it."

"What about her… you know?"

"What?"

"You know?"

"What?"

"For fuck's sake, Tar—do you want me to spell it out? What was her fanny like? Mouse's ear or Mersey Tunnel—excuse the pun."

"What the hell am I going to compare it to? I was a virgin, remember?"

"Fair point, mate," Jock says, shrugging.

THE CREW

"Oh, and another thing—it doesn't go sideways like you said it would on Chinese girls," Tar says seriously, as if he's just discovered a new continent.

"No shit, Sherlock! I can't believe you fell for that one!"

Tar laughs, his face crimson with embarrassment.

"Ahhhh, you bastard!"

"Very funny though, mate."

"For you, maybe."

"Anyway, how do you feel now you've done the deed?"

"LIKE I'M KING OF THE WORLD... KING OF THE FUCKING WORLD!" Tar shouts, thrusting his arms in the air.

Chapter 23
Nature Has the Answer

After a couple more beers, Jock and Tar take a taxi back to the yacht. Tar goes straight to bed, but Zecky is still awake, sitting on the edge of the quay with her legs dangling over the harbour wall, gazing at the moon as the taxi pulls up.

"You know I'm really going to miss you, Zecks, don't you?" Jock says, shifting up the quay to sit beside her.

Zecky takes a deep breath as she looks out over the harbour, then squeezes his hand and turns to face him. "I'll miss you too. This boat won't be the same without you."

"Do you really mean that?"

"Yeah, of course I do. You're a good egg underneath it all, and believe it or not, I've grown really fond of you. I must admit, though, you surprised me tonight."

"Why's that?"

"I didn't think you'd be back until morning."

"How so?"

"You know what I mean. You're single, it's Saturday night in Ibiza, and there are plenty of girls around. I thought you'd go and… play, so to speak."

"I looked after Tar and had a beer with him afterwards, but that's it."

"Why? What's changed?"

"I don't really know. I guess watching Tar and everyone else tonight made me think."

"In what way?"

"I suppose I don't want that promiscuous life anymore. I don't know why, but I just don't. It's fun when you're growing up because it's exciting, and you never know what's going to happen."

"Well, yeah, I guess it is. Otherwise, no one would do it, would they?"

"Yeah, but looking back, how many of those girls did I actually respect or care about?"

"Not many, I guess," Zecky laughs.

"None, actually."

"Why did you do it, then?"

"I've got needs, Zecks, and let's face it—if you're not in a relationship with someone on board, you rarely get to have sex, do you?"

"Is that why you had that one-night stand in Monaco?"

"Yeah, but I can't even remember her bloody name."

"Well, she might not remember yours either. Did you ever think of that?"

"Yes, I did. I've got to admit, it got me thinking."

"About what?"

"That. What's good for the goose is good for the gander. They could say the same about me. Is that really the life I want? Going through life without ever truly knowing or caring about anyone?"

"And vice versa."

"Exactly. And vice versa. At the end of the day, I don't want that for myself."

"My God! Could this be the sound of Jock maturing?"

"I've felt this way for a while, to be fair."

There is a brief silence. Zecky studies Jock's face, searching for any sign that he's joking—but there isn't one.

"That's the most sensible thing you've ever said to me, Jock. I never knew you felt like that."

"Neither did I. Would it have made a difference if I'd told you before?"

"A difference with what?"

"With us," Jock says with a grin.

"It might have done, yes."

That isn't the answer Jock was expecting. He had anticipated the usual flippant brush-off.

"Really?!"

Zecky lights a cigarette and takes a slow drag before answering. "Look, Jock, you and I have always been great friends, even if it looks different to an outsider. There aren't many people I'd trust more than you if the shit hit the fan."

"That goes for me as well. We do have chemistry, don't we?"

"Yes," she says, smiling.

"You've never told me that before."

"Well, you've never asked. You've just tried to squirm your way into my knickers—entertaining as that is."

"Anyway," she continues, "the reason I stayed up tonight was to have a bit of a think."

"About what?"

"Loads of things, really. But I didn't want you to leave without knowing what's going on inside my head when it comes to you."

"Shit! Should I dive for cover?" he says, giving her a playful nudge.

"We'll have to wait and see, won't we?"

"I'm really going to miss you, Zecks. I love you loads, you know that, don't you?" Jock says, looking down at his feet.

"I love ya too, Jock," she says, slapping him on the back.

Jock turns to face her, a serious look on his face. "No… you don't understand," he says nervously. "I really love you, and I have done for ages. I've just got a shit way of showing it. I suppose I've been fighting the feeling, if you know what I mean."

"I think it might be lust, not love, Jock."

"Lust is definitely there as well, but it's not just that. When I was sitting up at the bar with you tonight, all I wanted to do was take you to the beach and tell you how much I'm going to miss you. How upset I'd be if we lost contact. How I sometimes lie awake at night wondering what you're dreaming about and if you're warm enough. How great you make me feel when I hug you, even if it's just in a friendly way. And how I feel completely at home when I look into your eyes."

Another silence falls as they sit cross-legged on the edge of the quay, looking at each other.

"Well, what are you going to do about it, then?"

"I just needed you to know, that's all."

Zecky leans over, cups his face in her hands, and kisses him softly but deeply.

A look of shock crosses Jock's face as he tries to process what's happening. He's waited so long for this moment. Gently, he cups the back of her head with his hands and kisses her back. Together, they share a perfect moment beneath the starry sky, with the sound of the sea lapping against the quay.

"Do you want to come down to the beach with me?" Zecky asks.

"When?"

"Now," she says, kissing him again.

"You try and stop me," Jock replies.

* * * *

The next morning, everyone gathers for breakfast around the crew table. Jock and Zecky exchange little smiles and knowing looks across the table. They look a bit tired, and I wouldn't be surprised if they had been up all night.

Thrush comes down for breakfast, fishing for information about what time everyone got back last night while also moaning about various little things. He announces that the guests will be collecting their luggage from the yacht earlier than expected, so it should be packed and ready for collection by 3 pm. Their plans have changed, and they will be leaving the yacht today in Ibiza, as Mr Big is staying with acquaintances on the island. Thrush also informs us that there is a problem with the yacht's gearbox. The repairs will take about two days, so the yacht will remain alongside the quay until the job is done. This is also a factor in Mr Big cutting his charter short, even if only by a day.

The morning is spent on the usual cleaning and maintenance routine until the guests arrive to collect their luggage and say goodbye to the crew. Everyone stands in uniform on the aft deck, awaiting their arrival. They don't linger—just enough time to load the limo and shake hands with the crew. Mr Big personally thanks Zecky and expresses his gratitude to the boys for looking after them during the water sports. When he shakes Jock's hand, he produces a folded bar towel in the shape of an erect penis—the trick Jock had shown him. They joke for a moment before Mr Big moonwalks back to the passerelle and says goodbye. Unsurprisingly, he barely acknowledges Thrush.

Once the crew waves off the guests and their limo disappears around the corner, Thrush calls everyone down to the crew room. Everyone shows up except Olga, who is nowhere to be found. Without offering any thanks for our efforts, Thrush hands out the guest charter gratuity, then stands up from the table and leaves the room. As he reaches the door, he turns to Zecky.

"Could you come and see me in my cabin in ten minutes, please?"

"Sure. What's it regarding?" Zecky asks, looking puzzled.

"If you could just come up, please."

Everyone looks at her, wondering what he wants. It seems odd.

"What's that about, Zecks?" Rob asks.

"I wish I knew, mate. Haven't got a clue!"

"Have you upset him or something?"

THE CREW

"I don't think so."

I open my envelope and count the gratuity Thrush just handed out. Then I count it again. Something feels off, so I get the others' attention.

"Check your tip envelopes. Count what he's given you."

"Why? What's up?" Tom asks.

"It's not what I expected. I reckon it's hundreds short."

"You're kidding!" Tom says.

"No, I'm not. Just check."

Everyone quickly opens their sealed envelopes. As they count, disappointed expressions spread across their faces. The room falls silent. You could hear a pin drop until Rob breaks the tension.

"That's fucking shit! All that time and effort we put into the charter, just for this?" He slams the envelope on the table.

"Hardly seems worth it, does it?" Zecky says, shaking her head.

Rob scratches his head. "Mr Big seemed to have a great time, though. He left happy, and he wasn't exactly tight with his cash. I'm well surprised."

Zecky stands up with a big sigh. "Oh well, I'd better go see what Thrush wants. See you in a bit."

As she leaves, the mood in the room turns even sourer. It feels like all our efforts have been wasted. One by one, the others disperse until only Rob and I remain.

"You thinking what I'm thinking, mate?" Rob asks.

"Bloody right I am."

"What are you going to do about it?"

"What can I do? I don't know how much Mr Big actually tipped the yacht."

"Why don't you go up to Thrush's cabin and confront him?"

"And say what? 'Thrush, we all think you're a fucking thief—now cough up the rest of the tip and be fair!' I've got no proof. Until I find some, we can't do a thing. That fucker can get away with it. He's the only one who knows how much we were tipped."

"Why don't you ask to be kept in the loop about the finances?"

"I tried, remember? He politely told me to fuck off."

"He actually said that?"

"Not in so many words, but that's what he meant."

"Well, why would he do that unless he was hiding something?"

"You tell me."

A door slams, and suddenly, Zecky comes down the stairs in tears. Rob and I exchange glances before running after her. We find her on deck, sitting on a rope bollard with her head in her hands, sobbing. I sit next to her and wrap an arm around her.

"What's the matter, sweetheart?"

She takes a few moments to compose herself, dabbing at her streaky mascara.

"The fucking prick has sacked me."

Rob and I are stunned. If anyone's job on board was safe, it was Zecky's. She was great at her job.

"Sacked you?! What the hell for? You've done nothing wrong."

"I know!"

"What did he say?" Rob asks.

"He said he thinks it's time we go our separate ways."

"Did you ask why?"

"Of course I did. He just said that sometimes he didn't agree with how I did things."

"That's fucking bullshit, man!" Rob says angrily. "Hang on a minute… I know what's going on here."

"What's that?" Zecky asks.

"That fucker is trying to get rid of us all, one by one, to split us up. He wants to bring in a whole new crew that'll bend to his whim."

"Either that, or he's getting his mates in," I add.

"Another thing," Rob says, growing angrier. "Where the fuck has Olga gone? Don't you think it's weird she wasn't around when the tips were handed out?"

'You're right, Rob,' I say. 'Look at what's happening here. He treats us like shit, so some of us might start thinking there are better yachts to work on. The tips for the past two charters have been short. He got rid of the Chief Engineer a couple of trips ago to make way for his mate. Then he got rid of Jock, and now Zecks. Don't you see a pattern?'

'You've got a point. If he gets rid of Zecky, I bet you Olga will replace her as Chief Stewardess. That means she'll be in charge of the department and will get the extra cash. It'll be a cushy little number for them both.'

'That's exactly what I told him,' says Zecky. 'I said it doesn't take a genius to figure out what's happening here.'

'What did he say to that?'

'He just shrugged and said, "That will be all."'

'How long have you got, then?'

'Same as Jock—until the gearbox is fixed and the yacht leaves.'

'Right, that's going to be at least two days.'

'What are we going to do? We can't let him get away with this,' says Rob, looking at me furiously.

'Let me think about it for a minute.'

I walk around the aft deck, biting my thumbnail and pondering the problem. Rob does his best to comfort Zecky. She's in bits, and out of all of us, she doesn't deserve this.

After a few minutes, I rejoin them. 'There's only one thing to do. I need to find out exactly how much Mr Big tipped.'

'How are you going to do that? Call him up and ask?!' says Rob.

'That's exactly what I'm going to do. Zecky, do you still have his number?'

'You're kidding, right?' Rob stares at me, processing what he's just heard.

'Nope.'

'If Thrush finds out you've gone behind his back, you're finished, mate,' says Rob.

'By my calculations, we're all finished anyway. It's just a matter of time. Might as well go out in a blaze of glory. We can't let the twat get away with this—it isn't right. I wouldn't treat my fucking dog the way he treats the crew. Who does he think he is? We have to stick together. It's just him, but we are us. Loyalty and looking after each other—that's what matters.'

Zecky hands me her phone, and Mr Big's number is already on the screen. I press the call button and wait. After a few moments, he answers, loud music blaring in the background. He shouts at one of his bodyguards to turn it down.

'Hello?'

'Hello, sir. I'm calling from aboard the yacht.'

'Yes… what's the problem?'

'Sorry to bother you. I just wanted to check if you had a good charter and let you know we really enjoyed having you.'

'Great charter, great crew. I'm sure we'll be back.'

THE CREW

'That's great to hear, sir. I'm just going over the final bill, and I was hoping you could clarify a few items—we can't seem to find the paperwork.'

'OK... what do you need to know?'

'Could you confirm the total bill and the gratuity you left? It's just for records and office paperwork.'

'Hang on, let me check.'

After a minute or so, Mr Big comes back on the phone. I write down the figures he gives me.

'Yes, I can still hear you... got that... yes... and the final gratuity? Right... well, that's great. Thanks for that. Sorry to bother you, but paperwork is paperwork. Enjoy Ibiza, and hopefully, we'll see you again.'

I pull out my pocket calculator and do some quick arithmetic. I stare at the figure, then do the calculation again to double-check.

'That dirty, sly, low-down, robbing cunt!'

'I fucking knew he'd nicked some!' says Rob, standing bolt upright.

'How much are we short?' asks Zecky.

'Fucking thousands.'

'Thousands?! What are we going to do?'

'I'm going to call the owner and tell him exactly what's going on—the sackings, the stealing—everything.'

'You're calling the owner?! Mate, now you're really pushing it. Do you think that's wise?' asks Rob.

'Like I said, we've got nothing to lose. Any one of us could be next. Thrush can't be allowed to get away with this.'

'OK, it's your arse. But if you're calling him, calm down and sound professional.'

'Rob's right,' says Zecky. 'Don't go in all guns blazing. Just give him the facts. Now, hand me the phone—I'll get the number up.'

The boss's phone rings and rings. I'm about to give up when a voice answers.

'Hi, Zecky. Are you looking after my beautiful yacht for me?' He sounds in good spirits.

'Oh, hi, sir. It's me,' I say. 'I'm just borrowing Zecky's phone to call you.'

'Have you broken another one?! Christ, with people like you, I should invest in mobile phones! What can I do for you?'

'No… no, it's fine. Look, I know it's unusual for a crew member to call you directly, but I didn't have much choice.'

'That sounds a bit ominous. What's up?'

'There are a few things happening on your yacht that you should know about.'

'Like what?'

'We just finished the charter, and the Captain has sacked Jock and Zecky.'

'He's done what? Why on earth would he do that?'

'Nothing. Plus, the tips from the charter are really low again, and we suspect he's taken some of it.'

The boss is silent for a few seconds, processing what I've just told him.

'You had the same issue last time, didn't you?' he asks quietly.

'We did, sir. But we took him at his word and didn't question it.'

There is silence on the other end of the phone, and I can sense the boss beginning to fume.

"Have you got any evidence of this? And are you telling me everything?"

THE CREW

"As a matter of fact, I have. I've just got off the phone with the guest. I rang him to ask for a rundown of expenditure, and it turns out that what he gave as a gratuity is totally different from what we all received."

"How much less?"

"Thousands, sir. I'm sorry to bother you with this, but I thought you should know."

"No, you did the right thing. Right, mate, listen carefully. You're pretty lucky because, at the moment, I'm not really up to much, so I'll call my pilot to get my plane ready for tomorrow morning. It won't take long to get to Ibiza from Monaco, so I'll be there by lunchtime, all being well."

"You're coming down? Right... OK. Do you want me to mention it to the Captain?"

"No, don't say a thing. I want you to carry on as normal. Don't even mention it to the crew, except for Zecky and Jock. I'm glad you called because there have been a few discrepancies over the past few months, and I was going to check them out anyway. You've just brought that forward."

"OK."

"Remember, not a word to anyone else. I want to catch him off guard."

"No problem, sir."

"I'll see you around lunchtime, then."

"OK, sir... will do."

I end the call and hand the phone to Zecky. I'm a little worried that the situation will now escalate. I look at the sky, take a deep breath, and turn to Zecky and Rob.

"I'm not going to go into too much detail, but the boss is flying in tomorrow at lunchtime. He said I should only tell Zecky and Jock, probably because they're the only ones who have been sacked. However, you've just overheard me, Rob, so that goes out of the window. He doesn't want anyone else to know, so you've got to promise me you won't say a word. OK?"

"Yep, no worries. My lips are sealed."

"Right, let's get this yacht looking her best. Rob, get the boys together because it's all hands on deck today. Zecks, you'd better crack on with your stuff. If Thrush asks, just tell him you should be all set to leave the day after tomorrow in the evening. That way, he won't keep hassling you. Apart from that, just keep out of his way."

"Yeah, OK," says Zecky, jumping to her feet.

"By the way, I think we should all keep off the booze tonight to keep a clear head for tomorrow. And we should all stay on board tonight."

The crew spend the whole day cleaning and detailing the yacht, inside and out, to make her look pristine. After a long, hard day, everyone is tired, and a night aboard the yacht is welcomed. Most of the crew, except for Jock, relax in the crew room watching TV. Jock is out at the bottom of the quay, catching more fish. I wander over and sit next to him.

Jock turns and smiles.

"How's it going, mate?" he asks.

"I'm OK, big boy. How are you?"

"Never fucking better, mate. Do you want one of these?" he says, offering me a cigar.

"Don't mind if I do, mate, but don't you only smoke these when you're celebrating something?"

"That's right."

"Really? Considering everything with the tips and the sacking? I've known me and you to have better times, mate."

"Don't you worry, it's all going to work out fine. I'm celebrating two monumental things."

"What's that, then?"

"The first happened last night, and the second will happen tomorrow."

I smile knowingly at Jock. "Oh yeah? And what would that be?"

"The first thing is, Zecky and I got it on last night."

"I know, mate. I saw all the little sly glances at the breakfast table, and I overheard you talking before slipping off to the beach together last night." I put an arm around Jock's shoulders. "Do me a favour, though, mate. Don't go and hurt her. She's like a sister to me, and she's a bloody good catch."

"I've got no intention of doing that, mate. I care too much about her."

"I know. I heard what you told her."

"Yeah, well, we really had a moment last night. It was electric. We really connected."

"I'm glad, and I really hope it works out for you. I had a feeling about you two a while ago."

"Really? I didn't. I thought I'd never get anywhere."

"Just take it slowly, mate, one step at a time. So, are you ready now for the pain?"

"Eh?"

"The pain, mate! This isn't going to be just a one-night stand, you know. If you're going to have a relationship with this girl, she's going to make you grow like you've never had to before. With growth, there is always pain as you adjust and re-adjust. It goes with the territory."

"Oh, right. That's one of the things I've been thinking about."

"I'm glad you've thought about it. The rusty old edges will be smoothed out, and this time next year, I won't recognise you, mate!"

"She'll have a job on her hands. I've lived my single life the way I've lived it for so long, I'm going to need a bit of coaxing."

"Well, Zecky is a strong-willed girl with a good head on her shoulders, so if anyone can do it, mate, it's her. She'll turn you into a S.N.A.G. before you know it."

"A what?"

"A S.N.A.G… Sensitive New Age Guy."

Jock looks at me with a mixture of horror and disbelief. "This is me you're talking about, isn't it?" he says, bursting out laughing.

"Seriously though, mate, how are you going to deal with it?"

"What the fuck am I supposed to do after all these years? What is normality? I don't even know anymore. My life has been like a meal—my childhood was a shit starter that gave me a lifelong ulcer to live with. It made me grow a certain way."

"Everybody is a product of their environment, mate."

"Yeah, I know, but philosophically speaking, I've lived an extraordinary life—eating fucking spicy chilli in an ordinary world where potatoes are the norm. Unfortunately, life's dinner table doesn't serve my dish! Now I totally see why the courts in this country award money in divorces to keep people in the lifestyle they're accustomed to."

"How so?"

"Because it's fucking painful to step out of your comfort zone and live a life you aren't used to."

"Are you scared of change and being in love?"

"Fucking right I am! I feel naked and vulnerable for the first time in my life."

"Yeah, well, so will the other person if they're in love too. You'll sort it out—just stick with it. Do you remember what I told Tar? It's not the changes in life that are tough, just the transitions."

"Yeah, I guess."

"Talking of Zecky, has she told you what's happening tomorrow?"

"Yeah."

"All of it? About the boss coming down in the afternoon to see if he can sort out this problem with your sacking and the crew tips?"

"Yeah."

"Good. That saves me a job then. I just hope Thrush doesn't sweet-talk his way out of it. When his head is straight, he can charm anyone into thinking black is white."

"Maybe when his head is straight, but I doubt he can when it isn't."

"What do you mean, Jock?"

"I mean exactly that. We'll just have to tip the scales in our favour, won't we?"

"What are you talking about? Getting him pissed so he makes a twat of himself? He barely touches a drop, and there's no way he'll drink at that time of day. If you're thinking of getting him pissed before the boss arrives, you've got no chance."

"Who said anything about booze?"

I begin to feel a little uneasy. "Jock, I hope you're not thinking what I think you're thinking. You'll get locked up for that, and then your life really will be fucked."

"And what am I thinking?"

"Drugs? You're not thinking about drugging him?"

"Not with anything illegal."

"Well, anything legal is shit and wouldn't do anything, so you must be talking about narcotics."

"Take a look in the bucket behind you," Jock says with a grin.

I lean over and see half a dozen gold and white fish.

"What do you see?" Jock asks.

"Fish?"

"Correct. That's what I'm going to use to tip the scales in our favour."

"You're going to use fish to get him off his tits before the boss arrives?"

"Yeah, that's exactly what I'm going to do."

"What are you going to do with them? Beat him around the head until he's too concussed to speak?"

"Nope. He's just going to eat them."

I stare at Jock, waiting for more of an explanation. "I'm not with you, mate. How is eating those fish going to get him off his tits?"

"These are no ordinary fish. They're sarpa salpa, a species of bream. If you eat the heads or certain body parts, it's like taking LSD. The Romans used it as a recreational drug. Within minutes, you get vivid hallucinations—you start seeing and hearing things. He'll be tripping his tits off for about a day and a half, and there's no antidote."

"You're fucking kidding me, aren't you?"

"No, I'm not. I'm going to lace Chef's fish soup with it tonight, so if I were you, I wouldn't eat the soup at lunchtime tomorrow."

"How do you even know about this?"

"Because I've had it myself—on holiday in Corfu. I was off my fucking lord! I met some lads who used to fish off a peninsula near where I was camping. They were always there first thing in the morning and around this time every evening. I never understood why they put in so much effort until they told me about it. They gave me some and called it 'dream fish'. And to top it all off, it's completely legal."

"How are we going to stop the rest of the crew from eating it, though? We don't want everyone tripping their tits off when the boss arrives."

"Good point. I haven't figured that one out yet, and we can't tell anyone in case it gets out. The fewer people who know, the better."

"I couldn't agree more. Look, you'll just have to lace his meal only. The only way to do that is to help Chef serve it and make sure he gets the right bowl."

"Sounds like a plan."

"Jock, are you sure this won't do anything other than make him trip? I don't want him keeling over."

"Yeah, I'm sure. Apart from tripping my tits off, I was fine."

"If anything happens to him, I'll deny all knowledge. You know that, right?"

"Yeah, of course. But it's foolproof. I'm going to give Chef the fillets tonight—they're harmless. It's just the head and certain parts I'll grind up and slip into his soup. If he figures out later that he's been laced, there'll be no way to prove it. It'll just look like he accidentally ate the wrong parts."

"Fucking hell, mate, this is perfect!"

"Yeah, I know. Nature always has the answer, doesn't it?"

"Right, mate, are you coming in now? Most of the lads are in the crew room, and the girls are having a slumber party in one of the cabins. It should just be the boys in there, and the footy's on in half an hour. I've got a little joke I want to play on Tar since he got away with it today. Just go with whatever I tell you, OK?"

"Cool. I'll see you in there in ten minutes."

* * * *

Jock fillets the fish and puts it in the galley for the chef to add to his soup. Then he separates the heads and some body parts, grinding them into a mush to lace Thrush's soup with, before joining me and the boys in the crew room. As expected, all the girls are away at their cabin slumber party.

"Well, the footy isn't on for another twenty minutes, so what shall we do till then?" Jock asks.

"I don't know, really," says Rob. "What do you reckon?"

"There's not a lot we can do in twenty minutes, is there?" says Tom.

"Fuck it. Let's have a wanking contest. We've not done that in a while," I say, as casually as if I'd just suggested making a cup of tea.

Tar looks around the room to see if he's heard correctly, but everyone appears completely normal. Tom, Jock, Rob, Steve, and I are all in on the joke. We've pulled this prank on other young crew members before—with dramatic results.

"Did I hear you right? Did you say we should have a wanking contest?" Tar asks.

"Yeah, that's right," I reply, keeping a straight face.

"Here? Now? Are you crazy?"

"We do it all the time. It's just a bit of a laugh when we get bored."

"You're kidding, surely?"

"No. Obviously, we turn the light off so it's pitch black and we can't see each other."

"Yeah, the lights are off when we do it. We're not fucking weirdos, for God's sake," says Rob.

"Well… what's the point?"

"Money. We all throw fifty euros into the pot, turn the lights off, lock the door, then jerk off into our hands. The first person to come shouts 'bingo'. Once everyone's tucked themselves away, we turn the lights back on. Whoever finishes first wins the money. Simple."

Tar looks around at the five poker-straight faces at the table. Nobody cracks. "So if all of you throw in fifty euros, that's 250 euros for the winner?" he asks.

"It sure is," I say. "But I reckon we should make it more interesting. Let's make it a hundred each—winner takes five hundred."

"Five hundred euros?" Tar's attention sharpens.

THE CREW

"That's nearly half a month's salary for a cadet, isn't it, Tar?" Tom says, reeling him in.

"Yeah, it is." Tar is slowly warming to the idea—after all, it's a lot of money for a few minutes of effort.

"Well, there's my hundred," says Jock, slamming his money onto the table.

"And there's mine," I add.

"And mine," say Tom and Rob in unison.

Everyone turns to Tar, waiting to see if he'll take the bait.

"Are you in, then, Tar?"

"No… no, I don't think so."

"It's five hundred euros if you win. Just for having a wank, mate!" says Jock.

"I know… I know, and I'm tempted, but it's a bit embarrassing. Anyway, I don't have a hundred euros. I've only got fifty in my cabin."

"Oh, fuck it, that'll do, since you're on a lower wage. Are you in, then?"

"Er… OK, then. But the lights will be off, right?"

"Yeah."

"And you won't turn them back on until everyone's, you know… finished?"

"Of course. You'll probably win anyway, mate. Just think about what you got up to last night," Jock chuckles.

"Right, I'm in. Turn the lights off and lock the door, then."

Tom gets up, switches off the light, locks the door, and finds his way back to his seat in the darkness.

"OK, everyone, whip it out, and I'll give you the countdown," I say. "First one to finish shouts 'bingo'. Is everybody ready?"

"Yeah," they all chorus.

"OK, then. Five… four… three… two… one… GO!"

After a few moments, Jock, Tom, Rob, and I start making little grunting noises. Squelching sounds can be heard around the darkened room. Then, higher-pitched noises begin coming from Tar's direction—there's no mistaking who's making them.

At this point, Tom very slowly stands up and makes his way quietly towards the light switch.

The grunts grow louder, the squelching more frequent.

"Egggggh… euuuuurr… eeeeeurr… ahhhhhh… AAAAAH… BIIIIIIIIIINGO!" shrieks Tar.

At that exact moment, Tom flicks the light on.

Tar stands bolt upright, mid-orgasm, emptying the contents of his balls into the palm of his hand.

The rest of us sit there, fully clothed, grinning at him—our dicks safely in our pants. The squelching noises hadn't been us wanking, as Tar had thought. We'd just been holding our cheeks between our thumbs and forefingers, rapidly moving them from side to side.

Everyone—except Tar—bursts out laughing.

"BINGO!" we all yell.

Tar's pinkish hue turns beetroot red.

"Fuck off… FUCK OFF, would you?!" he shrieks, diving beneath the table to hide his embarrassment.

The rest of the night is spent shouting at the footy on the TV instead of shouting at Tar. Around midnight, everyone heads to bed. It's been a long day.

Chapter 24
What Goes Around Comes Around

The next day, everyone is up at the crack of dawn. The shore-side engineer begins work on the faulty gearbox but has to wait for a part arriving by plane later tonight. The crew ensure the yacht is immaculate for the boss's arrival—stainless steel rails gleam, varnished wood is polished, fresh flags are raised, and the paintwork shines in the sun.

By lunchtime, there is still no sign of the boss. Jock and I finish clearing up, ready to head below deck and put our plan into action.

"Are you ready for this, mate?" Jock asks.

"Ready as I'll ever be. Where's the stuff for his soup?"

Jock pulls a small, watertight plastic bottle from his pocket and shows me the contents.

"All I need to do is take the top off before I go into the galley to bring the plates down. Then, when I get the chance, I'll empty it into his soup."

"There doesn't seem to be much there, Jock."

"There doesn't need to be—it's powerful stuff. Just a few ground-up bits of body parts, so he won't notice. He'll be off his head."

"How much does it take to trip?"

"One fish would do it if you ate the right parts."

"How many fish did you use to make this little concoction?"

"Seven."

"SEVEN?!"

We head below deck and take our seats for lunch. Jock sits closest to the entrance near the galley, while I position myself to keep a good view of Thrush. A few minutes later, Chef calls down as usual.

"OK, lunch is ready—can someone give me a hand?"

"No problem, I'm on my way," Jock replies, standing up quickly.

He jogs up the stairs, adrenaline and nerves racing through him.

"OK, whose is whose?" Jock asks.

"These can go to anyone, they're all the same. I've got Olga's and the Captain's," Chef says, pushing past him.

Jock has to think fast. The plan will fail if he can't lace Thrush's soup, and the boss could arrive at any moment. It's now or never. Just as Chef passes through the doorway, Jock turns sharply, knocking the hot soup over Chef's hands. The bowl smashes on the floor.

"Oh hell! Sorry, mate. That was bloody clumsy of me. Look, I'll take these downstairs while your hands are full, then I'll come back up, OK?"

"Shit! It's burning my hands," Chef mutters, rushing to the cold tap.

Jock seizes the moment, slipping out of sight for a few seconds. He pulls the small bottle from his pocket, quickly empties it into Thrush's soup, and stirs it in with his finger before carrying the bowls to the table.

"What happened up there?" Thrush asks.

"We had a little accident with the soup—smashed a bowl. I'm just going up to sort it now."

As Jock leaves the room, he gives me a sly wink. The plan is in motion. Now it's only a matter of time.

Everyone continues their conversation with the usual politeness, mindful of Thrush's presence. I'm halfway through my soup when Jock returns, giving me a small smile as he sits down. About twenty minutes later, with Thrush halfway through his dessert, we notice the change. His usual intense, vermin-like stare softens into something more impassioned and expressive. His journey has begun.

THE CREW

Jock and I keep an eye on him as he starts twitching, glancing at things in the corner of his vision. He inspects the pattern on the table closely, mumbling to himself. The rest of the crew remain oblivious, chatting away as usual. The plan is working perfectly so far.

Thrush is engrossed in examining his reflection in the cutlery when Olga speaks.

"How's your dessert?"

"What?" Thrush replies, looking startled.

"Your dessert—how is it?"

"Dessert... fine... what?"

"What?" Olga repeats, confused.

"What did you say?"

A short silence follows before Olga calmly replies, "I just asked how your dessert was."

Thrush looks irritated. "I know you asked me that! I'm sitting next to you, for God's sake! What did you say after that?"

"I didn't say anything after that."

"I heard you."

"Heard what?"

Thrush sighs deeply, rolling his eyes before taking another mouthful of dessert. Then, leaning towards Olga, he whispers, "I'm watching you."

The crew finish their desserts and leave the room, puzzled by Thrush's odd behaviour. Most head to the open deck to enjoy the sunshine before getting back to work. Shortly after 1:30 p.m., I see Thrush resting his elbows on the handrail, gazing out over the harbour, lost in his own world.

I glance down at the gate at the end of the quay and spot two men walking through. The boss has arrived, accompanied by someone. I quickly move to the after deck to inform the others. Zecky disappears inside while Jock and I stand at the gangway.

As the two men approach, both wear serious expressions, focused as if on a mission. Jock and I step forward to meet them. The boss greets us with his usual friendly smile.

"How are you, boys?"

"As well as can be expected, sir. Good to see you."

"Likewise, lads. This is Graham," the boss says, introducing the other man. "He's coming aboard to check a few things and go over some paperwork with the Captain."

"Pleased to meet you, Graham," we reply, trying to conceal our nerves.

The boss leans in conspiratorially and speaks in a low voice. "I already know your side of things from our phone call," he says to me. "I've checked with the guests about the tip—it all adds up. There are a few more accounting discrepancies Graham needs to discuss with the Captain, but I doubt he'll be able to talk his way out of this."

"I doubt that very much as well," says Jock, knowing a little more than the others.

"By the way, Jock, as far as I'm concerned, your and Zecky's jobs are safe, so stop fretting, OK? And tell her straight away so she doesn't worry."

Jock visibly relaxes, and it is clear that a huge weight has been lifted from his shoulders.

"Right then, where is he?"

"I last saw him going into his cabin," says Jock. "He looked a bit worse for wear, to be honest."

"I see. OK, boys, I'll call you if I need you."

The boss and Graham walk up the passerelle onto the yacht and disappear around the corner.

I glance over at Jock, who has a huge smile on his face. "I bet you're as happy as a pig in shit, mate, aren't you?"

"Fucking right I am, but not just because I've kept my job."

"I know… I know before you even say it. Now you and Zecky at least have a chance of staying together a little while longer."

"Yeah, exactly. I feel like sparking up another cigar, mate."

"Not yet, Jock. It isn't over until that spaced-out fucker walks down the passerelle for good."

The boss and Graham find Thrush in the same state as he was at lunch. He has his back to them and is having a conversation with himself.

"GOOD AFTERNOON!"

Thrush almost jumps out of his skin as he hears the boss's booming voice behind him, among the many other sounds inside his head. He turns around quickly, looking as though he has just seen an apparition.

"Do you mind if I have a word with you in my lounge?" the boss says, leading him down the stairs.

After an hour or so, Graham walks the deck to find Jock and me working on the jet ski at the back of the yacht.

"I've got a message from the boss, and I'll quote him word for word: 'Go into his cabin, empty his wardrobe, pack his and Olga's bags, and order them a taxi for 3.30 pm.'"

Graham then disappears back into the lounge, where we see him going through paperwork with a very confused and aggressive Thrush. The boss looks like he would shoot him if only he had a gun.

Jock and I go upstairs to his cabin, where the door is open.

We find their suitcases and begin packing.

"Where's Olga?" asks Jock.

"Don't worry, mate. She went ashore, so she won't walk in."

As we go through the wardrobes, Jock suddenly stops in his tracks. He can't quite believe what he's seeing.

"I fucking knew it – the warped bastard! Tell me I'm imagining this!"

Jock can't take his eyes off something at the bottom of the wardrobe.

"What's up?" I ask, on my hands and knees emptying Olga's wardrobe.

A big grin creeps across Jock's face.

"You remember that conversation the girls had with Olga about men, sex, and all that weird shit when she came back pissed that night?"

"Yeah."

"And do you remember Zecky said Olga let slip that Thrush likes to dress up?"

"Yeah, she said leather was insinuated."

"Well, fuck me sideways, my old china – I've just found the motherlode!"

I peer around the door and can't believe what I'm seeing either.

"I always knew there was something very strange about that guy," I say as Jock reaches into the wardrobe and pulls out a pair of black leather shorts and a gimp mask fitted with a large snooker ball.

"It's like something out of that scene in *Pulp Fiction*," says Jock, examining the mask.

"I know! Who was that guy into all that gimp mask shit in the movie?"

"It was the owner of the shop where Bruce Willis and the big black gangster had a fight. His name was Zed."

"Zed, that's it. That's the captain's new nickname from now on."

"We'll hang on to these as a keepsake, mate," says Jock.

The packing takes only about fifteen minutes, and then Jock and I drag the cases down to the bottom of the passerelle. When the taxi arrives, Jock tells the driver to put the bags in the boot and wait.

"Where am I going?" asks the driver.

"Don't know yet, mate," I tell him, "but I think we're about to find out."

As soon as the words are out of my mouth, a commotion can be heard coming from the outside deck. Doors slam, and the boss can be heard arguing with Thrush. The voices grow louder and louder as they clearly square up to each other, making their way towards the passerelle.

Jock and I move onto the quay next to the taxi to get a better view. Thrush, in a world of his own, is barking at the boss as he walks away from him. At one point, Graham has to step in to separate them and keep the boss where he is as Thrush walks down the stairs and along the passerelle to the taxi.

"AND KEEP AWAY FROM THIS FUCKING YACHT, YOU THIEVING PIECE OF SHIT STONER!" shouts the boss as Thrush walks off.

Thrush stops momentarily and turns to look at Jock and me with his wide, saucer-like eyes before getting into the taxi.

"You two haven't seen the last of me – watch your backs," he says quietly and coldly.

Jock stares back at him just as coldly before replying, "Newton's Third Law."

"What?" replies a flustered Thrush.

"Newton's Third Law is something you should study. For every action, there is an equal and opposite reaction. What goes around comes around, you fucking sicko!"

Thrush snarls and mutters something before climbing into the back of the taxi, banging his head as he gets in. Just before the cab pulls away, I lean in through the window for one last word.

'By the way, we absolutely loved the mask and the leather. I think you'd look absolutely lovely in it.'

As the taxi disappears, the boss calms down a bit. He shouts from the deck to get my attention.

'Get back on here, you!'

'You'd better answer him, mate,' says Jock.

'Are you talking to me, sir?'

'No, I was talking to the seagull behind you! YES, YOU!!'

'Oh, right…'

'Now get your arse on here. And Jock, you get the beers in. In fact, get everyone up to the lounge. We're all going to have a drink or ten,' says the boss gleefully.

* * * *

For the rest of the afternoon and most of the evening, the boss gets drunk with his crew. Music booms, and everyone laughs, jokes, and dances. The tension has disappeared as quickly as Thrush had. The boss flies back to Monaco the following day, but not before ordering me to stock up the yacht as soon as possible. Another young captain has been found, and we are to prepare the yacht for an Atlantic crossing to Barbados, where the boss is planning a surprise anniversary party.

The future looks bright. We've all seen the last of Thrush, Tar has got laid, Zecky has kept her job and lowered her usual impeccable standards to let Jock into her life, and the engineers have finished working on the gearbox. The yacht is quickly stocked for the crossing.

* * * *s

As we head out of the harbour in the afternoon sun, Jock and I stand on the top deck, peering through binoculars at a figure on the breakwater.

'Is that who I think it is?' I ask.

Jock starts laughing. 'He's in the same clothes. He must still be off his tits!'

'How long do the effects last? It's been just over twenty-four hours!'

'One fish can keep you hallucinating for about thirty-six hours, but it depends on your metabolism.'

'How much did you put in?'

'All of it.'

'That's seven fish. Fuck me, Jock! He'll be off his lord until the end of the month. Jock, run down and get the shorts and the mask from the crew room. You know what to do, mate.'

The paraphernalia has pride of place, hung up in the crew room next to Thrush's picture on the dartboard. Jock writes something on an elastic card tag and fastens it to the mask. The end of the breakwater is coming up fast, and Thrush has spotted the yacht heading towards him, close to the end of the pier.

As the yacht sails past, the new captain sounds the ship's horn, and Jock hurls the leather shorts at Thrush. He then shows me the gimp mask with the heavy ball at the front, and I give him the nod.

'Go for it, mate!' I tell him, unfastening my trouser belt to moon Thrush.

Jock takes aim, mustering all his strength before hurling the mask at him. The heavy mask lands at Thrush's feet. He bends down to pick it up and notices the card tag with Jock's writing, which reads:

'You've got no hope if you've got no soul.

Lots of love,

Your dealer.'

As Jock walks back up the deck, Thrush disappears in the distance behind the yacht.

'So, mate, how was Zed?' I ask, grinning.

'To coin a phrase from *Pulp Fiction*... Zed's dead, baby... Zed's dead!'

www.ingramcontent.com/pod-product-compliance
Lightning Source LLC
Chambersburg PA
CBHW040107100526
44584CB00029BA/3854